D0419402

Read

– 9 JUL 2011

– 5 MA   '12   2 1 AUG 2019

– 1 MAY

              ? 2019

                 ?020

MAGGIE'S FARM

by JOHN SHERRY

THE PERMANENT PRESS
SAG HARBOR, NEW YORK 11963

By John Sherry:
The Departure
The Loring Affair
Pistolero's Progress
Maggie's Farm

Plays Produced:
Abraham Cochrane
The Icing
The Admissions Chairman
The Basket Case

Again to D.

Copyright © 1984 by John Sherry

All rights reserved including the right to reproduce
this book, or parts thereof, in any form, except for
the inclusion of brief quotations in a review.

International Stardard Book Number: 0-932966-50-0
Library of Congress Number: 83-063238

Manufactured in the United States of America

THE PERMANENT PRESS
RD2 Noyac Road, Sag Harbor, NY 11963

"In order to discover some of the major categories under which we can classify the infinitely various components of experience, we must appeal to evidence relating to every variety of occasion. Nothing can be omitted, experience drunk and experience sober, experience sleeping and experience waking, experience drowsy and experience wide-awake, experience self-conscious and experience self-forgetful, experience intellectual and experience physical, experience religious and experience sceptical, experience anxious and experience care-free, experience anticipatory and experience retrospective, experience happy and experience grieving, experience dominated by emotion and experience under self-restraint, experience in the light and experience in the dark, experience normal and experience abnormal."

Alfred North Whitehead: ADVENTURES OF IDEAS.

EX·PE′RI-ENCE (eks-per-i-ens; iks-) (OF.; fr. L. *experientia.* fr. *experiens, -entis,* pres. part. of *experiri, expertus.* to try, fr.. *ex* out + the root of *peritus* experienced.) 1. The actual living through an event or events; actual enjoyment or suffering; hence, the effect upon the judgment or feelings produced by personal and direct impressions; as, to know by *experience.* 2. State, extent or duration of being engaged in a particular study or work, or in affairs; as, business *experience.* 3. Knowledge, skill or technique resulting from experience, 4. The sum total of the conscious events which compose an individual life. 5. Something that is or has been experienced; as, his hunting *experiences.*—v.t.; -ENCED (-enst); -ENCING (-ensing). To have experience of or learn by experience; to undergo. —Syn. Know, suffer, have, undergo,—*experience. religion.* To undergo conversion.

Webster's Collegiate Dictionary—5th Edition

"I try my best
To be just like I am
Everybody wants me
To be just like them
They say, "Sing while you slave"
But I just get bored

So I ain't gonna work on Maggie's farm no more
No I ain't gonna work on Maggie's farm no more."

—From "Maggie's Farm" by Bob Dylan

CHAPTER I

Early in the game, very early, it was clear to me through some process that I do not wholly understand that stardom was to be the touchstone of reality to the members of my generation. Whether in business or art, science or technology, the unspoken understanding was: stardom is the key. The society in which we lived and with whose creation we have been involved clearly was going to settle for no less of a measuring rod. Equally clearly, neither was it much interested in anything more. It did not seriously occur to me as a boy to doubt the validity of such a concept. Like many another contemporary, I simply assumed that it was the way things were and, furthermore, assumed that the day of my own elevation to pre-eminence would be along in due course. That such a day did not arrive must, in some measure, be due to a certain amount of unconsciously ambivalent feelings towards the concept that I accepted so blithely.

On the verge of turning thirty in the year 1953, my attitude toward those matters had not changed appreciably. Nor, I must admit in all honesty as a child of my times, has it changed much to this very day as I begin this account of a rather peculiar and retrospectively blood-curdling defensive action undertaken in company with my wife between 1953 and 1960.

1953 found us in North Africa: My wife ensconced in a flat on the Rue Fernando de Portugal in Tangier, awaiting the birth of our first child; I working in Casablanca to pay for the flat on the Rue Fernando de Portugal and awaiting my own personal act of childbirth; the publication of a first novel, timed, by some oddity of chance, to coincide with the arrival of the child. With the dedicated illogic of the true dreamer, I believed absolutely that these events would have bearing upon each other or to be more precise, that fame and fortune were just around the corner and that the child would grow up secure in all things including the possession of a successful and clever father.

And so, arrive they did, child and book, almost simultaneously. The child, I am happy to say, turned out very well. the book fared less well, disappearing into the deep of oblivion with rude disregard for my hopes and dreams. An immense question of the age descended upon my shoulders in all its intolerable weight. And, despite the objections of those many people who take the opposite view, that question is not, Who am I? It is, What am I going to do?

In regard to the years leading up to that moment in North Africa, I had absolutely no regrets. I had fought in World War II and had been lucky enough to escape unscathed. I had spent a few cheerful, underpaid, hard-drinking years trying not to get ahead in the advertising agency business. And I had been fortunate enough to be taken to husband by a fine woman. Furthermore, on the ever-sound premise of, if not now, probably never, we had sailed away to Europe in time to enjoy what were probably the last three years of exhaust-fume-free Rome and tourist-free mediterranean Spain.

So, for the past, no regrets. But, for the future, profound trepidation. Some instinct warned me, for the moment, to avoid my native shores. I believed then as I do now that the United States is the true sausage meat machine for those who cannot vouch for their intentions in terms of actions. Which was my position in a nutshell. With the failure of my first book, the economics of the precarious trade I had chosen to follow emerged rudely from the warm dream world in which I had kept them hidden; the endearing and terrifying cries of our new-born daughter drove home the message: change, drastic, irreversible change had taken place. A wife who had been heretofore the sturdiest of economic bulwarks would now and hereafter require sustenance and care. By nature non-conformist and rebellious, I had, within the limits of my memory, considered myself free: a state of mind which, no matter how illusory, I was then and am now determined not to see terminated. However, the nature of the freedom which I had enjoyed up to that point was a jerry-built structure designed for the temporary housing of youthful exuberance and hedonism and glued loosely together by a mixture of defiance and lack of discipline. The freedom which exists inside necessity stretched out before me as an inpenetrable paradox. I was scared blue and held myself together almost wholly through the conviction that I must not allow that fear to infect my family. That same fear made me turn my back for the moment on the idea of returning home. I had no plan for survival and no appetite for the bohemian life; without one or the other, life, particularly in America, is thin ice indeed upon which to skate and the waters beneath it are deep and cold. My intention of pursuing a career as a writer did not change, but at that time it provided no help beyond psychic consolation. There were mouths to feed and nests to be built and I was not able to fool myself into believing my pen could immediately solve those problems. Fortunately there was some money. Not much, but enough to grant respite from immediate decision and commitment.

It was not, except inside my head, an unpleasant time. My wife was caught up in the happiness which the categoric demands of a newborn child inspires. After the accouchement, I quit my job at Casablanca and returned to Tangier to stew. When the flat became oppressive, I would walk down through the Medinah and meet Mac at a cafe in the Zocco Chico. He was an acquaintance from Casablanca; a gentle, intelligent pederast whose mode of life made my hair stand on end. He lived, in fact, in a male brothel off the Zocco, a circumstance upon which I did not let my mind dwell at length. Despite our disparate sexual proclivities, we had two things in common: he also was a novelist who had published one book which had failed and he also was giving serious thought to the possibility of returning home. Of gentle birth and puritan background, Mac was at war with himself. He had chosen to live in Morocco for reasons of sensual gratification of course, but he did not find his life meet. Curiously enough, some months later, shortly before I decided to bite the bullet of my own homecoming, Mac did return to America. His nervousness must have been even more extreme than he realized, for a rather pathetic circumstance occurred—one which was not without symbolic significance. While descending the gangplank at the precise moment of his disembarkation in New York, he fell and broke his leg rather badly. I visited him in the hospital for a moment shortly after this happened and he intimated that he would return abroad when he was released. But at the time of which I write, our meetings in the Zocco were soothing to us both. His nervousness about the future was wholly centered around the difficulties attendant upon being a pederast in the U.S.A. Mine was more prosaically based upon the need to be husband, father and breadwinner; we pretended politely to listen to each other's worries while each considered his own.

At this time also, I thought much of my friends. Friends is not really the correct term to employ but I know of no other. How can I explain these associations which had dominated my life and—I now suspect—stunted it? I must make a beginning of it now for the deadly intertwining of our lives to their virtual strangulation is a tragi-comic thread which will run through the time ahead. I must make a beginning by going back.

O'Hara and I were the first to meet. We could not have been more than nine or ten years old. We were classmates at the public grade school I attended near my parents' suburban St. Louis house. From this time, no strong physical impression of O'Hara remains except a vague remembrance that he was smaller than I. He was Catholic, a circumstance which I found exotic and disquieting; I remember being repelled by the appurtenances of that religion which adorned his bedroom as I remember a sense of exclusion when he would abandon our play to fulfill some religious duty. I cannot claim enough retrospective sentience to know why we were kindred. But we were so, immediately. He remained in that school for one year, perhaps two. He was then placed by his parents in a parochial school and so passed from my ken.

The school where O'Hara and I first met did not go beyond the sixth grade. I was then entered in a private coeducational country day school where my elder brother was already enrolled and about to begin his junior year. The beginning grade of the private school was the seventh. The normal nervousness of being thrown with a group of strange children was dispelled somewhat by catching sight of O'Hara. We were classmates again and kindred from the day of our first seventh grade assemblage.

Our friendship was undoubtedly strengthened by the fact that we who had something in common were venturing upon unbroken social ground of a complexity hitherto unencountered. It was 1934, a depression year. A large percentage of the parents of my classmates were badly strapped, my own among them. Many of us, I am sure, were there on scholarships of the "accommodation" variety. My elder brother was such a pupil, which was the reason I had been sent to the school. I was not—although I believe some sort of cut-rate tuition arrangement had been made. The financial status of my classmates at the John Burroughs School would have, I believe, broken down something like this: one third came from families which like my own were going through a serious financial belt-tightening due to the depression; one third derived from families involved in a push towards what is now known as upwards social mobility; the final third was drawn from backgrounds of genuine and quite breathtaking affluence. The father of one boy for example, was throughout my time at that school, listed annually in the newspapers as being among the ten most highly paid men in the United States. Another boy's father was president of the American arm of a large foreign-owned international oil company.

I sometimes marvel at just what an odd group the class of 1941 of the John Burroughs School was; odd and terribly tasty cookery. The eventual disposition of the few I know about frequently makes me smile. Some certainly are dead of war and other diseases; some, I know, gave up their grip on sanity. One girl of whom I was rather fond, ran, at one time, a plantation in Angola. (Her younger brother—in the class below me—outstripped her in reach, doing time later on in life for the murder of a mutual friend.) Another classmate—heir to a good deal of money—was for many years a perfectly contented Greyhound bus driver. Yet another, whose name I see occasionally in the newspapers, is Director of something called "A School for Peace" which is supported by the folk singer, Joan Baez. I know of four commercially published novelists among my former classmates and thank God I do not know all the eccentric works produced by them which remain unseen. Keep in mind that the total number of children gathered together that day we first assembled did not exceed 25.

11

Besides O'Hara and me, there were two others among that group who will entangle themselves with us in our mutual Gordian knot. (O'Hara's phrase.) Let me take Kate first. I can see her now clearly in my memory as we gathered in that schoolroom—it was, I remember, a biology lab; O'Hara and I sat together, each estimating our peers.

O'Hara's eyes, like mine, were, I am sure, drawn first and foremost to Kate. She was unquestionably the female star of the galaxy. Nothing is more purely romantic than the heart of an eleven year old boy and mine was, perhaps, even more so than most. Kate's appearance and aura fulfilled its sternest requirements. Stick-thin, blonde, uniquely handsome, haughty even then and, forgive me for using such an unfashionable word, patrician. There is no point in being reticent about the truth: both O'Hara and I fell in love with her then. And remained in love with her for many years. Ten, twenty, yes all of those, certainly; and still a few more. Kate and I would not even be close friends for another fourteen years; not until after my marriage. My wife so impressed her that she was forced to examine me, her predatory instincts alerted towards me for the first time in the many years we had known each other. Twice only in our lives did we stand at a point of danger. She came once to our apartment on 12th Street in 1950 for purposes of seduction, although whether conscious or unconscious on her part, I cannot say. My wife was away at work. Twice married by then; once widowed and once divorced, Kate did not have children with her, a rare occurrence. The strap of her slip was broken, she said, and she peeled off her sweater, asking me to pin it. Any old country drugstore cocksman would have had the situation well in hand in seconds, but I had lived with romance so long I could not realize that I was being offered flesh and blood. Thank God, for I had not the requisite knowledge or strength of character for allegiances other than to my wife. The second time we broke lances, we did so for good and Kate gets the credit for generous behavior. It was in 1954. Kate had returned to St. Louis and had been living there during the three years my wife and I (and O'Hara) were abroad. I went to St. Louis on a short trip in search of money to begin the events this book describes. Kate had invited me to stay with her during the few days I would be there. She had devised an odd

mode of life which perfectly expressed the fundamental contempt she needed to keep her ego operative. With studied,
stud-book hauteur, she occuped a rather proletarian flat in a
depressed part of the city. She made, in other words, full use
of her formidable social connections, but she made use of
them by making them come to her; it was both utilitarian and
stylish. The uncle who was then dean of her family frequently
had himself driven to her dingy neighborhood in order to
present various plans for her rehabilitation, all of which were,
of course, rejected. The uncle was of that class of man who
goes to Africa to shoot big game. I recall when I stayed with
Kate for those few days in 1954, she told me that he had
recently returned from a safari upon which he shot an
elephant. With a pause of exactly the proper length to let that
sink in, Kate added, "Even *he* knew he had done something
stupid." A stylish lady.

The money I had come for I did not get. I had not really
believed that I would; it would be many years before I would
return again exultantly to attend a funeral and close the books
on that account. So, no money. But inevitably love cropped
up. I say inevitably because, when a man and a woman have
given as much thought to each other as we had, it is very
nearly impossible to keep it down. Furthermore, I believe
that Kate had realized since our earlier encounter just how
extensive was the romantic attachment that I harbored for
her. By which I mean romantic with all the full-fledged Jean
Jacques Rousseau craziness. In such a situation, the depth of
female delicacy is beyond description. A woman, if she
chooses, can bring the shyest, most awkward and hesitant of
men to a sublime point of confidence. And they do so more
often than they are given credit for; women create more men
than they destroy.

What happened between us on that visit was simple, even
prosaic. We ate, we drank, we talked and we drove around
the city I had not seen in so many years. The casual physical
contacts of old friendship were more than casual and we both
knew it. It was not really fair. For either of us. She was very
lonely. And I was trying to keep my mind under control in
the face of the fear I felt for my contemplated plan of action. I
remember that on the penultimate night of my stay with
Kate, we went to a concert of eighteenth century music in one

of the quadrangles of Washington University. And suddenly the hand holding became sentimental, and having become sentimental became passion. We returned to her flat and faced one of those strange moments which mean commitment to another human being if it is carried to conclusion. I remember standing face to face on the verge of disaster. Kate smiled then and said, "No, we can't. It would be incestuous." It was so absolutely true and right that we both burst out laughing. And then inevitably we began to speak of Darroch, who had been her husband and was the father of one of her children, and who had been present in that biology lab in 1934 when we all first laid eyes on each other.

From the outset, my instincts instructed me not to take Darroch seriously. Then, after the war, I denied my instincts and took him seriously only to find, after watching his hands become more and more heavily coated with blood, that my instincts had been right from the beginning. He had, I suppose, more chances than any of us. The world, we are told, is for the very rich, the very pretty and the very witty. Darroch was certainly the second and capable of the third when he chose. Which is not often; he is a heavy man.

As Kate stood out from the others that first day, so did Darroch. He was a startlingly handsome boy and would become, in time, an equally handsome man. He was, from the first, secretive and deceptive; I was not really aware of the quality of his mind until after the war when, drawn together by common experience in different parts of the world, we would attend the post-war debutante parties together. The extent of his secretive turn of mind is indicated by the fact that I did not know until then that Darroch and Kate had begun sleeping together during our ninth grade year, and had continued to do so for many, many years thereafter.

I was expelled from John Burroughs at the end of the ninth grade for general unruliness and Darroch was dropped at the end of the following year for roughly the same reasons. He subsequently attended a Connecticut prep school not far from mine and we would make the journey from St. Louis to the East together. Only O'Hara and Kate remained to the end and graduated from John Burroughs. They were not close there; but they were intensely aware of each other.

O'Hara and Kate did not actually meet, in fact, between

1941, the year of their graduation from Burroughs, and 1954, shortly after I had paid my brief visit to St. Louis. During those years I was always in close contact with O'Hara. Frequently during the war, for example, I would spend my leaves with him in Carmel, California. He had escaped the draft and lived there throughout the war with a rather pleasant woman by whom he had two children. Whenever I visited O'Hara he would always be curious about Kate. And, after 1949 when my wife and I were close friends with Kate, she always expressed a reciprocal curiosity regarding O'Hara.

Kate's hard knocks began almost immediately after her graduation from Burroughs. To everyone's surprise, she married almost immediately. I knew her husband, Sam, and liked him very much. He was a grandee, a huge, impeccably tailored man whose handsome bulk contained an extremely gentle heart. I do not think Sam inquired too closely into the relationship between Kate and Darroch. Like most aristocrats, he operated from the fundamental assumption that his life would proceed along an ordered path. He was aware of Darroch however. I remember seeing Sam in a bar in St. Louis a few months before I entered the Army Air Corps as a cadet. He had just graduated from Princeton and was off to active duty with his R.O.T.C. commission. "What about this Darroch?," he asked me. I told him what little I knew, for Darroch and I were not then yet close friends. "Christ," Sam said with puzzlement in his terribly elegant accent, "he sounds like a man who doesn't even like shoes." It was impossible to dislike Sam. He was straight from the pages of Ford Madox Ford—like Tietjens, a personality out of place in time. From the first, the marriage of Sam and Kate showed portents of disaster. And yet their union seemed somehow perfect, both blue-eyed, both blond, both handsome and rich—splendid symbols of the Nordic, upper middle-class dream. Beneath the surface there were tensions. For openers, Kate's doting, gentlemanly father chose to die with fine Freudian fury an hour before her wedding at the Army post where Sam was then stationed. Within two years, Sam was dead from cannon fire in the Ardennes. Kate was left with a daughter and enough money to be more or less self-sufficient.

As soon as Darroch returned from his service with the Marines, he and Kate took up where they had left off before the war. They seemed to me to represent a true workability; both of Scots descent, both obdurate and both courageous. But the cocksman's virus was already gnawing at Darroch's vitals; it is a slow but virtually certain prescription for the death of a man's possibility. Did he really have possibility? I will never know, I suppose. But surely all of us must have possibility until the moment we choose to abandon it. Kate left no stone unturned, no card unplayed in her efforts to bring him to heel with life. She was at her finest then and, at her finest, she was one of the most courageous human beings I have ever known. To be trite, I honestly believe that Darroch was always her man.

By which, I mean that together, they would have represented a standard of excellence to which each would have been driven to conform; together each would have been more than he or she was alone. From some mysterious center of female wisdom, Kate knew this; could they have dealt honestly and generously with each other, they could have dealt more honestly and generously with their lives. Certainly, Kate was proud but, in my lexicon, pride can be made into a virtue if one is willing to undergo and recover from the fall which follows it. Had her first husband, Sam lived, I suspect that Kate would now be a reasonably contented society matron of the sort who appears occasionally in Vogue. But such was not to be the case and her preoccupation with Darroch was to lead her far afield from any preordained paths.

Inevitably, she became pregnant. Darroch agreed without fuss to marry her, giving due notice that he would leave her as soon as the child was born. As a point of abstract morality, I believe that Darroch had a certain right on his side; no man or woman should be forced permanently into marriage because of a biological accident. But children are not abstractions; they are flesh and blood who grow up and stand as symbols of things left undone. For better or for worse, their nurturing remains the basic matrix of human purpose.

Accordingly, Darroch and Kate were married. They moved to Woodstock, N. Y. and in that tolerant, bohemian place, the child—a second daughter—was born. At that time, I was working in New York for an advertising agency and I paid them a brief visit shortly after the child was born. True to his word, Darroch was preparing to depart.

He left almost immediately thereafter and returned to St. Louis. His father, a splendid, kind man, and probably the one human being Darroch came closest to loving in his life, was dying there of a particularly brutal, lingering disease. Darroch undertook a sustained death watch and, I believe, paid over the few remnants of his faith during it. Like Gautama, he emerged with an underlying conviction that life consists of sickness, old age and death; unlike Gautama, he neither had nor could he formulate a basis of faith to contain such terrible knowledge.

Between my childhood friend, O'Hara and Darroch, there was no contact during the years between 1941 and 1952. They met then in Rome and seemingly hit it off from the first. However, theirs was an exceedingly complex relationship. Years later, O'Hara published a rather odd and dreadfully boring novel whose central figure was a peculiar melange of the personalities of each. It was as if, from the moment of their meeting in Rome, each indulged himself with fantasies of what it would be like to be a composite of both. With O'Hara particularly it was a preoccupation of dangerous depth and complexity. There were elements of vicariousness in O'Hara's fascination with Darroch. And elements of jealousy. Jealousy certainly because of Darroch's long-standing relationship with Kate, who, throughout the years, had never ceased to be an element in O'Hara's total calculus despite the fact that neither jot nor tittle of concourse had passed between them. But there was jealousy present also of a more dangerous and schizophrenic variety. Both men were caught up in the fundamental fallacy of believing that the world could be tricked into giving them what they wanted. Loosely stated, what each wanted was stardom; to occupy a position where people would think about him and so grant him power. However, the rewards each expected from his dangerous dream were vastly different. O'Hara saw power as an aspect of function while Darroch, I now believe, only wanted from power such tangible things as money, women and drink. Paradoxically enough, each went out of his way to give the opposite impression; the intellectual proclivities displayed by Darroch were unremittingly metaphysical; he eschewed all advertent signs of dandyism. O'Hara on the other hand, was greatly concerned with style and trappings. Wanting more, O'Hara's motivations were more complex. His jealous envy of Darroch's physical stature and extraordinary nervous system drove him to toy with the idea that Darroch could perhaps be made to function as an extension of himself. But this was a mistake. Darroch was never malleable; his own appetites dwarfed any other reality. O'Hara's weapons against Darroch were basically irony and scorn and he was frequently terribly funny. No one enjoyed this more than Darroch who called O'Hara's sallies against him "fleabites" and chuckled at them with contemptuous pleasure. "The leader of the people" was one of O'Hara's sobriquets for Darroch. He was also fond of observing that Darroch "was the man who had invented the bad fuck". And I remember one day when they both had come to the small village in Spain where my wife and I were then living: We were all sitting on the beach chatting, except for Darroch, who was swimming about a hundred yards offshore. He swam, as he played games, with an indolent magnificence, a perfection of cordi-nation which almost seemed to flaunt itself. I looked up that day to find O'Hara watching him with fierce concentration. "Look at the son-of-a-bitch." he said, "he talks nothing but spirit and he won't move an inch for anything he can't eat, drink or fuck." Darroch's attitude towards O'Hara can be reported more simply. When I visited Kate in St. Louis in 1954, she showed me a letter she had received from Darroch written from Rome shortly after his encounter with O'Hara. It said: "I have run into our old classmate, O'Hara. He is a pale-faced, tricky bastard and I am a big red-faced, tricky bastard; we get along very well together."

These then were my "friends" and the friends of my wife also, because she had married me in the good old fashioned spirit of total acceptance and loyalty, not only to me, but to my associations. These were my friends and one other of whom I shall never be able to speak with objectivity because blood is a thick substance and he is my brother. Older than the rest of us by four years, he had nevertheless chosen some years before to cast his lot in with us and so, he too, was enmeshed in our Laocoon-like entanglement with each other. As I sat in Tangier trying to devise some intention for the future, they were all in London. O'Hara and Darroch figuring out their next moves in their quest for power, their

18

attempt to trick the universe. Only Kate had remained at home, waiting for her life to begin again. Soon, we would all go home. I must confess that I longed to be cavorting in London also. But I was not; I was in Tangier and I was the father of a child and I was faced with a question—no, *the* question—I could not answer.

The best immediate plan I could muster was movement. And movement is, at best, only a substitute for action. But Tangier, as the readers of Mr. Paul Bowles know, offers no hope of any sort; it is one of those places which is a final repository of inertia and despair. Where then? Rome, perhaps? Yes, Rome. It had fed us before and just might do so again. For the moment, it was still a waiting game.

CHAPTER II

We returned to Rome in autumn of 1953. Because Rome has been for me a city of such incomparable magic, I find there is a disinclination, a lack of longing to go there now; I have loved it so much in the past; I do not want that love lessened by the present. Prior to our return in 1953, my wife and I had lived there for close to two years. And they were, in the main, two very happy, carefree pre-parental years without undue financial strain or worry about the future. However, during our second residence, those murderers stalked my mind, knives drawn.

As it does sometimes during a time of tension, the mechanics, the administrative side of life which I hate and fear so bitterly, went surprisingly smoothly. My Italian was by then fluent if somewhat erratic, which helped. An advertisement in Il MESSAGERO led us to a first-rate furnished flat at a rental we could manage. Its location could not have been better, off the Via Flaminia on a lovely winding street called Viale Delle Belle Arti quite near the Villa Giulia and the Museum of Modern Art. From our windows, we could look out across the Borghese Park. On this visit, we were too broke and our tenure too temporary to afford an automobile, which was fine since the flat was a perfect starting point for walks. To penetrate old Rome, one simply walked down the die-straight Via Flaminia to the Piazza del Popolo and thence along the Corso, turning right at the Piazza Colonna into the past. If one wanted Via Veneto and its cafes, one climbed through the Borghese gardens past the splendid Renaissance elegance of the Piazza Siena and so to the Porta Pinciana. It was the first of these routes which beckoned most frequently; the cafes of Via Veneto seemed a doubtful source of response to my question of what to do.

It was a time of rigid economy; every Puritan edge of my character was, for the moment, honed sharp. While my wife and my mother (who was then with us) celebrated female mysteries with the baby, I would shut myself in the dining room in the mornings where I made a stab at writing a play much under the influence of Mr. Tennessee Williams. It was not bad but it was soon clear that I could not beat him at his own game and the project languished. In the afternoons, I walked and stewed, taking along, most days, our goofy Boxer dog and a hundred lire—enough to buy the Rome Daily American and a cup of coffee at some cafe. Socially, life was totally barren. O'Hara, Darroch and my brother were, as I have said, in London. Our other close Roman friends, Bill and Doris Murray, had returned to New York. A big day's social excitement would be to return to the flat to find my mother entertaining the local Episcopalian vicar at tea. Since dead, he was a likable man clearly under a certain amount of strain in mustering continued belief in the mysteries he promulgated. My mother gave him a copy of my late, ill-fated novel, which he read with enough interest to inspire him to dwell upon it, some weeks later, in one of his sermons. The gist of his remarks as reported to me was: the fellow who wrote this book is not as bad as he appears. I hope so.

Not that there was not, among the Puritan quills I was then extending, a deep longing for relaxation among the fleshpots. Unfortunately neither the money nor the personnel for such pursuits was available. I longed to have the telephone ring and hear the voice of our well-loved and frivolous friend, Frank O'Connor, blown in from God knows where, invite Dorothy and me out to do the town. I must digress now to give some slight flavor of O'Connor for he will serve as a frame of reference at certain moments in this chronicle:

It is strange that three of the four men I have loved most in my life have all been Jesuit-trained and Irish by blood. And, perhaps more important, apostates from their religion, to a man. Of the three, Frank's apostasy is the least formal and binding; he is likely to call for shriving upon his death bed. His view of life was essentially absurdist; he saw it as a voyage of brief duration and dubious value; don't be a fool, he would advise his assembled drinking companions, take the one with the big teats; or: it only hurts for a second. Terribly generous, there was also a quality of fundamental decency about him. Once, in Tangier, he announced to my wife and me that he was going to give a brilliant luncheon party for us. He did so, too, assembling at one of the odd, out of the way hotels he was in the habit of frequenting, as exquisite a combination of the refined and the raffish as I have ever encountered. That the company emitted a common aura of damnation lent spice to the lengthy, beautifully-cooked meal. To all except my wife and me, it was clear that a certain segment of those present harbored orgiastic intentions for the balance of the afternoon. Two limousines had been laid on to carry the guests away after lunch. The orgiastically inclined among us climbed into one, the remainder into the other. Not knowing whether we were afoot or on horseback, my wife and I climbed into the wrong car. Like a scene from an old Marx Brothers film, Frank climbed right in behind us and with consummate aplomb shepherded us through the limousine and out of the opposite door into the non-orgiastic car. I do not believe any human being is corrupt who goes out of his way to prevent corruption in others. But perhaps, after all, his intentions were selfishly motivated. A pair of innocents can pretty well put the skids under an orgy.

Oddly enough, the very thing I hoped for would occur. Frank would turn up in Rome within a very few weeks. By that time, I would have hit upon the answer to our future and would be trembling on the brink of commitment to it. The rounds of gaiety with Frank and his debauched circus would have a beneficial effect upon pushing me to a decision. But, for the moment, the social pickings were slim and unrewarding. I continued to walk and ponder.

The dilemma was this: I was completely without training in any crafts except writing and the operation of a Norden bombsight. There was slight market for the latter certainly. The market for the former, however—if one were not too choosy—was practically limitless. Advertising, public relations, radio, TV—all those segments of what is loosely known as the communications industry—beckoned to any aspirant who could provide even a semblance of talent. I wish to make it clear at the outset that I do not carp at these pursuits; lengthy discussions of the moral dilemma they present are a terrible bore and generally lead nowhere. My hesitancy about trying to re-enter that world stemmed less from a distaste for it than from a fundamentally healthy fear of extending my energies to reach for rewards I did not really want. The payoff in that world, it seems to me, is iron-bound membership in the great American middle-class—St. Paul's for the sons and Farmington for the daughters; a great circle course back to the point where one began. Traveling in circles offers only a limited amount of experience and experience is the real clay from which one is fashioned. To be lucky enough not to be born in a ghetto or a jungle and then merely to concentrate on staying even is not much of a game. Life without the embellishment of some creative admixture is a pretty boring business. And I knew myself well enough to be chary of my ability to retain balance in any situation which did not provide a rich tapestry of experience. My Scots-Irish heritage provides vast reservoirs of rage and spleen and drunkenness; the quickest way to open their floodgates is to embrace a course of action which is neither believed in nor desired. Yet the first rule even for a tentative aspirant to manhood is: fulfill your responsibilities to those you love. I have never known a man who funked that one to survive. And my time was running low; unless I could contrive or encounter a more peculiar and rewarding plan, my destination was pretty well going to have to be Madison Avenue with all its real or imagined dangers.

The idea came, as such things so often do, from an oblique direction. In Rome at that time was a friend of my brother's, a serious, rather ascetic Englishman named Haddam. He was employed temporarily by the U.S. Embassy or perhaps the U.S. Information Service, I was never sure which. Whatever the precise nature of his employment, it was not taxing; he was usually free in the afternoons to chat and I fell into the habit of stopping by his office once or twice a week. Because he was a completely serious man, there was great solace in the occasional hour I spent with him. He too faced an uncertain future; the job he held (which, I believe, had something to do with statistics) clearly did not constitute a career. One day when I was quizzing him about his plans, he remarked idly that he had often thought of returning to England and getting a small farm. It almost went by me completely and then, a moment later, my mind went into reverse and I thought: no, I

24

don't think somehow that you will do that, my friend; but I might; I just might.

As a sort of test, I attempted to ignore the idea during the days ahead. I found that I could not. It both lingered and persisted. However, I kept my own counsel as far as the distaff were concerned. I was not about to paint myself into any corners. Feeling rather foolish, I began to browse amongst the books on farming in the U.S.I.S. library. The section did not run to much beyond the works of the late Louis Bromfield. All agricultural neophytes should be warned that these are dangerous books; dangerous because they make farming sound so idyllic. They do so because Bromfield genuinely loved farming and was good at it. Together, he and I tramped the fields of his Ohio farm. We increased our yields and replaced top soil by using cover crops. And we experimented with something called kudzu vine. I am sure that I was the only man dreaming about such matters from a bench in the Piazza Navona or while strolling on the Celio in the hush of dusk. I frequently found myself laughing at these daydreams. Still, there was a curious sensation of health attendant upon them. The terrible fears of a future dictated purely by circumstance receded to a manageable distance.

I was fascinated that the idea of farming should be able to possess me. My experience of farms and farming was slight. As a boy, during summers spent on the island in Lake Ontario where my maternal Grandfather maintained a summer home, I had worked with the threshing crews occasionally, providing, I am sure, more of a hindrance than a help. That island was so bucolic, so far outside the streams of change that, even in the thirties, the horse and buggy was still the staple of transportation. Each evening, one of my tasks was to fetch the milk from a farm about a mile away. And there were pleasant memories of sitting in the farmer's cool milking barn while he and his daughter hand-milked their twenty cows, occasionally pausing to squirt a stream of milk into the mouth of some waiting barnyard cat. But I did not—indeed, knew not how to participate in the milking. I liked the farmers on the island but they considered me, as I did them, inhabitants of another world. My grandfather was aloof and autocratic and scarcely paused to speak with the natives as his chauffeur-

25

driven car took him to and from the ferry which served the island. A certain distance between us and the locals was generally preserved. No, there was certainly nothing in the past to explain my present preoccupation.

Exhausting Louis Bromfield, I gave thought to a more serious quest for information. Rome, happily enough, is a fecund source of farming lore, due to the permanent presence there of the United Nations Food and Agricultural Organization. It is located in a lovely, gleaming-white Tufa building near the Terme di Caracalla. I went there one day and was passed from hand to hand until I fetched up in the office of a gentleman I shall call Dr. Black. He was a courteous man, a North Carolinian who had been associated with agricultural schools of various southern universities. I hardly looked the part of an aspiring farmer and by the time I had given him a brief resume of my past and told him what was on my mind, I am inclined to think the suspicion that he was faced with a madman must have crossed his mind. However, as I was to learn often during the coming years, one of the endearing qualities about Southerners is that they do not care very much whether you are crazy or not as long as your manners are passable. Dr. Black also assumed that my interest in the subject was that of an amateur, a potential gentleman farmer who would never have to depend upon farming for his living. My view of the situation at that point was, to be frank, roughly the same; the slight flirtation I had begun with farming was based upon a hope that I could use it as a means of taking up the slack while I cracked the literary case.

During the coming months, I would meet with Dr. Black, a number of times; he was of inestimable service to me. First of all because he took—or, at least, pretended to take—me seriously. Second, because he led me to become specific in my thinking about the general area in which I might consider farming and the precise type of farming which I might do. Because of his own experience, he was, of course, most knowledgeable about the southeast, an area comprised roughly of Virginia, North Carolina, West Virginia and Tennessee. He was the only mentor available to me for the moment and I, quite naturally, took on his coloration. I began to confine my dream-farming to that general area, particularly to North Carolina, a state whose beauties and agricultural

26

potentialities he extolled. As to the specific type of farming he felt most feasible: it was the raising of beef cattle. In this, I later discovered, he was wrong. But for the moment, his word was the gospel; I farmed away happily, raising my annual crop of calves on the Palatine hill and along the Via del Babuino. In my saner moments, the truly preposterous aspects of the situation brought forth some rather hollow laughter. Nevertheless the scheme was difficult to dislodge from my head.

A rough general plan began to outline itself. Clearly it was madness to think of returning to the United States and immediately set about buying a farm—even if I could somehow manage to find the money to do so, an eventuality of which I was by no means certain. Both as an earnest of faith and as a way of finding out some things, I was going to have to find some sort of farm employment. Just how I could set about finding a farmer amiable and eccentric enough to take on a thirty year old, one-book novelist with nary a callous to his hands, was a question into which I was not yet prepared to inquire too closely. At the same time, I knew that the amount of time during which I could confine my thoughts to my imagination was limited; my Calvinistic heritage instructed me that more lives are lost through dreaming than in any other way. I also suspected that the exposure of my dreams to the women of my house would provide some sort of test; women are stern judges of possibility. Therefore I hung back from that moment, hesitant and afraid.

One day in the Cafe Greco off the Piazzi di Spagna, I bumped into Lisette O. down from Milan on a modeling assignment. In spite of their fundamental incapacity to get along together, she and my friend O'Hara had lived together during most of the preceding three years, joined by God knows what sexual or intellectual affinity. Lisette was a wild likeable soul, one of those who are incapable of taking thought for the morrow. Half Polish, half South African, born in Penang, she was a beautiful girl then at the very top of her career as a mannequin and about to begin the downhill slide. She was surprised to find Dorothy and me in Rome and I invited her to come to our flat the next day for drinks. Then, on a whim, I swore her to secrecy, and told her I was playing around with the idea of returning home to be a farmer. She received the idea with perfect seriousness and I knew that, by showing my hand even to Lisette, I had moved one step closer to reality.

It was almost as if, in meeting Lisette, the signal had been given for the party to begin; the last party we would enjoy for many years. For Frank O'Connor telephoned the next morning. I asked him to come along for drinks that afternoon. Frank sounded uncharacteristically worried and said he had something he wished to speak to me about.

He arrived the next afternoon looking rather distraught. Lisette was already there. The two had never met although each had heard much of the other from O'Hara. It was immediately apparent that Lisette was interested and her character, mixture of courtesan and adventuress that it was, did not allow her to dissimulate. Frank, on the other hand, was brusque and preoccupied. He passed her by with a brief how are you, and crossed to my mother to extend his full range of courtliness. My mother always found Frank disquieting and always succumbed to his charm. Whenever they met, she would view him with an air of distinct disapproval which would disappear rapidly as he drew her into the net of his complicated Irish nonsense.

He soon withdrew with me into a corner and produced an imposing looking document which he gave me to read. It was a letter from some California lawyer advising him of his recent inheritance of a huge tract of land in that state. Beyond the fact that he was most certainly rich enough to live on a rather grand scale without working, his finances were a mystery to me. As mine must have been to him—for his distraught quality, it turned out, stemmed from a temporary need for money. I explained that we were hanging on by our fingernails. I asked him if his situation was serious and he replied that it was nothing that time would not cure. He sighed then and said, "Two thousand a month going out and fifteen hundred coming in; there's some kind of a bind coming." With that, he shrugged off his cares and we spent a couple of pleasant hours. He and Lisette left together finally, having clearly reached some sort of understanding. We made arrangements to meet the next day. Lisette had to return to Milan the next day to fulfill some modeling assignment. During the next two weeks, she would bombard him with telegrams.

And so a round of gaiety began which lasted two weeks. Frank's traveling companions were stellar examples of what he usually referred to as "my set": Lord R., an English novelist of the middle reaches and his friend David, an aging writer of travel books, whose debauched appearance was such that it suggested purity. There was little in the world that his hooded old eyes had not seen and nothing in which he had believed. Like many very corrupt men, he was almost wholly without ego. I liked him and never ceased to marvel at a world which could have brought him and me into social juxtaposition.

I cannot defend the pleasure I once took in the company of unabashed hedonists; it is simply a fact. I suppose it lies in the time-tested attraction of opposites; for I am, in spite of frequent attempts to avoid it, one of those who believes that the work of the world must be done.

One night, dining at Ranieri, I told Frank the story of the smart pills. He complained bitterly, saying that "a prepared story is an abomination in the sight of God". Nevertheless, I persisted. No habitual teller of jokes, I agreed with him; yet this was perhaps a bit more than a joke. It seemed apposite to the present:

A poor southern man is in the habit of frequenting the local cafe. There, nightly with awe and wonder, he watches a very rich man cavort. Consumed with envy for the other's big car, fine clothes and beautiful girls, the poor man finally screws up his courage and approaches his nemesis. "Man," he says, "tell me somep'n, whut makes you so smart?" The rich man takes a pill from a case, swallows it, and disdainfully replies, "I'm smart, man, 'cause I take an occasional smart pill?" Intrigued, the poor man says, "How much you gettin' fo' them pills?" He is told they cost fifty cents apiece and, after due deliberation, he pays over half a dollar and receives a large brown pill which he swallows. Making a terrible face, he says, "Man, that is one bad tastin' pill and man, I don't feel one bit smartuh." "Well man," the pill purveyor says with even greater contempt, "you don' get no smartuh on jus' one li'l ole pill; you gotta eat a few". Whereupon the poor man digs down into his overalls, brings up all the money he has, which is two fifty, and buys five pills. By the time he gets the last one down, he is sweating and his eyes are watering with the effort. "Man," he says, "These pills is jus' awful tastin'; why, they taste to me jus' like rabbit shit". "Well, there you are, man," the pill salesman says triumphantly, "you is gettin' smart already".

As my wife and I went the rounds with Frank and his companions, I began to get the same insight as the poor man in the story. Too much laughter, too much food and too much drink had the predictable effect of making my dream about a farm assume a greater urgency. As Frank's time in Rome became shorter, I was torn between a desire to see as much of him as possible and a horrified disgust at our wastrel ways. The night before he left, we reneged and remained at home. The drunken phone calls importuning us to join them began late in the evening. They came from a place which only Frank could have discovered. It was called, "Bob's Flying Restaurant" and was located, God help me, in the main railroad station. It was the name of the place, of course, which so bemused Frank. He had developed an entire fantasy about "Bob" whom he had never laid eyes on. In response to any quandry, Frank was likely to say, "We'd better see Bob about this". This last night, the phone calls finally became so oppressive that I got angry and told him he was waking up the baby and everybody else in the house. I hung up to a hurt silence. A few minutes later, the phone rang again and I went wearily to answer it prepared to deliver a real blast. "Listen," he said in tones of great portent, "I've got something to tell you: Bob's a wop." I hung up, laughing.

With a mixed feeling of relief and sadness, I picked Frank up the next day to see him off. The first person I saw as I entered the lobby of his hotel was Lisette. Beautifully turned out as always, she was clutching a small parcel. I asked her where on earth she was going and she replied that she was going back to Tangier with Frank.

"What's that?" I said, pointing at the parcel.

"My luggage."

"What's in it?"

"The damnedest looking nightdress you've ever seen."

David, the old writer and I took them to the station in a

30

taxi. Never had I watched a train pull out with such a mixture of pleasure and sadness. David and I rode the first part of the short trip back to the Piazza de Spagna in silence. Then I told him about my intention of becoming a farmer. He said a curious thing; one of those remarks from semi-strangers which hang on and provide strength in times of weakness.

"Oh, I should think you'd always be all right," he said, "after all, you're a man of spirit."

I had a letter from O'Hara in London shortly after that. He was planning to return to the States; he said; so was my brother. Darroch, it seemed, had already returned—to St. Louis, of course— beginning again his odd, compulsive hegira between St. Louis and New York. It would go on for many years. At this point, however, I had the feeling that Darroch was giving thought to fulfilling some of his primary obligations; he was, after all, the father of a child by Kate, who had waited in St. Louis for the preceding three years in the hope that he would return changed enough so that they could take up the threads of their lives together. It was not a forlorn hope because Kate is not a forlorn woman; misplaced, is probably the proper word. While O'Hara's letter dwelt much upon these matters, I did not then realize the passionate interest in their resolution which gripped him.The hallmark of O'Hara's mind is not deviousness but complexity, the ability to project events to an extent where they become abstract and have no real relationship with the original premises of their projection. "It's always stranger than you think," was a dictum he was fond of repeating. True enough; but it is dangerous knowledge to support unmatched by faith.

Throughout O'Hara's letters and those of my brother during this time, ran a thread of preoccupation with the workings and the meaning of our own country. Our basic attitude towards America—inherited from such disparate sources as Hemingway, Henry Miller, Mencken and Mark Twain—was one of fundamental scorn; that it was a pretty good joke. What few pitiful efforts we had made to meet our country halfway had been such ludicrous failures that we were prone to believe all the hope which American proffers with such profligacy contains about as much real sustenance as a cone full of cotton candy at a country fair. I could not then see what arrant nonsense this was. I could not even recognize, for

31

example, the latitude we had all been granted in the realm of choice. None of us was rich, yet all of us had rattled around the world without restraint to our hearts' desires. None of us was yet capable of recognizing that we were children of a country which offers its citizens a degree of freedom unparalleled in the history of the world. And none of us was yet capable of realizing that that lack of recognition was tantamount to the invention of a personal tyranny. Our minds worked like Rube Goldberg machines, ceaselessly trying to invent a world which would conform to them, rather than deal with the one that was there. Fly now, pay later, has a moral and a spiritual backlash as well as an economic one.

The plans of both O'Hara and my brother were nebulous and vague. They talked of going to Washington, D.C., but exactly what they intended doing there was not clear. The vagueness of their intentions, however, had the effect of making me concentrate upon turning my plan of being a farmer into a reality.

A month or so later, a rather cheerful thing happened: my novel was sold to the paperbacks for five thousand dollars of which sum I got half. It doesn't seem like much now, but it was more money than I had had in a lump in my life, and—more important—it was money I had earned from writing. On the negative side, it was a bit of a two-edged sword, strengthening my feeling that I could approach farming in the spirit of amateurism.

At any rate, the moment eventually arrived when I decided to lay down my hand. Half prepared to be hooted to death with laughter, I announced to my wife that I was seriously thinking of trying to be a farmer. Her reaction was the single one that could have taken me by surprise. She did not bat an eyelid—her only question was: when do we start?

We sailed for Naples a few weeks later.

CHAPTER III

By the time our boat arrived in New York, my brother and O'Hara had fulfilled their plan and had rented a house on the outskirts of Washington, D.C. It had been arranged that we would go there after our arrival and Dorothy and the baby would stay with them while I scoured my circumscribed area of the south looking for a job on a farm.

We remained in the environs of New York City for a few days first, staying with my wife's sister in New Jersey. There were a few pressing administrative problems to take care of, notably the purchase of an automobile. Trying as always to strike a balance between the demands of style and practicability, I bought a splendid Ford station wagon, one of the last if not the last, model to be made with a body of genuine wood. It antedated those steel monsters designed to appeal to the burgeoning rash of suburban euphoria and pleased me mightily. It was, alas, doomed to come to a grotesque, comedic end, but for the moment, we were content. Luckily—as I did not know a tappet from a piston—it was sound; its previous master seemingly having been a gentle one.

I spent one rather dreamlike day in New York City. I went alone, Dorothy having elected to remain and gossip with her sister. I made arrangements to have lunch with my old friends, Pennebaker and Douglas Wood, at a restaurant in the West Fifties. But first I fulfilled the ostensible business reason for the day; to pay a call upon Hiram Haydn, the editor of my novel. He was still at Bobbs-Merrill then but would move shortly to Random House. He had brought on a star turn in William Styron's first novel, "Lie Down in Darkness" and his publishing career was very much in the ascendant. Our meeting was not a success; I was truculent and unsure of myself as

33

one is prone to be with a still-undigested failure under one's belt. And, foolishly enough, I was somewhat prepared to blame Haydn for the failure of my book; one's subjective essence is a treacherous quality. We parted uneasily, Haydn assuring me that anything I did in the future would receive total consideration. He was politely interested, no more, in my plan to be a farmer. It was, I had discovered by then, a quest too far removed from what passes as reality, to interest others much. I suffered then from a fallacy which has still not been entirely rooted out: that my life is as interesting to others as it is to me. "Don't bother me," Frank O'Connor had said once when I was pestering him about his hopes, beliefs and dreams, "The only thing I know about people is that they think they're pretty good."

On the way to meet Penny and Douglas, I anticipated what would almost certainly be a bibulous luncheon by taking on a few drinks. I must confess that the city frightened and unnerved me. Its hardness and its frenetic energy had been forgotten during three years in Europe's softer, more ambivalent psychological climate. I remember that day turning to look at a pretty girl as she passed and, as a result, caroming into a fellow pedestrian approaching from the opposite direction. As I turned instinctively to apologize, his lips bared themselves in a snarl. I felt a flash of anger which passed away as soon as I looked into his eyes. They were wide with terror. It reassured me somehow that the farming quest was right and proper.

In that inhospitable frame of mind towards New York, I came to the restaurant where we had arranged to meet. It was dusty, empty, obviously defunct. Is this a joke, I wondered, have I got the place wrong? Then I saw with relief that there was a message to me inscribed in the dust of the window; come to G's, same place uptown one block. I obeyed and found them gathered around a table. It was a happy reunion. With them was Douglas' fiancée, a magazine editor with whom I was not acquainted. They would marry and then divorce. Douglas would die as would she. And Penny would achieve a portion of the stardom we all sought.

Those things were far away and problematical that day. It was a long, wet and cheerful meal. Finally, Douglas and his girl went away. Penny, then working for an advertising agency and not taking it too seriously decided that a return to his office was unthinkable; the day was shot. We decided to visit our old friend, Barbara Hale, then convalescing from her second bout of TB in an uptown hospital. We took a case of beer with us, smuggling it up the back stairs. The visit was not a success. We were too loud and Barbara did not find me sufficiently vehement about Senator McCarthy. Eventually, we were asked to leave by a crisply starched nurse who found our boisterousness unsuitable to the sick room. On the way out, we stopped to see my friend Mac from Tangier. He was concealing his true nature and fearful that I would make some ribald reference to his pederasty. "They're not on to me here," he said glancing nervously around. (I could not help thinking of an afternoon he and I had once spent drinking together in the small Moroccan town of Berrechid—known as, Bearshit, of course, by all English speakers. Within an hour of sitting down at our cafe table, Mac had been surrounded by small Berber boys. "They were on to me in a matter of minutes," he said, his eyes twinkling happily.)

The next day we drove to Washington in our splendid wooden car, the baby cooing away happily in the back. Without too much difficulty, we found the house that O'Hara and my brother had rented. It was rather a charming house, located in Maryland on the periphery of suburbia not far from the banks of the old Cumberland Canal.

The week I spent in that house before taking the road south was not what I would call a happy time. There was one fistfight of a rather half-assed variety from which I emerged with a black eye. Now, I believe the strife which came to the surface was territorial in origin; the presence of Dorothy and the baby excited it; particularly in O'Hara, for whom life without a woman was not only physically difficult but symbolic of defeat. It was not that O'Hara was bothered by any imperative need to possess Dorothy physically (although he certainly would not have been averse to such a thing). It was rather that the very trust she granted me filled him with despair; it was the one basic, all important gift which his various women had always withheld from him and which I believe it is safe to say they always will. I remember one brief interchange while we were staying with O'Hara in Maryland which threw a harsh light on his interior workings. He was attempting, with frequent success, to get at me through questions aimed at Dorothy and couched in tones of weary contempt. "What *is* it that you see in him?" he asked her one day. Her answer, given after due deliberation was: "He's fun to sleep beside." O'Hara grew silent and, a moment later, left the room. He was, above all things, precise in his use of the language. Had she said, "sleep with", he would have hooted with laughter and considered his ploy to have been a total success. But in her use of the word "beside", Dorothy reminded him that woman's love is rooted in trust and, in doing so, laid bare the essential cancer of his being: the fear that he would never be loved by a woman. O'Hara was wise enough to know that a woman who does not rest easily by a man's side is planning either her own escape or his destruction.

Have I loved O'Hara? Perhaps it is one of the questions I am trying to answer in setting down this record. Shared experience is a strong glue and we have been through much together. He did not meet Dorothy until shortly after our marriage. We traveled then to San Francisco where O'Hara was living. It was our intention to settle in that city but somehow the chemistry was not right. One either believes in California or one does not. My own feelings about it have always been perfectly expressed by Darroch's terse judgement: "It's too far away". Admittedly, we did not try terribly hard to find a foothold in San Francisco; when O'Hara (with whom we were staying) brought up the idea of going to Mexico, we fell in with it. We had wild plans of finding employment there and settling down. None of which worked out. It was a trip which ended up leading us far afield.

O'Hara, Dorothy and I had set out for Mexico during midwinter of 1949. Our combined assets totalled about two hundred dollars plus the decrepit Ford convertible in which Dorothy and I had driven west. Mexico threw us off as definitely as had San Francisco. The letters to such dignitaries as Diego Rivera with which O'Hara had armed himself produced nothing beyond polite invitations to tea. After two weeks, our money nearly gone, we streaked for the border, frightened lest we be stranded in that violent, colourful land whose language we did not understand.

It was during those days and the days which lay ahead that I took my first fumbling steps towards being married. The

ceremony had taken place two months before, but that formality is, at best, only a symbolic beginning. I marvel still at
the faith which could lead my wife to place her life in the
hands of a man whose nearest approach to an intellectual
position was anarchy and whose announced determination
was never to work another day at a steady job. I had told her
of my desire to be some kind of a writer of books and, in all
honesty, I felt a strong measure of confidence in my ability to
do so. The specific evidence of such a bent, however, was
lacking. But my wife's childhood—so awful to me that I still
stand in awe of it—had provided her with a lodestone of
character which has brought me back from many wrong turn-
ings. Her mother dead when she was nine, her father a
hopeless drunken derelict, she had been wholly on her own
since she was sixteen, earning her way through the small
Lutheran college she attended, with jobs as a waitress. That
strange place (attended also by Fitzgerald's Gatsby) attempted to inculcate a standard of moral rigidity so high as to
be almost abstract. (Girls—and I do not joke about this—
were earnestly enjoined by the Dean of Women to turn all
photographs of their boyfriends to the wall while undres-
sing.) At the time when O'Hara and Dorothy and I set out
upon our travels, she was a human being whose potentialities
were greatly obscured by prejudices and rigidity. O'Hara,
nihilistic by nature and anarchistic by design, had been pal-
ling around with people like Henry Miller when my wife was
toting in the blue-plate special. Being a beautiful girl and
aware of it, she was beyond any real harm from him, but,
from the first, he poked constant and merciless fun at her.
Frequently angry with him to a point of violence, she nevertheless used his knowledge and intelligence as a grindstone to
whet her own. As he became aware of her ability to keep the
gold and throw away the dross of their conflict, a respect for
her was born which rapidly became friendship. By the time
we reached New Orleans on our feckless flight from Mexico,
both solidarity and cameraderie existed among us. It was a
good thing, for some terribly hard and terribly funny times
lay ahead of us.

I fear that the impression I am giving of us is that of Jack
Kerouac people; pre-beat, stone-age hippies. Nothing could
be further from the truth; there was not a bohemian bone in

any of our bodies. The area of unreality in which we operated was more dangerous than that. And yet, I am still somehow sympathetic to it. Like so many of my immediate generation, we were all Ernest Hemingway's children. We wanted the festival at Pamplona for the first course and the Nobel prize for the second. We didn't know yet that dessert would be the business end of a shotgun shoved into the mouth, but I imagine we would have shrugged it off if we had. Our desire to escape the strait-jacket of our middle-class past was so desperate that we had stopped to formulate no values for the future. That, I now believe, was the process in which we were engaged; the process in which all mankind is engaged. Blake's axiom, "If the fool would persist in his folly he would become wise," may contain the kernel of the only truth there is.

Penniless when we reached New Orleans, we did a thing which now seems totally lacking in common sense but which, according to the peculiar arithmetic we were then employing, did not seem remarkable. We sold the car for 175 dollars and paid one month's rent on a magnificent flat in the Quarter. Since the monthly rent was also 175 dollars, this left us with nothing but the sparse gleanings of pockets and pocketbooks, with which to eat. We began a search for work but it was not forthcoming. An appeal to my family brought only a stony rejection; the fecklessness of the preceding few months had been remarked. My stock in that direction, never more than moderately high, had sunk out of sight. O'Hara had had no concourse with his family for many years. Dorothy had only one tappable aunt who alas, had been tapped already from San Francisco.

O'Hara and I turned out to be pitiful failures at finding work. My wife, more adept at survival by far, eventually found a dreadful job whose precise details I have always held at arm's length. It had something to do with selling coffee or tea. While we waited out her first paycheck, I experienced real hunger for the first time in my life. It was while I was seeking work, and I became faint on a street in downtown New Orleans; faint and so dizzy that I had to sit down on a fireplug. When it happened, I was laughing at myself but the situation nevertheless seemed so desperate that I left my fireplug and went to the nearest Air Force recruiting office to inquire into the possibility of getting my commission back. A year later, the Korean war would have begun, and such a request would have been granted with celerity and dispatch; for the moment, thank God, I was rejected.

O'Hara had convinced me that, barring all else, we would be able to get work as longshoremen, a calling he had followed sporadically in San Francisco. But we were not in San Francisco; we were in the South and in the South, nothing is more suspicious than a white man with the wrong accent and a troublesome veneer of cultural pretension. As longshoremen, we were a total bust.

The hilarious evening of my wife's first payday arrived. We were a long way from starving but we were dammed hungry. With great anticipation, we bought a huge package of stewing meat and vegetables. O'Hara, who fancied himself as something of a cook, volunteered to cook the stew; Dorothy and I breathed over his shoulder with jealous anxiety. At a crucial moment, O'Hara fumbled the salt cannister into the stew pot. Momentary rage and sadness swept over us all. We were on the brink of mutual recriminations when the humor of the situation struck home. Under normal conditions, the stew would have been so salty as to be uneatable; as things were, we wolfed it down, returning to the pot for thirds and fourths.

Our search for employment finally led O'Hara and me to the nadir of experience: door-to-door salesman. Can anyone really call himself an American, I wonder, who has not dipped into that grotesque world? Deciding to take this momentous step, O'Hara and I dressed ourselves carefully in our best suits and reported to the place indicated in the newspaper advertisement. During the walk there, we laughed and joked with sardonic bravado but each, deep in his heart, felt that he was taking a definitive downward step on the scale of human value. Our firm was called The Realsilk Corporation; our wares: ladies stockings. The assembled applicants were a seedy lot—many, I am sure, driven there by complex sexual fantasies of favors casually bestowed by randy housewives. I myself confess to having allowed my mind such salacious play. About twenty of us assembled in a sort of classroom, the air thick with fear. Each face wore the studied unconcern of a man in the waiting room of a whorehouse; each pair of shifty eyes betrayed the knowledge that their owner's present position was somewhere near the bottom of the heap. Embarrassingly enough, our jocularity dried up; I felt my own eyes grow shifty and looked over to find O'Hara licking his lips apprehensively. The strange virus of competition infected the room. Would we be chosen? Or would we be rejected and so know that we had been beaten by better men? A rapid, cursory screening process ensued. We all breathed more easily as a few obvious derelicts were sent away, reassured in the human way because we were not at the *very* bottom of the heap. We were to undergo three days of intensive training in the peddling of our wares. Our mentor now entered, confident and assured—a man who clearly knew the secrets of the universe. A slight sigh of awe swept across the room; men reduced to such a position as ours can believe in anything.

And, in truth, those fellows who muster the beaten and the botched to move their wares are not without interest. Terrible top sergeants of a nether world, masters of certain rude psychological techniques, they know how to instill a spurious hope, fan the coals of dying avarice and generally foment a highly temporary Kamikaze spirit of do or die. Generic descendants of W. C. Fields and the snake oil pitchman, they are American to the core. Our man spent the balance of the day painting a rosy picture of our futures; the sky, he frequently told us, is the limit. In spite of any particle of common sense that I possessed, I found myself tempted to believe. As we walked home that afternoon, O'Hara and I were subdued and spoke of other things, each nurturing his own private Horatio Alger dream. Many great men had, after all, begun at the bottom.

Our training proceeded and our euphoric glow continued warm; we rose early and shaved carefully anxious lest we miss a single particle of the wisdom being proffered us. Much reference was made to our "sales kits" which we would receive on the final day of our training. With the aid of such a magic box of tricks, it was intimated, no housewife's door would be proof against our assault. Certain fundamental techniques were covered: the foot in the door, the pearly white smile which melts the heart. On several occasions, I surprised a fellow trainee as he practiced a sickly grin. The virus of competition was carefully nurtured by our instructor; vague, rather sinister references were made to fundamental inequalities of talent and determination which existed among us. These, we were warned, would determine the apportionment of "territories;" a good man would get a good territory, an average man an average territory; the dregs (among which I hoped desperately I would not be listed) would receive territories spoken of in such terms of gloom that one could only imagine some terrible slum wrapped in penury, vice and violence. One frequently heard such remarks as, "God," I hope I get a good territory," during the hourly breaks in which we smoked a cigarette. Hope filled the room along with a certain miasma of suspicion; we were, after all, men who were preparing to vie for prizes. That dank sea of McGuffey's Reader cliches which exists in the subconscious of every American, rose to engulf us; all early birds got every worm; for the rest, defeat, despair and deserved oblivion. O'Hara and I were cool towards each other; we might turn out to be men of differing caliber—in which case, of course, an adjustment in our mutual regard would have to be effected. Each night, as we crept off to study our instruction manuals, my wife examined us with an air of wonderment.

Finally, the day of graduation arrived. We sat breathless with anticipation as our instructor announced in portentous tones that the assignment of "territories" would begin. My heart sank as O'Hara's was the first name called. Green with envy, my heart dark with bitterness, I watched O'Hara advance to receive his accolade. His face wore the dazed, fulfilled look of a successful mountain climber.

"O'Hara" the instructor said in stentorian tones, "I like the spirit you've shown here; I like the cut of your jib." He paused then to let the full portent of his words assume effect before saying, "I'm giving you the Garden District for your territory". With a brisk, definitive gesture, the instructor planted a large green flag in O'hara's lapel which bore the legend: "All Signs Ahead Say Go". Clutching his dreadful looking fibre sample case, O'Hara strode from the room, his step firm with determination. My turn came soon; the ritual was repeated. I left to board the streetcar which would take me to my "territory".

My "territory" turned out to be a neighborhood with such a massive lack of distinction that it remains in my memory only as an amorphous blob of small, squarish ranch houses—

what O'Hara had always called fuck boxes. During the long street car ride, I had rehearsed my recently-mastered techniques: the knock, the foot in the door, the pearly white smile and the announcement that I was bearing "a free gift," a small cardboard kit of darning wool worth pennies. The same combination of fear and anticipation gripped my bowels that I had felt on the way to bomb Cologne; I would surely triumph.

Three hours later, I sat disconsolately in a bar nursing a glass of beer that I could ill afford. The pages of my order book were virgin and unmarked; I had not made a single transaction. Furthermore, I had been chivvied about and warned off the premises by assorted drabs and unfriendly householders until my spirit had finally snapped. Even my "free gift" had been spurned in most cases; on only two occasions had I been able to dispose of one. I could see no comic side to things; failure, bitter failure, was my lot. The boy who had sat on the old dock on Amherst Island in Canada and dreamed of conquering the world as he watched the sunset, sat now in this dingy bar with his sample case at his feet, and faced the fact that he could not even sell a pair of socks. Worst of all, that concommitant of failure—fear of being passed-by by better men—haunted my mind. By now, I was certain, vast fleets of trucks had taken to the roads laden with socks to fulfill O'Hara's successful sales contracts in the Garden District. Sadly, I left the bar to board the streetcar for home.

The emptiness of our flat depressed me further. I had half-hoped I might find O'Hara there, wallowing in a like condition. No joy, I was alone gripped by the guilt of a small boy playing hookey in an empty house. Unable to stand the sight of my dreadful sample case, I hid it under the bed and then lay down, one arm across my eyes, to compose self-justification for my failure: a half hour passed which did not ease my mind. Then I heard a heavy step at the bottom of the stairs which led up the outside of the house to our flat. My mind was suddenly flooded with a wild surge of hope. I listened carefully to the sound of these unknown feet. They were slow and leaden; the tread of a doomed and despairing man. I held my breath, my hope growing as a key was inserted in the lock. A moment later, O'Hara appeared in the doorway of the bedroom. His jaunty flag bearing its hopeful message of "All Signs Ahead Say Go" drooped from his lapel in a dispirited angle; his sample case dangled from one lank arm. We stared at each other for a long moment before he said, "Nothing?"

"Nothing," I replied, feeling better already.

"Not even one pair?" he said, his eyes beginning to gleam.

"Not even one pair. You?"

"Nothing. God, it was awful."

We began to laugh simultaneously; it was laughter of such intensity that I was rolling around on the bed and O'Hara was clutching the doorjamb for support. Each time it threatened to fade, one of us would recall a particularly noisesome incident from the day's experience and our laughter would begin again.

My wife was much relieved upon her return home that evening to find that our foray into the world of commerce was ended. Whatever else we were, she had never doubted the fact that we would come to a bad end as door-to-door salesmen.

The end of our meteoric careers with the Realsilk Corporation signalled the beginning of a period of acute demoralization which, understandably, would soon begin to communicate itself to Dorothy. Our efforts to find work became more and more desultory and finally ceased altogether. The days passed dreamily, ruled by increasing sloth. Our moral state was inexcusable. O'Hara and I rose late and passed the balance of the day playing chess, reading novels and strolling about the quarter, involved in long discussions designed to prop up our sagging egos. Partly as a supplement to Dorothy's pitifully small wages, partly as a rather petulant gesture of defiance, we took up the practice of petty pilferage. O'Hara was the possessor of a long black overcoat. He had introduced passages into it which led directly from the pockets into the lining. We would sally forth for our afternoon stroll around the Quarter and return clanking with contraband. It was only a matter of time before we would get caught.

It happened, in fact, on the same day that we had a terribly curious encounter. At that time—and for that matter, today—I had little acquaintance among the world of the celebrated. This was not true of O'Hara. During his years in Carmel, he had moved among the greater and lesser literary lights of Carmel and the Big Sur; people such as Henry Miller and Frieda Lawrence. He also had some slight acquaintance with the English critic and novelist, Cyril Connolly, a fact which has bearing on what I am about to relate.

Both possessed of vague, inarticulate literary yearnings and friends since boyhood, O'Hara and I shared a mutual and passionate admiration for certain writers. High on the list was the late Evelyn Waugh. It is an admiration—on my part, at least—which has not diminished through the years. I have read and re-read everything by him and about him. The concensus of opinion among the works which throw light on his personality maintains that he was a sour, misogynistic and unapproachable man. One of the few people who knew him well and wrote about him, and does not take this view, is his son, Auberon, who remembers his father as an affectionate and satisfactory parent. I am sure Waugh did not suffer fools gladly but, for that matter, who does? I believe he was the pre-eminent comic genius of the century and a comic genius, living, as he does, in an upside down world, is bound to be a bit eccentric and ingrown. But I am inclined to believe Auberon Waugh is closer to the truth about his father than many others. Our meeting with Waugh in New Orleans was exceedingly odd.

As I recall, it was on Bourbon Street. Walking along, engaged in some pointless discussion, O'Hara and I were distracted by the appearance of a very exotic couple approaching us about a block away.

"My God," O'Hara said, "it's Waugh."

And indeed it was. We examined him with great curiosity as he approached. He was a figure as ill-suited to the French Quarter of New Orleans as one can possibly imagine. Waugh was, of course, a sort of dandy; his style was an odd mixture of Winston Churchill and the Duke of Windsor. He wore a square black bowler hat and a wide and very loud raglan greatcoat of horse-blanket tweed. A walking stick swung from one hand and he seemed to radiate an aura of the past he so passionately preferred to the present. He was, in a word, an exceedingly forbidding figure. So forbidding that I could not believe my ears when O'Hara said, "Let's brace him". Then, I thought, what the hell, if O'Hara is crazy enough to do it, why not?

By that time, we were past them. I was so busy looking at Waugh that I paid little attention to his wife and I remember her now only vaguely as a rather reserved lady dressed in black with a definite twinkle in her eye. Waugh took no notice of our scrutiny, staring stonily ahead as he walked. Having taken our insane decision, the problem was to put ourselves in a position where we (or rather O'Hara—I was frightened to death of the entire business) could accost Waugh without seeming more blatant than necessary. Accordingly, we abandoned our shaky dignity, turned right, and scampered back along the next street parallel to Bourbon Street. When we emerged back on Bourbon Street once more, Waugh and his wife were approaching us as before, about a half block away. When the distance between us lessened to five feet, O'Hara spoke. I am still awed by his temerity. In a somewhat quavering voice, O'Hara said, "Mr. Waugh."

Waugh neither broke stride nor looked at us, simply raising one hand to his square bowler and saying, "Howdja do." But O'Hara was tenacious; he made one last desperate bid as Waugh had progressed to a point some five or six feet away.

"Mr. Waugh," O'Hara called, "We have mutual friends."

It did the trick. Or, to be more precise, it was the thin edge of the wedge, for I am inclined to think Waugh's reply was intended to brush us off and put us in our place. At O'Hara's call, he stopped, turned, and fixed him with a very steely eye indeed. His reply was guaranteed to frost a Polar bear: "Indeed," he said, "How are they?" By this time, poor O'Hara was reeling like a punch-drunk fighter. My own inclination was to cut our losses and run. But O'Hara was game to the end. "Yes," he said, "Cyril Connolly."

I will always wonder why Waugh decided to relent. Certainly the mention of Connolly's name made him pause to look at us. Having looked, the artist's unconscious process of screening phenomena must have taken over. Two rather odd fish had swum into his net and he was going to have a leisurely look at them. We chatted for a few minutes after having exchanged names and having been introduced to his wife. He was, he told us, lecturing in various American cities, under Roman Catholic auspices. I could scarcely believe my ears when I heard O'Hara ask the Waughs if they would like to come by our flat that evening for a drink. I was even more

45

appalled when they accepted with obvious pleasure. We parted cheerfully, having made a date for six o'clock.

"Are you crazy?" I said to O'Hara after the Waughs had gone, "We have no money, no drink, no glasses to drink out of except jelly glasses, and you've just invited Evelyn Waugh and his wife around for cocktails."

O'Hara counseled calm and suggested we take inventory. A careful search of all our pockets produced exactly one dollar and seventy five cents."

"Sherry," O'Hara said, "It'll have to be domestic Sherry."

In view of the endless wine snobbery in *"Brideshead Revisited,"* it was an appalling prospect. Still, we had no choice; it was the best we could possibly do. We discussed trying to steal some whiskey or gin and vermouth but our nerves were not up to it; from petty theft to the stealing of liquor would be graduation to an ionosphere of crime. Glasses, materials for some sort of canapes, we could pilfer, but we were pretty well stuck with domestic Sherry.

Our one dollar and seventy-five cents barely covered a bottle of mediocre New York State Sherry. We deposited this in the flat and hurried off to downtown New Orleans to complete our "shopping".

All went smoothly at first. Some of the objects we needed were unwieldy, however. We lifted half a dozen sherry glasses from a dime store and slowly accumulated such things as olives, crackers, caviar and a jar of paté. Flushed with success, we started home to prepare our party. It was then that we made a mistake.

As we passed a neighborhood store where we were in the habit of dealing, O'Hara suggested that we enter and have one last look around for delicacies which might appeal to our illustrious guests. We did so and as we browsed, we stopped by a display of soap. O'Hara asked me if we were not short of it and I replied that we were. He began loading up. Without looking at me, he suddenly said, "The guy saw me". "Put it back then," I whispered. He did so, and we discussed the problem *sotto voce*. We were both loaded with contraband but only I had things from this particular store in my pockets. O'Hara's loot was all from different sources. The proprietor was showing absolutely no interest in me but he was following O'Hara with an eagle eye. We decided that I should try to leave the store and I did so unmolested. From a doorway across the street, I watched as O'Hara approached the counter to pay for whatever token purchase we had made. After ringing up the single item, the shopkeeper said, "Now what else have you got in your pockets?"

"Nothing," O'Hara replied.

"Don't fool around, I saw you take something back there."

"The fact remains that I have nothing of yours in my pockets."

"Well, you can just turn them out and we'll see."

"What if I don't?"

"I'll call a cop."

O'Hara slowly began to empty his pockets. It was a wondrous collection including the six Sherry glasses but O'Hara was on firm ground. What he displayed was obvious contraband, but equally obviously, it had not been stolen from *this* store. The shopkeeper was understandably furious. They stared at one another for a moment, and then O'Hara began to replace the various objects in his pockets with great deliberation. At the end, he very nearly went too far. Before leaving the store, he turned and said, "You realize, of course, don't you, that you could get in very serious trouble, accusing people like this. I shouldn't let it happen again if I were you." The shopkeeper's ears began to glow but he held his silence as O'Hara swept loftily from the store. "Close call," he said when I joined him around the corner.

Knees knocking together, we hurried back to the flat to prepare our meager festivities. It was then about five o'clock and Waugh and his wife were due at six. Dorothy rarely reached home later than five-thirty. This day of all days, it turned out that she had been asked to stay on at her job for a couple of hours. Five-thirty came and went, and there was no sign of her.

Finally, the Waughs arrived. I am happy to say that he took the bitter pill of the domestic sherry like a man. Perhaps our carefully arranged platter of stolen hors d'oeuvres helped take the curse off it.

It is rather anti-climatic to report that I recall no memorable remarks falling from the master's lips. It was, however, a friendly, pleasant hour which we spent together; there was not a single sign of the novelist's fabled waspishness. I am

47

sure the poor devil was looking forward to tucking into a flock of dry martinis; the social pickings of a lecture tour under Catholic auspices, no matter how rewarding to the soul, cannot have been terribly exciting. However, he did not seem to have a bad time, working on the New York State Sherry with a will. I shuddered to think what he would have thought had he known the tawdry history of the viands upon which he munched. Clearly, he was making some sort of attempt to classify us, and, equally clearly, having little success. Two young men in a very stylish flat with no visible means of support; what were they? He finally gave up and resigned himself with literary small talk. I spent most of the hour chatting with Mrs. Waugh. It turned out that she was acquainted with some English people I had known during the war; this discovery gave us a more or less firm social footing upon which to proceed. Finally, the Sherry bottle near empty, they took their leave.

Ten minutes after their departure, my wife arrived home. She examined the husks and remainders of our little party and demanded to know what had been going on. We told her that Evelyn Waugh and his wife had stopped around for a drink. Her disbelief was immediate and sarcastic. It took us, until nearly midnight to convince her that we were telling the truth. When she finally did swallow it, she was understandably rather grumpy at having missed the fun.

The month for which we had paid our rent on our flat in the Quarter was now coming to an end. There was no possibility that we could scrape up another month's rent; Dorothy's wages were barely enough to keep us eating in a substandard way. Some sort of decision would have to be made as to the future. It seemed to fall upon my shoulders to make it. We were all apathetic but my apathy was not quite so pronounced as that of Dorothy and O'Hara. Finally, I persuaded them that we must try to get back to New York where I had some friends and Dorothy had a sister and there was some chance of finding work. We scraped up enough money for three bus tickets to New York. There was a bit left over which we invested in a great bunch of eggs which we hardboiled to keep us going during the long ride. It was a beaten and shameful trio that finally arrived in Manhattan. O'Hara and I were twenty-six years old, Dorothy twenty-four. The time had clearly arrived for me to pull up my socks and for Dorothy and me to cut loose from O'Hara. I remembered how, when O'Hara and I were about fifteen, his father had paid a call upon my father at his office, bearing the message that he felt O'Hara and I were a malignant influence on each other and that they should agree to keep us apart. My father pooh-poohed the idea, saying that he was fond of O'Hara and if O'Hara's father was not fond of me, that was his business. My father's reply was the more generous but I have often wondered whether O'Hara senior's proposal was not the more sentient.

Twenty-six is an age of great resilence; I did manage to get my socks pulled up. But there has never been any doubt in my mind that my wife was the glue which kept them there.

My brother had recently sailed for Italy where he was enjoying a carefree bohemian time in Rome living on the proceeds of a very successful little radio show packing firm he had started after the war. O'Hara was anxious to join him there. I introduced O'Hara to Barbara Hale, whose war with T.B. had not yet begun. Barbara was in possession of a small inheritance and at loose ends after the recent termination of a lengthy and disastrous love affair. Within two weeks of their meeting, Barbara and O'Hara embarked for Italy also. It worked out well for Dorothy and me; we inherited Barbara's flat on West 12th Street. By that time, I had got a job at a midtown advertising agency. The fecklessness—for us, at any rate—was at an end.

Before a year had passed, I had left the agency, had a novel on the stocks and a publisher's contract for it. (We too then sailed away for Europe.) It was during that year in New York that we became close friends with Kate. We also saw much of Darroch, who, prior to his departure for Europe, was living in a small flat in Chelsea, chasing the girls and trying also to establish himself as a writer.

It was a good year and a key year; the slight success of grasping a tenuous professionalism helped make it so. But by far the most important thing about that year was a marriage which finally became a reality. Crooked wheel that it is, we nevertheless gambled on it and won. We discovered that we could make it together.

CHAPTER IV

The essential strategy of my search for a farming job had been derived from my kindly advisor, Dr. Black, of FAO in Rome. He had given me various letters to specific people in the area I was going to comb but he had also warned me that these would be, in the main, people connected with the academic aspect of farming, who, he hoped would pass me on to others more directly concerned with its practical aspects. Dr. Black had told me that the County Agent would probably turn out to be my most valuable avenue of approach and in this he was correct.

For the benefit of those who, like myself a year earlier, do not know what a County Agent is, I had better provide a brief definition of his function. The County Agent is an employee of the United States Department of Agriculture who operates in an advisory capacity to the individual farmers of the county for which he is responsible. If he is a good County Agent, this means that he deals on a highly personal level with as many farmers as he can, encouraging a spirit of experiment and the adoption of modern farming techniques. At the time I set out on my farming quest, my attitude towards any manifestation of bureacracy was one of total disbelief and disdain. The limits of my experience stemmed from war, the advertising business and sitting around in barrooms; all, with the exception of the first, rather abstract pursuits to say the least. It had never really occurred to me, for example, that in the history of the world, my country was the first one of any size, scope and power to have cracked the fundamental case of feeding its citizens. The astonishing American agricultural success is due to numerous factors to be sure: the essential fecundity of the land, high incentives, mechanical sophistica-

51

tion and so on. However, it is also due in large measure to a functioning bureaucratic process which never loses sight of its objectives. Stated in the simplest possible way, its objectives are to produce the maximum amount of food using the minimum number of people who are getting paid the highest possible return for the labor in which they are engaged. I know nothing about the upper levels of that bureaucratic process; however, I do know from experience that it works very well at the grass-roots level. Which is to say, the level of the County Agent. In my travels around the South, I met many of these men and an astonishingly large percentage of them are enthusiastic, knowledgeable and energetic. And terribly helpful. It was one such who eventually put me onto my future employer, as strange a man as I have ever encountered.

All in all, I must have roamed through my four chosen southern states for about three weeks. It was a largely unconscious but essentially accurate instinct that had made me choose the South as the area in which I intended to settle. The reason is a very simple one: the South is—or was— economically sub-marginal from an agricultural standpoint. It is open to invasion by the inexperienced, which highly evolved agricultural areas such as Iowa or Wisconsin are very definitely not. My ingrained knowledge of this fact left me, I now realize, in a curiously schizophrenic emotional position regarding the South. Because I was determined to settle there, I had to spend a good deal of time conning myself that I liked it. The truth is the exact opposite and I may as well set it down here and now: I hate the South. I hate its sloth, its weary cynicism, its hypocrisy, its stone age religious bias, its preoccupation with class distinction and, most of all, I hate the dreadful, ingrained guilt of the southerner which he does little or nothing to alleviate. I've never had to bother reading much Faulkner because I know he's right. George Bernard Shaw's remark when finally trapped into commenting on "Ulysses" works perfectly when applied to Faulkner: "It's about the way it has always seemed to me" said Shaw, the seething love-hate he felt for the Irish, being one himself, bubbling furiously to the surface. It always takes one to catch one. And I have to admit with an exasperated sigh that I am, in some measure, a southerner. St. Louis is a peculiar, ingrown, strangely sophisticated city which has been fed from many different directions; but, in the last analysis, it is, psychologically, a southern city. I can understand perfectly the mysterious mixture of sadness and fierce joy with which Sherman put the land to the torch on his march south; and the contempt with which Ulysses S. Grant must have acccepted the surrender of Robert E. Lee's gentlemanly sword. There is a passage in the Bible which has always typified the South to me psychologically. It is when Lot, that best of fellows ends up in a cave with his daughters after a lifetime of chasing after something for nothing. "Thus both daughters of Lot were with child by their father. The elder bore a son and called him Moab. He is the father of the Moabites of the present day." That's my South: the land of the Moabites of the present day.

Which is not to say that Moabites are not fascinating or likeable; they are both. It is not southerners but the south which fills me with such a desperate desire to escape. The job I finally found threw me right into the midst of as fine a nest of Moabites as the original gang in the cave. The patriarch of the clan could have been taken directly from the pages of T. S. Stribling.

Towards the end of my three weeks' jaunt, I came to the city of Statesville in North Carolina. I was, to put it mildly, beginning to loose heart; many County Agents had presented me to numbers of farmers but I was too odd a duck for them. The combination of inexperience and a background as a writer required more imagination to bet on than most possessed. It was, I think, a penchant for mischief on the part of my future employer which eventually brought about my hiring. And a penchant for mischief is certainly a product of imagination.

In Statesville, I sought out the county agent and presented my spiel; it had become pretty pat by then. The county agent was a pleasant young man about the same age as I. He ruminated for a few minutes and then said with decision, "Let's us get in my car and go out and see a man I know named Casey Crawford." The way he spoke, our destination seemed only a hop, skip and jump away but it turned out to be a drive of nearly an hour to the neighboring town of Mooresville, an undistinguished Southern milltown upon which the hand of change lay lightly. During the ride, I had been roughly briefed by the agent as to the nature of Casey

Crawford's farming operation. It was, to say the least, atypical. Crawford, it seemed, was a road building contractor in a small enough way of business so that he still took on jobs such as building fishponds for farmers. His inventory of machinery consisted of three or four bulldozers, some ramshackle dump trucks and a small drag line. His labor force was a group of about ten Negroes augmented, occasionally by other Negroes which he took on for bigger jobs. He also ran a beef cattle farm; it was this farm which was the object of our visit.

We found him sitting on a nail keg in front of the machine shop where his machines were serviced and repaired. He was, so help me God, whittling on a stick. I always called him Mr. Crawford but I will refer to him here as "Mist Case," the title bestowed on him by his Negro employees and most of the other people in the town. Mist Case was a tasty dish: He was a small, rotund but very powerful man of an age somewhere between fifty-five and sixty. His unvarying costume was khaki shirt and trousers all surmounted by an odd little hat turned up both in front and back, which he wore tilted forward on the front of his head. It was a comedian's hat; Mist Case was a fairly straight Mack Sennett turn with some complicated Southern overtones. His eyes, when they suddenly darted at one from beneath the comedian's hat, were very shrewd. When not in the company of his Negro laborers, he was usually bored, I later found out. (In the flatland South, the Negroes do everything; they not only do the work but provide the jokes and the music and generally shore up the culture of a very shaky scene.) Such was the state of Mist Case that day we first met; his hands were all away on a job and he sat lonely and bored upon his nail keg whittling. His eyes began to gleam as the County Agent made his pitch for me. Mist Case was fundamentally amused by life and open to experience; life had brought him a writer of books who wanted to be a farmer and he sensed immediately the opportunity for practically unlimited fields of fun. I might add that I never took a round off him—well, maybe one, but I shall come to that later on.

When the County Agent had finished describing my quest, Mist Case looked me over, his eyes twinkling happily.

"So you one of them book writuhs. Goodness gracious me,

54

beats me how a feller goes about writin' one of them books."
His tone made it clear that he regarded such a pursuit as a
complete waste of time but was nevertheless pleased to be
faced with a fellow so foolish as to have carried through such
an outlandish project.

He came rapidly to brass tacks: "Got me a little farm out-
chere with a few cattle on it. Caint tend to it propuhly myself.
You think you'd lahk to take a crack at it, eh?" I said I would
and he got up off his nail keg, saying, "Less jus take us a drive
on out theah an' look things ovuh."

"His "little farm turned out to be four hundred acres while
his "few" cattle turned out to be a couple of hundred pure-
bred whiteface cows and heifers. However, the place was far
from being fancy; the only house I could see was derilect and
unliveable and the barns were either falling down or leaning
one way and another. The fences appeared new and good and
there was a large new silo but, for the rest, the place was a
mess. We walked around examining the cattle, I trying not to
appear as ignorant as I felt. In his quick, decisive way, Mist
Case made a proposition: two hundred a month and a house
for me and my family. I asked him where the house was and
he said, "Got me a little house in town do jus' fine."

It was all about as far from anything I had envisioned as I
could imagine; but then, reality usually is. Anyway, I jumped
at it. We drove back into Mooresville and looked at the
house. It was an appalling shack which backed up on the
dolor of Mist Case's machinery yard. There was no bathroom
in it, a problem which he dismissed airily with a brisk, "Put
you in a bathroom in a couple of days."

I balked. By that time, I was getting as interested in Mist
Case as he was in me, even though I realized with a certain
misgiving that my interest was that of a novelist rather than
neophyte farmer. I suspected even then that I would learn
precisely nothing about farming if I went to work for Mist
Case. No matter; we needed a Benz chamber to make the
transition from depth to surface and this looked as though it
were going to be the only one that would offer itself. But I
was damned if I wanted to live in a shack surrounded by
rusting bulldozers. More important, I did not want to be that
closely under Mist Case's thumb. Even then I was instinctively alert to his capacity for mischief but I saw no reason to

put myself in a position where he had me available for torture on a twenty-four hour a day basis. He gave in quickly, saying, "Got me anothuh little house ovuh on Main Street do you jus' fine."

We looked at that one and it was not too bad; one half of a white frame two-family house in a nice shady yard well back from the street with a magnificent oak tree in the front yard. (Later on, that tree would save us serious injury, if not our lives: a noise like the crack of doom had awakened Dorothy and me one morning at about four o'clock; I found the driver of a trailer truck dazed and bleeding trying to ring our doorbell. He had left the road at full speed and only the tree kept his truck from plowing right into our bedroom. After we had got medical help for him, I wandered out to examine the wreck. Beneath it, almost hidden by the bulk of the trailer was an old jalopy with four dead Negroes in it.)

Now, Mist Case and I struck our bargain. We arranged that I should return with my family four or five days hence. The County Agent and I drove back to Statesville; he, highly pleased with the success of his catalytic effort and I game but slightly apprehensive.

Back in Maryland, I found my wife champing at the bit; while the three weeks with O'Hara and my brother had not been unpleasant for her, she was anxious to be gettting on with it. Both O'Hara and my brother were, for the moment, men without plans or a discernible future. My brother would soon return to Europe. O'Hara must have been thinking things over very carefully; inside a few months, he would hand us all an unexpected—and seemingly cheerful—surprise. Within a couple of days, Dorothy and I loaded the station wagon with our belongings and the baby and took the road south for Mooresville. With us still was our Boxer bitch Gordo. Poor Gordo; born in Spain, ex-citizen of Morocco and Italy, she was now thoroughly confused and suspicious of each new move.

In Mooresville, we settled into our new house without much difficulty and I began my apprenticeship under Casy Crawford. It is clear now that it was more an apprenticeship in the mores of the flatland south than it was an apprenticeship in farming.

I have mentioned previously that Casy Crawford's farming

operation was atypical. The reason is simple; it bore no relation to economic reality. It was, first of all, a hobby for Mist Case and, second, a tax dodge. But those things do not necessarily make a farm economically unreal; many such farms are beautifully run and incorporate interesting and experimental techniques. What made Mist Case's farm a total Alice in Wonderland operation was that it was not self supporting in any department. In the David Harum sense of the word, Mist Case was an extremely cunning man; cunning and hopelessly out of touch with the times. If he has not come to grief by now with the U.S. Government, I should be surprised. For example, he paid absolutely no attention to the rules regarding the payment of withholding tax for his employees. I have heard his son, Shorty, warning him that this would lead to trouble but Mist Case simply shut him up with a brisk patriarchal hand, saying, "Pshaw, Ah don know nothin bout them damn fools in Washington; Ah jus pays off in good green money an that's the end of that." And he greatly enjoyed pay day, warning each Negro in jocular tones against misbehavior as he thumbed the bills off a large roll. He was not a mean man and the wages he paid were high by local standards. His view of Negroes was the prosaically southern one that they were incapable of taking care of themselves. Accordingly, he owned the mortgages upon nearly all the houses in which his hands lived; which meant, of course, that they paid for a certain protection against disaster with a sacrifice of their essential freedom. Thereby, helping to maintain the shaky Southern status quo.

His unwritten bargain with his hands was to keep them steadily employed. From this fact stemmed the first reason for the unreality of his farming operation. On a given day, any hands not needed on whatever earth-moving contracts being fulfilled would be sent to work on the farm. Therefore, such time—and money-consuming tasks as the building of new fences were accomplished by use of a large gang of laborers and charged off against the contracting business. This, I soon found out, made me into the overseer of a group of Negro hands and led, inevitably, to my downfall for reasons I will presently explain.

The other fact of unreality concerning Mist Case's farm was that very little actual farming went on there. The cattle had to be looked after, of course, but this amounted to little more than feeding them, spraying them, and seeing to it that the calf crop was looked after. During the relatively short time I worked for Mist Case, the feeding part of the program was not necessary, we were far enough along into the spring so that the cattle were on grass. Mist Case did little actual farming because it was cheaper and more efficient for him to take payment in kind from the various farmers for whom he did earth-moving work. He would build a fish pond, for example, in return for which the farmer who wanted it would see to it that Mist Case's silo was filled with corn. Other work of that sort would be paid for by the delivery of large loads of alfalfa hay. The spring that I went to work for Mist Case he had planted 40 acres of corn for silage, but even this would be harvested by a farmer who owed him money. The actual inventory of machinery on Mist Case's place was pitifully small: a Ford tractor with a mower attachment and a wagon and some rusty old spike harrows. There was also a woebegone horse about the place whose virtues Mist Case never tired of extolling.

The routine of my days varied according to how the Negro labor force was engaged on a given day. I would report in the morning to Mist Case's machine shop exactly like all the other hands. If it was a day on which there were men to spare, I would load the ones assigned to me into a truck and we would repair to the farm and carry on with whatever large continuing project, such as fence building, was then in hand. If, as frequently was the case, there were no hands to spare, I would spend the day on the farm taking care of various minor projects that I could handle myself: building loading pens or keeping the pastures mowed back. Then there was the constant business of keeping track of the cattle and seeing to it that those cows about to calf were separated and put in a small calving pasture near the barns. It became increasingly clear to me during the time that I worked for Mist Case that any sort of beef cattle operation would forever be beyond me in scope; to be profitable, such an operation requires a great deal more land than I could ever get together the money to buy.

The purpose of Mist Case's farm was not the raising of beef for market but the breeding and raising of pure-bred Whiteface cattle to be sold as breeding stock. The bull calves were castrated shortly after birth with a hideous little machine which was the subject of much coarse joking among the hands. They were then weaned and sold off at the local market as veal or to be raised and fattened for later sale as prime beef. The heifers were all kept, raised and subsequently bred. The theory being that, over a long period of time, stern annual culling and the use and purchase of finer bulls would eventually result in a herd which would produce prize-winning animals at the local fairs and so attract potential blood stock purchasers to the farm. When I worked for Mist Case, such an ideal state was far, far in the future. Records had been poorly kept or not kept at all and the quality of the bulls used for breeding had not been high. However, shortly before my advent, Mist Case had invested an astonishingly large amount of money in a vast polled (hornless) Hereford bull, a dull-eyed lackadaisical beast with a long pompous name. To see him climb ponderously aboard some cow or heifer was a sight which gave Mist Case great pleasure. "Looky theah," he would shout gleefully, "he gon poll them cows; he gon poll them cows for shuh."

Besides his bulldozers, his family and his cattle in about that order, what interested Mist Case most in the world were Negroes. They were always referred to as "nigguhs" and they were, for him, the fundamental source of all material and spiritual well-being. The ability to function within the confines of that endless minstrel show which is the South, the ability to burgeon from their labors and still maintain the tenuous illusion of control; these were the requisites of manhood and reality to Mist Case. When he realized that I was not the master of these techniques and never could be, Mist Case conceived an essential contempt for me that he took little trouble to conceal. He regarded me more and more as something of a nigguh myself; albeit, a totally unsatisfactory one who was white, would not be worked like a dog, did not play the clown and used long words that he did not understand.

The relationship between Mist Case and his Negroes was a delicate balance which had been worked out during centuries of impossibility. There was no conscious cruelty on his side of the scale just as there was no conscious contempt on theirs. He expected a certain amount of work from them and a certain amount of amusement and he was aware that he could only obtain the latter at the expense of the former. They, on the other hand, were content to use their great psychological expertise towards his diversion in order to keep their physical labours within reasonable limits.

The natural leader among the group of hands that were usually under my supervision was a young man in his early twenties named Clem. He was a good looking fellow, strong as a bull and a tireless worker when he wished to be. Clem sensed immediately that I could be seduced by his idiom which was breezy and employed most often in discussions about the opposite sex. To Paul, a younger and less confidant colleague, Clem said one day, "Boy, how dat good lookin' sistuh you got?" "She fine," Paul said, bashfully. "Yo Pop, he still away up at de jailhoue?" "Yeah, he be away fo a while longuh." "Well, you tell dat gal dat de sugah man be roun' one a dese evenins, heah?" "Don' you come messin' roun' wit no sistuh of mine, boy," Paul said. Chuckling happily, Clem replied, "Oh yes, de sweet sugah man, he be roun'."

Near quitting time one Friday afternoon, Clem confided his intentions to me: "Jus' one little ole half hour, Mist John, and Charlotte, heah I come. Them ole Charlotte gals bettuh watch out 'cause ole Clem, he comin' to town. Fust, I goes home and puts on the pants to mah blue suit; not the coat, Mist John, 'cause if you puts on de whole suit they thinks you is jus' some ole country boy; den I puts on mah new sportin' shirt and Charlotte look out fo ole Clem." Knowing that I could be lured into such conversations at will, my authority was slowly and steadily undermined.

All in all, I must have worked for Casey Crawford for about three months. During this time, I became steadily more convinced that I was marking time and learning little of genuine value to me should I ever have a farm of my own. Which is the real reason I finally resigned. However, there always has to be a signal in matters of timing and Mist Case supplied one by instigating a comic ploy designed within the labrynthine passages of his Southern mind to test my metal.

He had, as I have mentioned, an aged, rather recalcitrant horse about the place who dwelt in some equine elysium of plenty to eat and no work to do. Horse-preoccupation having been left out of my make-up at birth, this beast and I had little to do with each other. He was, however, fated to be instrumental in the final joust between Mist Case and me.

Mist Case arrived at the farm one day bored and, as usual on the lookout for mischief. He interrupted me at some unimportant task and we chatted idly about various jobs he felt should be taken in hand. Finally, we hiked over to examine the forty acres which had been planted in corn. The young corn shoots were up only a few inches and Mist Case examined the field appreciatively. In truth, it was a fine stand of corn and I felt at peace with the day until I saw that sudden gleam appear in Mist Case's eyes which invariably heralded some preposterous suggestion or command. In his best hick vein, he began to ruminate upon the value of old fashioned farming techniques.

"Young stan of cohn lak that needs harrowin' raht bout now," he said, thoughtfully, "Thing is, young cohn lak that so tenduh that it needs nice slow, careful harrowin'."

By the time he continued, I was braced for what was to come; "Tell you whut," he said, "you jus' git that good ole hoss of mine an hahness him up to them ole spike harrows; you'll find some hahness an a singletree ovuh to the bahn."

I was tempted to protest but some foolish devil of pride made me keep silent. Then too, there was not much time in which to protest; it was Mist Case's practice to leave the scene quickly after he had conceived what he felt to be a good joke. A moment later, he drove off in his pick-up truck and I was left drearily contemplating the prospect of catching an animal I feared and distrusted, dressing him in some apparatus I did not understand and plodding wearily behind him for what seemed it would be weeks. Let all those who operate within the limits of suburban perspective be warned that forty acres of corn is a hell of a lot of corn.

Somehow, I caught the beast, diagnosed the proper placement of his harness and, filled with mutual distrust and antipathy, we advanced upon the vast expanse of cornfield. The sun was well up in the heavens by then and the heat of the late spring North Carolina sun is no joke. By the time the horse and I had done two rows, I was drenched with sweat. The horse, predictably enough, performed as if he had been given private instructions by Mist Case. He either went too slow or too fast and I floundered in his wake idiotically, shouting gee and haw with little or no result. Every now and then, he would come to a full stop to examine me contemptuously. I kept it up for an hour before thoughts of revolt began to stir. To quit, was an idea I did not seriously consider; I was taking his money and it was clear that I owed it to Mist Case to harrow his cornfield. What rankled was the horse and all that pure poppycock about the need for the horse's use. If the keys were still in the tractor (and Mist Case was perfectly capable of having removed them), I could somehow manage to rig the rusty old harrows behind it and complete the field in a few comparatively comfortably seated hours instead of the days of torture which lay ahead.

The keys were still in the tractor and, moments after making that discovery, the horse was back in retirement and I was proceeding with my task in the proper manner of 20th century man. By the end of the working day the job was done and well done; the nascent weeds uprooted and the young corn untouched. Childishly, I could not resist stopping by Mist Case's machine shop on the way home. Enthroned upon his nail keg, he eyed me happily. "Git yuah cohn done?" he asked, fully aware that one man walking behind that dreadful horse would need at least a week to complete such a task.

"Yes," I said.

"Whut?" he said, looking startled.

"I used the tractor."

"Bet you done rooined that purty young cohn."

"Go take a look," I said, enjoying myself.

"By Gawd, I jus' will. Come on."

We drove out to the farm together, Mist Case clucking away like a frustrated hen about his ruined corn; I, benign and imperturbable. So impertuable, in fact, that Mist Case had lost all hope of finding his corn damaged when we arrived. Nevertheless, he walked the rows carefully searching for bent or broken plants. There were some, of course; but no more than he would have found had the job been done using his damnable horse. When he finished his inspection, he muttered something about, "Looks all raht but t'woulda been a bettuh job if you'd used that ole hoss".

However, he was cheerful as we rode back to town; that joke

had not worked out but, no matter; there would be another joke along soon.

Shortly after that, Mist Case and I parted company. We did so on the best of terms and I continued to rent his house on Main Street. It was only a week or so later that I went to St. Louis on my ill-fated quest for funds to purchase a farm.

CHAPTER V

In a play of mine, a scene occurs in which the members of an upper-middle class family are attempting to dodge discussion of the subject which interests them most: money. The mother puts a stop to this by saying simply, "Money is always interesting." In my experience, her remark is true; money *must* be interesting in order for me to have spent as much time thinking about as I have during my life. It is a process which has given me much pain and much pleasure.

Due to a certain profligacy on the male side and a certain malfunction of the breeding mechanism on the distaff, my patrimony (or rather, my portion thereof) remained lodged in the viselike grip of a spinster aunt during most of my life. I have devised many a scheme in my time to jar it loose, but in the end, only death could turn the trick. The anatomy and history of that patrimony have always bemused me because, to my knowledge, neither contains even a suggestion of any creative act; buy low, sell high were the conditions of its birth, and preoccupation with chimerical rainy days the condition of its nurturing. When I say patrimony, I refer only to that derived from the paternal side. From the maternal side, I inherited opportunities for experience, openness and a sense of style and, as a result have never felt that I was owed anything further. Since youth, I have been convinced that I was owed much by the assorted mortgage-holders, penny-pinchers and Franklin D. Roosevelt-haters which made up the majority of the paternal side. From this group, I carefully except my own father who was much to my taste. It was his father who put together the nucleus of the rather large sum of money which was to drive me mad with rage during most of my young manhood. This gentleman's name was Josiah

Sherry and he died when my father was sixteen years old. He was a grain speculator who, I have been told, had grave ups and downs but managed to leave a goodly sum of money even though he perished at comparatively low ebb. This eventually filtered down to my father and his three sisters, each of whom received about one hundred thousand dollars upon the death of their mother, a much-admired lady who died before my memory began to function. Only one of the three sisters had issue; a daughter who died and a son, a cheerful chap who, where last I heard of him, was circumnavigating the earth in a trimaran of his own construction. The remaining two sisters did not breed. The elder was a nonentity who married and kept house for her husband and her younger sister all her life. Thus they lived in one of those commonplace, middle-class and thoroughly sexless *menages a trois*. And when I say sexless I mean sexless. Although it is the most dangerous thing a man can do, I would be willing to bet every cent I've got that the younger sister, Susan, died an intact virgin. Unlike her elder sister, however, she was no nonentity.

Largely because she eventually became the repository of most of the money in my family, Susan was always of great interest to me. But, my fascination with her by no means stemmed completely from that. It stemmed also from the fact that she inspired in me as strange a combination of intense dislike and intense respect as I have ever experienced. She was an educated woman, an early graduate of Vassar and a brilliant teacher of mathematics who retired at 65 as assistant principal of a large metropolitan high school. At 70, she still had enough gas left to go to Japan where she taught mathamatics at Kobe College. This was during the period when we were living on 12th Street in New York while I was writing my first novel. Dorothy was doing her best as a breadwinner and I cannot lay claim to real penury. However, we sailed awfully close to the edge. When a medical problem drove us over the edge, I remember writing to my aunt with the suggestion that, since she was going to leave me some money some day, she might as well fork over a little now. Back from Japan came an extremely high-dudgeoned blast inquiring what possible right I had to make any assumption whatsoever regarding her testamentary intentions. Her objection was, I suppose, well-founded; nevertheless, it had the

66

effect of strengthening my dislike. The measurement of any potential act of charity was, in her mind, rectitude rather than need. She belonged to that class of person who views all recipients of welfare as avaricious, slothful and dishonest.

She did not believe in essential freedom. It was this aspect of her make-up whence my unchanging dislike stemmed. And by essential freedom, I mean simply a basic belief that freedom must be pursued by humankind within the confines of the terrifying paradox that it is unattainable. Essential freedom is an attempt not an attainment. Birds in the bush did not exist for Susan. And even those few brightly coloured birds in the hand which are available to human beings, struck her as being basically futile. The quality of her spirit was as poor as the quality of her rationality was high. As a teacher she was incomparable in her subject; when I was floundering helplessly with algebra as a boy, she drove with a few deft strokes a basic understanding of the subject into my head. So my savage dislike was always balanced by respect for her. And that respect was curiously tinged by nostalgia, an awareness of all she had missed in life and a knowledge of what she might have been. Once, on a whim, I sent her a copy of a fine book by Colin Wilson called, "The Outsider". I received a letter in return which asked, "Do you think I have been anything but an outsider all my life?" She was like a piano sprinkled with dead keys, devoid, like most of her race, of any understanding of or need for the creative act.

My application to her for enough money to buy a farm was rejected without any hint of consideration. It came as no surprise to me to find that I had traveled to St. Louis in order to be fed a bad dinner and subjected to an evening of homilies about the aimlessness and futility of my life. Interspersed throughout as juxtapository warnings were anecdotes about various local losers among her acquaintances who were fighting sad and hopeless battles for survival. False teeth clicking happily, she recounted tales of spinster daughters supporting aging mothers by taking in laundry and men reduced to penury through sickness and infirmity; only those poor unfortunates who had been struck down and definitively mangled by life were examples of morally right and proper need. I listened quietly; my name was Sherry too and I understood the rules of the game: ask and ye shall be refused and listen to a lecture in the process just for good measure. Yet, oddly enough, it would be Sherry money which would buy my farm in the end. It came through no good offices of Susan, but it was Sherry money nevertheless.

With that balloon definitely busted, I turned my head back towards specific farming information. There is in St. Louis, a rather interesting organization called the Doane Agricultural Service which deals in the management of large farms for absentee landlords. A person, for example, who inherited a large farm and who had no experience in farming could hire the Doane Service to provide personnel to run his farm subject to policy decisions made by the Doane office in St. Louis—which office would then carry out periodic inspections to see to it that those policy decisions were being carried out. My friend Dr. Black in Rome had spoken of this organization with respect and one of the things I had on my mind in going to St. Louis was to pay a call at their offices in the hope that I might find someone whose brains were both pickable and amenable to being picked. As luck would have it, I did, in fact, encounter such a fellow.

His name has long since departed from my memory although his appearance remains clear. He had what I always think of as "Astronaut" good looks, crew cut, well-scrubbed and given to an idiom of speech which replaced the word "very" with the word "real". For example, in Astronaut parlance the phrase "very good" is religiously replaced by the use of "real good". My man was about my age and he struck me immediately as knowing his stuff. He was a graduate of a good agricultural school, had grown up on a farm and, even now, happily ensconced on a policy level with a good firm, he showed a hankering to return to actual farming himself. It was this quality which induced me to pay such careful attention to him. After we had talked for perhaps an hour and he had a fairly clear idea of my intentions, he got out a map of the southeast and spread it on his desk. He then placed his finger on a specific area and said, "If I were going to buy myself a cattle farm, I'd go somewhere right about here."

I looked down at the map and saw that his fingernail was resting on a town called Wytheville, the county seat of Wythe County in the southwestern part of Virginia, quite close to the borders of North Carolina, West Virginia and Tennessee.

68

So do our destinies make themselves manifest. I decided then and there to drive directly to Wytheville on my way back to North Carolina.

The reasons for his choice seemed to me to be both sound and informed. The land in that area was natural blue-grass land which could be brought back by the proper use of fertilizer, even though it had been badly treated. It was also, relatively cheap land due to much of it having been badly farmed for crops instead of used for livestock as it should have been. Furthermore, it was an unsophisticated area in which most of the farms were too small to warrant the investment needed to make them pay even if the wherewithal for such an investment were forthcoming. Which, in most cases, it was not; cash is a scarce commodity in Southwestern Virginia.

A day or so after my talk with the young man at the Doane Service, I drove back to North Carolina by way of Wytheville, Virginia. When I was still a hundred miles from Wytheville, it was hard for me to believe that I would find anything there which would strike my fancy. My approach was through the narrow valleys of the West Virginia coal country, which is, I imagine, the most depressed economic area in the United States. Even though the mines are now largely inactive, thick coal dust seems to lie over everything; the very air reeks of poverty, ignorance, despair and violence. The last city of any size which I passed through in West Virginia was the city of Bluefield, a curious microcosm of urban corruption with which, later on, I would become familiar with through our daily newspaper, the Bluefield Daily Telegraph, a journal which chronicled a world more strange to me than Mars. (One highly typical front-page story which sticks in my mind concerned an eighty year man who poisoned a family's well and killed off the entire family out of pique because he could not induce a sixteen year old daughter of the family to sleep with him.)

As I passed through Bluefield and began climbing the Appalachian range which would lead me to the valley between the Appalachians and the Blue Ridge Mountains, I was appalled at the dreadful misjudgment of the young man whose advice had led me there. To my mind, the country through which I had driven was, not fit for human habitation. It stank of inequality and bore the physical and psychological scars of all areas where wealth has been removed from the earth to the enrichment of the few and at the expense of many. Yet, as I drove across the last twenty-five miles of mountains, the feeling of dolor passed away. The defunct coal mines thinned out and then ceased altogether. The country was wild but it was clean and beautiful wildness. Then I emerged into Virginia and the valley, and my faith in my young man's judgement was restored. It was August then and the fields on each side of the road undulated with ripening corn and small grain. The high mountains were now in the distance while the immediate country was hilly though still arable. But the brutal little secret rocky valleys of West Virginia did not persist beyond that final mountain range.

The town of Wytheville was only a scant twenty miles further. I arrived there about dusk and got a room at the town's major hostelry. The evening was spent walking about the town and chatting idly with whatever locals I could cause to fall into a conversation. I could force myself into no great raptures about the town of Wytheville itself. We have all seen fifty towns much like it. As is true of most Virginia towns, there were a few houses of genuine beauty, but in the main, the town was standard Americana, a scene reminiscent of those on the covers of the Saturday Evening Post during the Thirties and Forties.

Wytheville was the county seat of Wythe County; George Wythe, the namesake of these quantities, had been a Virginia jurist and one of the architects of the Constitution. I was instructed in these matters by a gentleman in the lobby of the hotel; he also advised me about a real estate man I might contact if I were interested in buying property in the area.

Bright and early the next morning, I presented myself at the real estate office. Having no money, I was bluffing shamefully but I was anxious to see just what was going in the way of farm land in the vicinity, and its approximate price. The realtor could not have been more pleasant. We set out in his car to have a look at various places he had listed. It was a discouraging quest; mountain people to whom the possession of the land is all important are a strange mixture of shyness and pride. The farms we visited that morning were of course

70

for sale and the people were furtive and ashamed because of it.

Late that morning, the realestate man stopped his car on the bend of a country road, saying "I doubt that this will interest you but we might as well take a look." At first sight, I agreed with him. The house was set back from the bend in the road about 100 feet. It had once been white clapboard but was now so badly in need of paint that it had weathered to a dingy grey. The design was one encountered frequently in that area, a two-storey house built in the shape of an L with a long veranda running across the front. If one stood facing the house, the ground dropped away to the left at quite a sharp angle of descent for about 200 feet where a clear mountain stream gurgled busily by. A dirt drive ran from the main road down past the left of the house to a small patch of creek bottom about the size of a football field. Part of this was a small pasture; the rest was fenced off for a large vegetable garden. Adjacent to the garden was a tumbledown barn, its nucleus a log cabin which had been abandoned as a habitation when the main house had been built around the turn of the century. The pastures and fields of the farm were hilly and rose steeply to the right of the creek bottom land. Clearly, the land had not been worked for many years. It was rough land, covered with broom sage and cedar saplings. Another dirt track led off up a defile providing some sort of access to the fields for machinery. It was the last sort of place which should have interested me, but it did, immediately, for the simplest reason in the world: it was beautiful. Interior voices were whispering furiously that beauty was a damned silly basis for buying a farm; I listened only fitfully.

When my interest remained alive after going through the house, I began to be seriously worried. The house was dreadful. In only two rooms the kitchen and the back bedroom above it, was the plaster sound enough to be saved; the remaining four rooms (living room and dining room below, two bedrooms above) would clearly have to be stripped down to the bare studs and re-covered with sheetrock. There was no bathroom and the only source of heat was a large coal and wood burning range in the kitchen. Even basic plumbing was lacking; the only water available was raised from a cistern beneath the kitchen by use of an old fashioned hand pump. About the best that could be said for the house was that it was sound. It was set upon a good solid stone foundation and showed no signs of sagging or structural collapse.

I did not bother that day with any careful examination of the land. It was something which I wanted to do at my leisure and I made up my mind then to return the following day. As we drove away, I quizzed the real estate agent about the size and probable price of the place. Its total acreage was ninety and the price being asked by the owner was eleven thousand dollars. The real estate agent thought it could be bought for about eighty-five hundred dollars. I asked if it would be all right for me to return the following day in order to walk around the land and he replied that it would be; the family in residence were not the owners but related to the owner, a widow who lived some distance away.

We spent the balance of the day looking at other farms but none struck me as possible. They were all either too small and poor or else beyond my reach financially. By the end of the day I had to face the fact that the Kegley place, as it was called, had lodged itself rather deeply in my mind.

When I awoke the next morning, it was still firmly entrenched there. I lay for a while in bed letting my imagination have free reign as to what lay ahead of us should we actually succeed in finding the money to buy the place. It was a dangerous process; my imagination is vivid and the potential trials and tribulations of owning and caring for that much land made me sweat with apprehension. I was still Ernest Hemingway's child but the festival at Pamplona and the Nobel Prize seemed to be receding from my grasp at an alarming rate. And what was replacing them with frightening rapidity and urgency was a mode of life which was largely unknown and correspondingly terrifying. Lying in bed that morning, my ambivalence towards the entire project assumed such staggering proportions that I examined my basic sanity with care. Biting off more than I could chew or swallow seemed a pale phrase to describe what I was contemplating. Still, driven by God knows what devils of pride or stubbornness, I finally climbed out of bed and drove to the Kegley place for an extended walk over its land.

A few months earler, I had plodded the streets of Rome

amusing myself with an entrely theoretical view of being a farmer. Now I was actually walking upon land which might possibly be my own. In Rome, I had known nothing; now, in all truth, I knew very little more. But a little bit more is better than no more. The talking, the reading, and the few months working for Casy Crawford had alerted me to the truly definitive mistakes I might make. These, it seemed to me, came under three headings. The first was simply the quality of the land itself. Properly treated, could it be brought back? Could the poor land growth be choked out by the application of suitable top dressings? Judging by the appearance of the neighboring fields under cultivation, the land seemed basically all right. This, however, was a question I could seek help in answering. the local county agent would advise me I knew, and I could also obtain through him a chemical analysis of the land's potentiality. The next point of real importance was the question of whether or not the land was too steep to be worked by machinery. If and when I ever made an all-out commitment to farming on a professional scale, I would have to grow both alfalfa hay and corn for silage and there must be enough reasonably level land to allow the use of a hay baler and a silage chopping machine. On Crawford's farm, I had fiddled around with machinery enough to be fairly certain that the Kegley place was feasible from that standpoint. The final question seemed wholly ludicrous at this point, but I knew it was not. It was simply: could the farm be expanded? If you buy a suit of clothes that is too big, something can be done about it. But if the suit is too small and the seams cannot be let out, it has to go to the rummage sale.

I had quizzed the real estate man about this extensively the previous day. There were, in fact, two possible avenues of expansion for the Kegley place. The adjoining farm across the creek was for sale and comprised about seventy-five acres. That farm was not being worked but it also was not in bad shape, the pastures having been better cared for than those of the Kegley place. It was owned and occupied by a young man about my own age and his wife who were not, strictly speaking, rural people at all. The young man, Bill, worked in a Wytheville store of which his father was part owner and qualified both economically and by background as a member

of the Wytheville upper middle class. Bill's mother and father
and younger brother lived on a piece of land which backed up
on his. Their place was not a farm at all but an astonishingly
charming small country house complete with beautifully laid
out gardens and a swimming place created by damming up the
creek. It was an extremely strange show to find tucked away
up that valley where, to a man, the families subsisted on food
of their own growing and meat of their own killing.

On my rounds with the real estate man the previous day, I
had considered Bill's place as a possible purchase but had
decided against it because the price was too steep for me. Bill
and his wife had made numerous improvements in their
house. Its nucleus was an old log cabin which they had expanded to make a place of considerable charm. Needless to
say, it possessed all the amenities in which the Kegley place
was so sadly lacking. The important thing to me was that it
was available. In the unlikely eventuality that I should ever
want to expand, I could either buy his land or make some
arrangement with him whereby I could rent it. There was also
another possibility of future expansion to the north of the
Kegley place in a piece of land of about seventy-five acres
which joined on the Kegley farm. In spite of the fact, that, at
that point, expansion seemed problematical to say the least, it
was reassuring to know the basic situation was amenable to it.

All in all, I must have trudged and pondered over the Kegley place for about four hours that day. Having not a dime
towards its purchase at that moment, I could not help feeling
a little foolish and I frequently laughed at myself as I would
assume some time-honoured agricultural ritual such as squat-
ting and letting the soil run through my fingers. But by the
time I left that day, I had made up my mind to bring Dorothy
to see the place as soon as possible, and if she concurred, to
move heaven and earth in order to buy it.

In the private recesses of my own mind, however, I must
confess that I had made no real commitment to farming the
place on a professional scale. I saw it still as a haven where,
safe in the possession of a few chickens, some hogs and perhaps a cow, I could make a last ditch stand with my type-
writer and bring fame and fortune to bay on my own terms.
Am I alone I wonder, or is it a common human characteristic
to back into action with one's eyes fixed in a mesmerized stare

upon some steadily receding goal? So, perhaps, do we con ourselves into trying.

It was a couple of weeks before we were able to return *en famille* to examine the Kegley farm. Dorothy packed a picnic lunch and she and I and our baby daughter Linda, set out in high spirits. It was not much more than seventy miles from our place in North Carolina up to Wytheville and it was a fine late summer day for the outing. The Kegley place was at its best that day, hiding its many fearful flaws behind the benefice of a fine season. I fully expected that my wife might question my sanity when she saw the place I had in mind to condemn her to live. But she was not fazed; the same qualities of peace and beauty which had gripped my fancy gripped hers also. We ate our picnic by the softly bubbling creek and decided we would try to buy the place.

Having agreed in principal, we returned to Mooresville to work out the means. Waiting for us when we got back was a letter from Kate in St. Louis which contained a rather interesting surprise. The return address on the back read Kate O'Hara. Inside, she had written, "As you will see from the envelope, some changes have been made." She and O'Hara had gotten married. They were planning to go to Scotland for inadequately explained reasons. It seemed that they were removing themselves pretty definitely from our orbit. Nothing, as it eventually turned out, could have been further from the truth.

CHAPTER VI

On the subject of money, the last chapter began and on the same subject shall this one continue.

At the point where I now found myself, I had chosen a course of action calculated according to my lights to maintain a momentum of growth. However, without a capital sum of money, I could not possibly implement that course of action. With my aunt disqualified, there remained only one possible source: my mother.

After leaving us in Rome, she had gone to England to tour the West Country with friends and to spend the remainder of the winter and spring in London. Now she had returned to America and taken up residence in a curious community near Asheville, North Carolina, called Montreat. A thoroughly metaphysically oriented woman, she had chosen, not surprisingly, to settle down in a thoroughly metaphysically oriented community. Headquarters of the southern synod of the Presbyterian church, Montreat is a lovely but dead little town ruled by a jealous Presbyterian God. To call it square would be a total understatement. Its psychological aura is that mixture of sincerity and impertinence best expressed by the character of its most celebrated resident, the Reverend Billy Graham. It was a place which gave me the absolute, thoroughgoing blues but it suited my mother to a T. Widowed then for five years, she lived in Montreat in a huge old hotel which was owned by the Presbyterian Church and which operated as a resort hotel during those months when it was not being used as a site for ecclesiastical conferences. There, in her own way, my mother enjoyed herself; in meditation, in driving about the countryside in her car, and in having many conversations with fellow residents whose subject matter was entirely predictable.

One of the reasons she had chosen Montreat was that it was within striking distance of the place Dorothy, the baby, and I lived in Mooresville, and likely to be within striking distance of wherever we might eventually settle. Thus there was a certain amount of intermittent concourse between us. Dorothy and I would sometimes drive to Montreat to see her, or vice versa. Occasionally we would meet half way between and picnic along the roadside in the mountains.

My mother, knew and approved of my farming aims. I had reported my aunt's refusal to advance me funds and Mother had received that news with disgruntlement. There was little love between my mother and my aunt and there had been even less between Mother and my father's eldest sister. The eldest sister had predeceased my father by a relatively short period of time. One third of her estate had passed to my father and this passed in turn to my mother upon his death a year later. My mother had no illusions about her possession of this money; she knew that, had my father predeceased his eldest sister instead of the reverse, my mother would have been cut immediately from the succession and the money would have gone directly to my brother and me upon the death of my father's eldest sister. Thus, in a very real way, my mother considered my brother and me to be the rightful owners of that inheritance. Legally, the money was entirely hers. Morally, she believed, it was ours.

After Dorothy's and my visit to the Kegley farm near Wytheville, I told my mother that I had found a place that I would like to buy. She was curious to see the place and we made a date to drive to Wytheville together. Surprisingly enough, she was as taken with the Kegley place as were Dorothy and I. There was not even any need for me to ask her for the money to buy it. She volunteered it immediately, with a bit more thrown in to get us started. On our way back to Mooresville, I stopped at the real estate man's office and instructed him to offer eighty-five hundred dollars for the Kegley farm.

Having the actual wherewithal to buy the farm and having made the offer, the real fingernail-biting now began. It would be nice if I could report complacently that my apprehension had to do solely with the possibility that my offer would not be accepted. The truth is that my anxiety stemmed in equal measure from the fear that my offer would be accepted. Dichotomy, ambivalence and all the other words coined to describe the cleft within human intentions were directly applicable to my state of mind. Ninety acres of worn-out, grown-over land; a frame house in an appalling state of disrepair; neither livestock nor machinery; I asked myself over and over in hollow tones whether, in all honesty, I was completely sane. The blind circumstance to which I had so cockily refused to abandon my life now seemed awfully warm and appealing. My doubts were so profound as to be nearly unbearable. I longed to voice them to my wife, but again a peculiar atavistic sense of manhood bade me be silent and told me it would be wrong to infect others with my fear. Night after night, I would wait until my wife's even breathing assured me that she was asleep and then creep from bed to sit by the window and wrestle with my confusion through the long, soft southern night. And there by the window one night, I was rewarded by undergoing something that I can only describe as a mystical experience. I write those two words now with a slight smile of embarrassment and self-derision, for time has worn away all tendency to believe in things supernatural or seek fundamental causes in metaphysical speculation. Yet, strangely enough, while my tendency to believe or disbelieve in God has waned steadily, the fervency of my belief in faith itself has grown. Although I do not proselytize about it much, it seems clear and sensible to me that God is not, should not, and cannot be an operative component of faith. The very idea that faith has a conscious, external source is a contradiction in terms; faith is the absolute, and the ability to maintain it in the face of growing consciousness is the evolutionary test.

Years ago when we lived in Spain, we were acquainted with a man we called, "Sailor", a monster of crossed wires whose nickname we had given him in parody of all his mixed-up swash-buckling fancies. Sailor had a little red sports car in which O'Hara, Darroch and I set forth with him one evening for a night of carousing in Malaga. The Sailor had taken too much to drink before our departure and halfway along the road, he became ill and stopped the car on the side of the road. O'Hara said, "For God's sake, Sailor, if you can't drive the bloody car, get out from behind the wheel and let someone do it who can." The Sailor's reply was plaintive and, it has always seemed to me, curiously pertinent to the human condition: "I can't ride and I can't drive," he moaned and then demanded more alcohol.

Such was my state when my mystical experience overtook me. While I purposely make light of it, I believe it was genuine. I can't ride and I can't drive, said the Sailor and, indeed, in differing degree, so say every mother's son of us from Jesus Christ to the tenement resident throwing the brick through the store window during the annual summer riots. This is, make no mistake, an agony, a true agony the inability of which to bear is common to all of us. Some of us may do it more frequently than others but we all crumple under that agony from time to time. In the final act of the most dramatic life ever devised, Christ speaks his famous words: My God, why hast though forsaken me? So, in one form or another, do we all. The agony of not being able to drive and not being able to ride becomes unbearable.

But what if, for reasons manifold and strange, the agony is contained? Depending upon the motivation of such containment, the result can be either madness or vision of a hitherto unencountered clarity. This, it seems to me, is the ground of mystical experience. The mystic supports his agony in the light of some real or imagined positive aim; he allows the fires of ambivalence to roar unchecked within the confines of his own mind. Nothing goes on forever and those fires must exhaust themselves with the very ferocity of their own heat. That strange moment is when the mystical experience occurs; that is when the peace that passeth all understanding descends. It is neither more nor less than the complete and utter cessation of all doubt. It is therefore a momentary triumph of faith, a personal peak among the myriad quantum mechanics of the universe.

This is what I believe happened to me that night as I sat by the window of our house in Mooresville quaking with fear. There is nothing noble about such an experience, nothing for which credit can be taken. I had simply—and for reasons I still do not wholly understand—contained an agony until the opposing forces which had created it had exhausted themselves, giving birth to a unity of purpose I had not possessed before. My fears vanished and the future, while far from clear, was open. The sensation I experienced that night was the furthest thing in the world from euphoria. It was simply a tremendous, all-enveloping sense of peace. I had made my offer on the Kegley farm and that was that. However it turned out, I would do the best I could. I returned to bed beside my wife and slept as I had not since offering to buy the farm.

I was not such a fool as to believe that the feeling of peace and happiness would continue. Doubt can cease but doubt can be born again. But peace did persist for an astonishing amount of time. Until the matter was settled, I found myself able to function. I spent two rather happy weeks writing short stories and then the telephone finally rang and it was the real estate man saying that our offer had been accepted. We had bought the farm. I would be a liar if I did not confess that doubt was immediately born again.

The usual minor delays of closing a property transaction followed. It was actually the end of October before we were able to take formal possession of our farm. The day we did so was a far cry from the placid, summer beauty of our first encounter with the place. A light snow—the first of the sea-son—lay on the ground. Even the first fine flush of ownership could not conceal the dreariness of the prospect.

Before our arrival, I had arranged that the coal cooking range be removed from the kitchen and replaced by an electric stove for cooking and a kerosene space heater for warmth. Those two things represented the sum total of improvements effected. For the rest, water was still obtained from the cis-tern via the hand pump in the kitchen; of hot water, there was none except that which was heated on the kitchen stove. The basic bodily functions were taken care of according to time of day or inclination, either by use of a pot or the crazily-tilted two hole privy located twenty-five yards up the hill behind the house. Our few belongings such as a pair of twin beds, the baby's crib and a chair or two, I had transported to the farm the day before. For chairs, we used the three seats from the station wagon which I had removed from it in order to make room for transport. Oh, it was a charming sight which lay before us; the brothers Collier would have felt at home. We had no long term plan; only a general intention to rehabilitate the house. Thus, we confined our living space to two rooms:

the kitchen and the room next to it which we thought of rather grandiosely as the "dining room". In both rooms the plaster was badly cracked and our combined living and sleeping room was festooned with peeling strips of dreadful water-stained wall paper reminiscent in pattern of aged mattress ticking. But these factors of depression were nothing compared to the odor of the place. How is it possible to describe the smell of a hill-billy farmhouse in which home-cured and canned hog meat have been cooked three times daily since its construction? It is with me still; worse than unpleasant, it was tinged with a rich aroma of defeat. Mixed with it was another, genuinely nasty component which was, as yet, unidentifiable. It was all so unpalatable that for a moment I was tempted to weep. Dorothy, undaunted by dirt, and sensitive as always to my moods, took one look at me and said, "You get the kerosene stove going while I make out a list of groceries we'll need from Wytheville. Then you go into town and do the shopping while I get this place straightened out a little bit."

With the stove lit, and warmth beginning to penetrate the icy rooms, I shamelessly made good my escape. It was all so awful that during the fifteen-minute ride into Wytheville, I had one genuinely serious moment of temptation when I thought of cutting and running. Anything was better than what we were faced with. I would be a gaunt, shame-ridden Somerset Maugham character drinking away his life somewhere east of Suez while people whispered the terrible story of the woman and child he had abandoned on a bleak Virginia hill farm. Junking this dream reluctantly, I proceeded gloomily instead to the local A & P, where I loaded up with many cans of flatulent, non-perishable foods. The purchase of one essential perishable item for the baby depressed me further: milk. How is it possible, I asked myself, for a man to think of himself as a farmer when he is carting home milk from the A & P? Even more morosely, I took the road home with my groceries. I knew it would all look even worse to me at second sight. The ride back to the farm was an even gloomier one than the ride to town.

And then, when I parked the station wagon on the bend in front of the house and prepared to carry in the groceries, there was a surprise; I took on a small amount of hope. Dusk had come, and a soft light which emerged from the front window of the dining room cast its glow on the light coating of snow that covered the ground. When I pushed open the door leading from the front hall to the dining room, I could scarcely believe my eyes. At the most, I could not have been gone more than an hour and a half. And in that brief span of time, Dorothy, drawing on some mysterious fund of feminine energy and talent, had removed the curse from the Kegley house. To begin with, both kitchen and dining room were now as clean as soap and water and elbow grease could make them. Several cans of Airwick had been brought into play and the sour aroma of old, indifferent cooking was now held in check. The beds were made, some sort of curtains had been rigged and the room was now lighted by two shaded lamps. The baby was cooing away happily in her crib with a bottle, and even Gordo, the goofy Boxer, had assumed an expression of tenuous hope. Over this scene of domestic *legerdemain* floated the strains of La Traviata playing from the portable phonograph. Dorothy had given the lie to old Edgar Guest in spades; unbelievable as it sounds, that sorry old house had been turned into some kind of home.

We dined on canned pork and beans and, afterwards, smoked and discussed the priorities of our next day's effort. The two most pressing were getting some sort of refrigerator and taking some steps toward installing a system of hot and cold running water to serve the kitchen. After determining upon those improvements, we took a flashlight and timidly prowled through the rest of the house. The two rooms in which we were dwelling were paradise compared to the others. In none of the rest was the plaster conceivably salvagable. And, in their cold, unlighted and unheated gloom, the dreadful acrid odor we had noticed earlier seemed more pronounced. We returned soon to the comparative warmth and comfort of our "apartment"; it did not seem wise to tempt the weakening of our spirits by remaining too long in those desolate chambers. But I knew we must make a start upon their rejuvenation without too much delay; their presence was too great a reminder of the impossibility with which we were surrounded. Finally we slept—feeling that if we had failed to triumph over the old house, we had, at least, stayed even with it. Dorothy's transformation of the two habitable rooms had given me heart and, in the way of women, having given heart to me, she was able to take it back for herself. There was too much to be done to admit of moping; forward momentum had to be established immediately. The necessity within which I hoped to find freedom had pinned me down at last.

During my school years, I had been a dedicatedly recalcitrant student—one who could be described in the present educational jargon as a "super non-achiever". After having been dropped from both John Burroughs in St. Louis and my prep school in the east, I had, in fact, only managed to graduate from a St. Louis public high school because of the war's advent. At the time the Japanese attacked Pearl Harbor, it was clear that, barring a miracle, I would fail my senior year for the second time. So certain of this was I that a month or so previously, I had taken the necessary exams to qualify for enlistment as an Aviation Cadet in the Army Air Corps. In the Japanese attack, I knew I had my miracle; it was less in the spirit of patriotism that I awaited notification of my acceptance as a cadet than in a spirit of counting on the patriotism of the educational authorities. I suspected that they would get themselves into such a fever of desire for carnage that the first few declared candidates for bloodshed would receive special dispensation. Such, happily enough, turned out to be the case; I was indeed accepted as a cadet and the school authorities allowed me to receive my diploma. In a class of 419 students, my ranking was 419th. In terms of the first shall be last and the last shall be first, I have always been tempted to claim Christian sanction. Fortunately for the position in which Dorothy and I found ourselves now, there had been one glaring inconsistency during my educational record of non-achievement: carpentry. At John Burroughs, we had been required to attend manual training courses for a couple of hours a week and I had found that the neat, unarguable logic of squaring boards and knocking them together had appealed to me. This in turn, had been augmented by hobnobbing with the resident carpenter at my grandfather's place in Canada. Therefore, while out of the race with Chippendale, I was still a fair, if amateurish, hand with tools when Dorothy and I moved to our farm.

There were, things I could not do of course; both fine masonry work and plumbing were beyond me. Fortunately, one of our neighbors about a mile down the road was a jack of all trades who, along with a partner, undertook small contracting jobs ranging from remodelling to the building of houses from scratch. He was also unfailingly kind to Dorothy and me during the ensuing years. I called on him the day after our arrival and he accompanied me back to the farm to have a look at our plumbing problems. They were not excessively complicated. All that was needed was to dismantle the hand pump bringing up the water from the cistern, replace it with a small automatic electric pump and water tank for pressure and then lead the system through an electric water heater and across the kitchen where we would install the sink. He promised to take the job in hand for us just as soon as I had assembled the various needed components and he was as good as his word. Within three days, we had made the gigantic stride forward of having hot and cold running water in the kitchen.

With that key advance, we had, in a manner of speaking, consolidated our position and were now ready to attack the house. The first step was sheer, simple destruction. Starting with the living room (or to be more precise, what we intended to be the living room), I took a pick axe and drove it into the wall to knock and pry loose the old plaster and lath. As I opened a hole in the wall, the peculiar acrid odor we had found so unpleasant became even more pronounced. Behind the plaster, to a height of about five feet from floor level, the walls were packed with a strange gritty substance rather like very coarse sand. Dorothy and I examined it carefully and came to the totally mistaken conviction that it was mouse guano. Relieved that we had found the source of the smell, we went back to work knocking down the walls. At first, there was in the work that element of satisfaction which accompanies the tearing down of anything old and worn out in order to make room for the new. In the face of the sheer physical unpleasantness of the task, that soon palled. The dust raised by the combination of "mouse" guano and old plaster made it impossible to swing the pick for more than half an hour at a time. We worked with handkerchiefs tied around our faces. After taking down a section of the walls, we would allow the dust to settle for a while and then go back and load the debris onto a wheelbarrow and carry it off. This went on day after day; our rate of progress was discouragingly slow. But it was a question of first things first; we could not proceed with our remodelling until all the rooms in which we were not actually living had been taken down to the bare studs. On warm, sunny days when we could no longer face the dust and stink of plaster removing, we would alternate our labours by chopping cedar saplings from the fields behind the house.

As this seemingly endless task went on, the question of bringing home milk from the supermarket every two or three days continued to rankle. I forced myself to broach the question of getting a milk cow. Dorothy agreed that this was a sensible plan but she wondered if I knew how to milk a cow. I looked wise and mumbled something about how I thought I could figure it out from having watched the farmer on Amherst Island when I was a kid. She looked dubious but nowhere near as dubious as I felt. As I nerved myself to begin the search for a cow, I quietly began investigations towards getting my hands on some sort of do-it-yourself book about how to milk the animal. I soon discovered there was no such thing; it became crystal clear to me that I was thinking of bridging a gap across which society had thrown no guide lines. Obviously, one was expected either to *know* how to milk a cow or not milk a cow at all. The only other answer was to arrange for some sort of private tutorial sessions in cow milking, a plan which struck me as being both too ludicrous and too harmful to my pride to contemplate. Nevertheless, the need for a cow both as source of milk and as symbol of my earnestness regarding the farm persisted. Following my usual bent, I backed into the project.

My casual enquiries finally led me to a very pleasant dealer in livestock. I visited him at his farm. He listened to my requirements and assumed a dubious look.

"What you want is a family cow the way I see it."

"That's right," I replied, feeling reassurance at the coupling of the two words.

"Good family cow's hard to find," he said.

"Oh, I know that," I said, fervently hoping that he would never manage to find one.

"I don't know as I can do much for you, Mr. Sherry, but I'll surely keep my eye out for a good family cow."

I went away happy. Family cows were in short supply therefore honor had been satisfied. Thanking my lucky stars that it was all turning out so well, I stopped by the supermarket for another load of milk.

To days later, our newly-installed phone, rang. It was the friendly livestock dealer.

"Mr. Sherry, I got you the prettiest little Jersey cow you ever saw in your life."

"Wonderful news," I said, trying to conceal the tremor in my voice.

"When you want I should bring her out to your place?" he asked enthusiastically.

"Oh, any time that suits you," I said, trying to match his tone. What I really wanted to say was, "About five years from now".

"Listen," I said, trying to sound calm and casual, "This cow . . . what I mean to say . . . this cow . . . is she . . . has she. . . ?"

"You mean, has she come fresh yet?"

"Yes, that's what I mean." I was not sure I really understood the term "fresh". However, it sounded as if he had told me what I wanted to hear. Fortunately, he clarified his remark.

"No, she ain't had her calf yet. Appears to me to be about a week before she'll come fresh."

A week! Quickly, I took heart. Anything could happen in a week: Atomic war, flood, fire, tornadoes—anything. With a week of grace, surely I would be able to figure a way out of the situation.

"How'd it be if I brought her out in the morning then?" the livestock dealer asked.

"Fine," I said heartily, "I'll be waiting for you."

"What was all that about?" my wife wanted to know.

"Cow," I said, a shade paler than usual, "New cow. Coming in the morning." Feeling very rural, I added, "She won't come fresh for about a week though."

"What's that mean?"

"She won't have her calf for a week."

"You mean we're going to have a cow *and* a calf?"

"So it seems."

87

"I thought we were going to get just a plain cow."

"Well," I said with a certain tone of superiority, "cows do have to have calves, don't they?"

"Are you nervous? You certainly look nervous."

"Of course, I'm not nervous," I said with what I hoped was a sufficient show of conviction. Inside my head, I was repeating the phrase, "a week". I had a week's grace. Like a condemned prisoner, I did not really believe that the moment would actually arrive when I would mount the gallows. That night however, I slept fitfully.

At the crack of dawn the following morning, a horn sounded in front of the house. I staggered to the window and peered out blearily. A large covered truck like a moving van stood before the house. Clearly, my new cow had arrived. I threw on my clothes and hurried out.

"Mornin," the livestock dealer said.

"Mornin," I replied, trying my best to maintain a suitable rural calm.

"Funny thing about that little old cow," he said, "I would have bet my boots she wasn't gonna come fresh for a week or two."

"So you said," I replied, icy fingers clutching at my heart.

"Be durned if she didn't throw that calf last night. Bull calf, I'm afraid. Sorry about that."

I could not believe my luck had deserted me so cruelly.

"You mean there's a cow and a calf in that truck?"

"Take a look."

Heart quaking, I walked to the rear of the truck and peered in over the tail gate. What was actually in the truck was a very pretty little Jersey cow and her new-born calf. What seemed to be in the truck was a combination of Cerberus and the Loch Ness Monster with its young.

"Ain't she a beauty?" the livestock dealer asked enthusiastically.

"She certainly is," I lied.

"Where do you want her?"

"Down at the barn, I suppose."

He pulled his truck into the dirt drive and moved slowly along it towards my tumbledown barn. I followed morosely on foot. Courage, I told myself, forward and don't show the whites of your eyes.

We unloaded the cow and calf and ensconced them in a sort of loose box within the barn, nailing a couple of planks across the entry so they could not escape. I now abandoned my pride.

"What do I do now?" I asked the livestock dealer, a note of desperation in my voice.

"Well, you know how to milk a cow, don't you?" he asked in some surprise.

I could not bring myself to admit the truth. I lied in my teeth and said that I did. The livestock dealer undoubtedly had begun to suspect the truth. Fortunately, he was a gentleman.

"I brought you along a couple of bales of alfalfa hay that'll see you through the next few days. You just give her some hay and leave her alone with the calf for a day or so. She won't be ready to milk till then. For the first day or so, she won't give nothin but colestrum so you just let the calf have that. If her bag seems to be getting too full, just relieve the pressure my milking some of the colestrum out on the ground."

I nodded as if he were not suggesting feats as far beyond me as a ten-second hundred-yard dash. We unloaded the bales of hay and then went back to the house to conclude the financial aspects of the transaction. As the livestock dealer folded away my check in his wallet, he said, "You got yourself a fine little family cow there, Mr. Sherry. You ain't gonna have a bit of trouble with that little old cow." I nodded bravely in agreement and he took his departure. For the balance of the morning, my wife gave me a wide berth, aware that I was contemplating my own personal Golgotha.

During the morning, I made several visits to the barn. The cow and her calf seemed to be getting along as well as could be expected. In truth, Vacca (as she came to be called) was a small cow even for a Jersey; to me, she appeared to be the size of a full grown moose and I though I could detect a baleful gleam of resentment in her dark brown eyes. God, how I hated and feared that cow and the life that had brought me to such a pass.

During the course of the day, we had one or two casual visitations from neighbors who wished to examine our cow. Although we had been in residence little more than a week, we had been visited several times by neighbors tendering small gifts with the quiet, inbred courtesy of hill people. We were as strange to them as Martians but the advent of the cow seemed to enable them to place us in a more operative perspective. The concensus of opinion among those men who came to look over our cow was that we had made a good purchase. Then, late during the afternoon, as a neighbor and I were examining the cow, he said, "I'll tell you somethin, Mr. Sherry, that cow don't look right to me. In fact, that cow looks downright poorly."

I looked at the cow and realized immediately that he was right. The cow had suddenly grown very unsteady on her feet and, as we watched, she slowly sank to the ground. Panic rising rapidly, I asked the neighbor what he thought the trouble was.

"Probably milk fever," he said.

"What do I do?" I asked, trying to keep my voice from rising.

"Well, you got to get the vet. He'll give her some kind of shot and she'll likely be all right."

"What if I don't?"

"She could die on you. No, you better call the vet. One thing though, Mr. Sherry is that milk fever shows you bought yourself a pretty good cow. Sorry cows just don't get milk fever."

Clutching this frail reed of consolation, I telephoned a veterinarian and explained the situation. He said he would be along directly and was as good as his word. Having examined the cow, he concurred with my neighbor's diagnosis: it was milk fever. He explained that this was a sickness resulting from calcium deficiency and prepared a hypodermic containing a massive injection of calcium. The cow responded with amazing rapidity to the treatment. Within two hours, she was back on her feet, eyes alert and showing interest in her feed. The vet told me that what my neighbor had said was true by and large: that only cows of high quality tend to come down with milk fever.

Carrying a lantern, I examined the cow one last time before going to bed that night. She seemed fully recovered and her calf was working away busily on her bag. It did not seem too distended. I decided that I could give myself one more day's grace before trying to milk her.

I passed the next day absentmindedly knocking down old plaster walls. But my heart was not in the task; I was much preoccupied with the coming ordeal. My thoughts were a mixture of those of a young knight preparing for his first tournament, and a terminally-ill patient putting his affairs in order. In the afternoon, I drove to the local farmers' co-op and purchased a very professional looking stainless steel milking pail and a three-legged stool. It seemed unfair somehow that I should be forced to pay for the implements of my own torture. Still—as I was beginning to repeat to myself like a litany—nobody had forced me to this dreadful pass; I was there solely of my own choosing.

The next morning, I dawdled over my breakfast as long as possible even though I knew the business could not be postponed indefinitely. Finally, I gathered my new pail and stool and remarked to my wife with what I hoped was suitable jauntiness that I guessed I'd better go milk that cow. She smiled encouragingly but there was a certain tightness about the smile which deprived me of its solace. It was about half past seven when I set out morosely for the barn.

Both cow and calf appeared to be in good shape. The calf was butting and sucking away lustily at his mother's bag while she munched placidly away at her hay, showing no effects whatsoever from her siege of milk fever. As I entered the stall, they both turned to examine me. I could not help feeling a certain sarcastic sense of "Get him", in the cow's calm gaze.

The first problem was to remove the calf from the immediate scene of operations; my confidence was frail enough to start with, without having the calf butt away at his mother's bag as I attempted to milk her. I removed the lower rail from the entrance to the stall, manhandled the calf outside, and then replaced the rail so that he could not re-enter. The calf took immediate umbrage at this and began to bawl loudly, a disturbance conducive to the peace of mind of neither me nor the cow. I then loaded up the cow's manger with fresh alfalfa hay and made her fast enough with her halter rope so that she would have a limited amount of play

91

while I tried to milk her. The fresh alfalfa hay, would, I hoped, prove succulent enough to the unfortunate beast to conceal her owner's ineptitude. Having accomplished those small tasks, I went out and sat on the creek bank to smoke a cigarette and examine the sky for signs of succor. None were forthcoming. Finally, I took my pail and stool and advanced to the fray.

It seems odd now to think that I could have ever been afraid of Vacca who became, later on, such a pet. She was, in fact, a perfect love of a cow, the most gentle beast imaginable. Bad-tempered cows are not uncommon and, in time, I would own a few. If Vacca had turned out to be such a beast, I am certain it would have coloured my entire attitude towards milk cattle forever. However, as I made my highly tentative entry into her stall that day and stealthily placed my stool by her side, I was convinced that I was dealing with a bad actor and that I would be seriously kicked within seconds. Vacca made a few abortive motions with her leg which sent me scurrying for cover, but after about fifteen minutes, I managed to overcome my terror enough to sit beneath her on my stool. Still far from trusting me totally, the beast at least no longer seemed consciously malevolent.

Planted insecurely on my stool beneath the cow, we exchanged one long glance composed of supplication on my part and contemptuous curiosity on hers before she turned back to her manger. The moment seemed auspicious and I laid tremulous hands upon the two teats nearest me. Holding them gingerly, I began to make tentative up and down motions such as I remembered the farmer in Canada having employed. Even though her teats had been dripping milk when I took to my stool, precisely nothing now happened as a result of my ministrations. Still, I was rather pleased with myself. I was, after all, seated beneath the cow, actually pulling on her teats—and this was, in my heart of hearts, further than I ever thought I would get. A slight tinge of euphoria was born; it seemed to me that I looked both competent and professional as I pulled away at the poor beast's teats in what I felt was the approved manner. I increased the speed of my motions and smoothed out their tempo. Still, nothing happened; Vacca turned to examine me wonderingly a time or two before turning back to her hay in seeming resignation to her proprietor's ineptitude. I jogged along happily for a while, certain that things would turn out all right. But they didn't; not a single drop of milk appeared. A feeling of leaden fatigue began to attack my forearms.

Milking a cow (or not milking a cow as I was then doing) places an almost unbelievably arduous strain on the arms of anyone not accustomed to it. Some months later, Darroch came to visit us on the farm, bringing with him some archery equipment whose virtues and beneficial effect upon the soul he was then extolling. A far more powerful man than I, he warned me rather contemptuously that the bow required extreme pressure to bend and that anyone such as I who was not used to shooting the thing would not be able to do it. He was absolutely right; my brother, who was present also at the time, tried to bend the bow and succeeded only in getting it half way back before his arms began to shake and then collapse. Conditioned, by that time, to the twice daily milking of a cow, I was able to bend the bow without strain.

Now, as my untrained arms jerked and hauled upon poor Vacca's teats, the strain proved too much. My arms began to tremble and I had to desist. I crawled out from beneath the cow and went to sit beside the creek again to smoke another cigarette and try to figure out what I was doing wrong.

What I was doing wrong—or, to be more precise, what I was not doing at all—was based on complete ignorance of how a cow's lactation system functions; I did not get very far in my diagnosis of the trouble, therefore. No one had told me that there is a certain amount of voluntary cooperation required on the part of a cow before she can be milked. A cow must be induced to "let down" her milk, particularly when she is in strange circumstances (as Vacca certainly was), or after calving when she is tense and upset. This can be accomplished by bathing her bag with a warm cloth. Once she has "let down" her milk, the problem is simply one of squeezing the milk from each teat, using one's hand as a pump and then relaxing the pressure for a second while the teat refills itself. The jerking and pulling motion I was using may have seemed terribly stylish to me but what I did not know was that it couldn't and wouldn't extract one drop of milk from that poor cow. Having no way of knowing any of this, I returned to the wars on the same old terms. With exactly the same deplorable lack of results.

Thus I strove for what seemed an eternity, pulling and hauling until my muscles would no longer stand it, resting for a while and then pulling and hauling some more. As my frustration grew, so did my anger. Although, it was a brisk morning, I was stripped down to my shirt and wringing wet with sweat. The only positive benefit accruing was that it was beginning to dawn on me how fortunate I had been in drawing such a good-natured and long-suffering cow. Vacca was, indeed, a family cow. She continued to view my macabre fumblings with mystified and resigned eyes.

Finally, through sheer luck and fatigue, I cracked the case. The muscles of my hands and forearms became so cramped that I could no longer use them with any effect. In desperation, I reached out with only my thumb and forefinger and gently ran them from the top of her teat to the bottom. I had unwittingly stumbled upon a technique known as "stripping." With no hope that I was doing anything still other than going through the motions, I did this a number of times. I could hardly believe my ears when I heard the ping of a feeble stream of milk hitting the bottom of the empty bucket. Unbelievingly I continued as the streams of milk grew stronger. An understanding of the entire process suddenly flooded my mind and I changed naturally from the "stripping" motion to a squeezing motion. The milk now hissed merrily and foamily into the pail. In half an hour, I had actually succeeded in milking the poor cow dry. I had begun the attempt at seven thirty in the morning. At twelve thirty that afternoon, I staggered back up the hill carrying a full pail of the richest milk I have ever seen. Never, before or since, have I been so proud of myself.

Our ownership of the cow provided certain benefits as real in the psychological sense as they were in the physical sense. We now had unlimited milk; the humiliating visits to the supermarket were over. Jersey cows are noted for the extent of the butter fat content of their milk and that which I obtained from Vacca was literally too rich to drink. At an auction, we bought a second hand electric churn for five dollars and Dorothy began to skim the cream from the milk and put it aside in a crock. Before too many days, Dorothy was turning out more butter than we could possibly use, as well as buttermilk and cottage cheese. We soon discovered that only a small fraction of the cream obtained sufficed for our needs and that it was possible to sell the rest in Wytheville. Every week, we carried a gallon or two of cream to town. The actual amount of money we got for it was negligible—about five dollars a week. For purposes of morale, however, this little bit of money was invaluable. Pittance though it was, it was a pittance being earned by our farm and thus an augury for the future.

More important, there was now some form of animal life on the farm: the place ceased being a total abstraction. And life has a way of turning into more life. My mind now began to toy with the idea of hogs. No garbage truck calls in the hills of Virginia and the disposal of excess and leftover food presented us with a real and rather messy problem. Pigs are, of course, natural garbage disposal units so I hied myself back to my friendly livestock dealer to discuss the purchase of a couple of shoats. In due course, they arrived and I installed them in a pen near the barn where I built them a small shelter sturdily, if rather sloppily constructed by affixing boards to Locust posts sunk in the ground. We subsequently raised these pigs to maturity, had them slaughtered and cured at the local locker plant and enjoyed our own bacon, ham and sausage for some time as a result. However, this was our sole venture in pig raising; hogs did not bring out the best in me.

They fascinated me, I admit. Many a time, I have let an hour go by as I leaned idly on the rails of their pen watching them. The affection and reverence I felt for Vacca, as a source of both good nature and good things was entirely reversed in the case of the pigs. My attitude towards them was Shavian in concept and one of basic horror. Pigs are brutish, insensitive and concerned only with eating their way to their own extinction. Worst of all, they brought out a streak of cruelty in me that I had been unaware of previously. Never having before displayed sadistic tendencies, I now found myself going out of my way to give one or the other a kick. Once, later on, when a stray hog got into our garden, I shot him in the rear end with a shotgun full of birdshot and I confess shamefacedly that I enjoyed his squeals of pain as he ran away. This rather worried me until I unwittingly discovered that pigs tend to bring out the worst in everyone. Reading a farm magazine one night, I came across an article called, poetically enough, "Take It Easy On That Hog". Its point and purport were that this pig-hate I felt was so common that farmers were cutting their own throats by bringing hogs to market whose hides had been damaged by senseless acts of violence. Somehow the knowledge that pigs were universally detested enabled me to curb my dislike of mine and I was kinder to them after that. But I decided that I wanted no more pigs in the future.

Shortly after buying the pigs, I made one other foray into the purchase of livestock which eventually turned out to be rather interesting. Our land, as I have said, was poor, overgrown and in need of lime and fertilizer which we would eventually apply. I had been told that sheep or goats would eat a great deal of those poor land growths which a cow would disdain. Goats somehow did not seem our speed at all. However, I talked over the idea of sheep with L., the livestock dealer, and he agreed that a few sheep might be profitable and would certainly benefit the land. Accordingly, we bought and installed fifteen ewes and a ram. They were silly animals, appealing from a distance but noxious upon closer acquaintance. They required little or no maintenance, however; even during the winter they live almost completely off the land; an occasional bale of hay thrown into the fields when there was snow on the ground was all they needed to survive. ((It is rather interesting to report that those sheep were an amazingly profitable venture. I paid $300 for the lot and kept them through the winter, spring and most of the following summer. When I finally sold them, I found that from their wool, the lamb crop and the resale of the ewes and ram, I had made over $700.))

By then, we had been on the farm for a little over a month. Our house was a shambles but it was slowly coming on. And our farm contained one cow, sixteen sheep and two hogs. We also possessed a second-hand Ford tractor and mowing machine which had been given us by my mother. All in all, it was quite a jump from washing down the cannelloni with Frank O'Connor at Ranieri in Rome less than a year before.

96

CHAPTER VII

For all my sixteen sheep, two hogs and one milk cow, the view of my function to which I still held firmly was that of a novelist. At this stage certainly—and it appeared, for a long time to come—the farm was going to be at best a way of life rather than a means of providing. To make progress, to improve the place little by little, was obviously going to expend more money than it would bring in. Convinced that I could write myself out of this financial bind, I now set to work furiously on a second novel, spending a few hours each morning on the task. The hope centered on the project was so great as to totally preclude objectivity, but on the whole I was pleased with it. My rough plan was to labor on with it until I had approximately 80,000 to 100,000 words down on paper and then send it off to Hiram Haydn at Random House and sit back and wait for a contract, an advance against royalties, and words of praise and encouragement.

Our days assumed a pattern: rise early, milk the cow and slop the pigs and work on my novel until I ran out of steam. By then, Dorothy would have finished her household chores and we would work on the house the rest of the day, stopping to do the evening milking. After this, we would read or watch the television set for awhile and go early to bed. For people who were essentially sociable and used to some pretty rich social action, it was a curiously barren time. It was impossible to pretend that we were on the same intellectual wave length as the hill people among whom we lived. It would have been nice if our neighbor, Bill, had turned out to be congenial, but he did not. In truth, he drove me up the wall; he was a convert to Mormonism, a religion whose adherents practice

97

prosyletizing as an essential part of the discipline of their odd convictions. Poor Bill; I now realize that he and his wife were probably as lonely as Dorothy and I; the difference being that, while Dorothy and I longed for concourse with O'Hara and Kate and Darroch and Frank O'Connor, Bill and his wife longed for the company of fellow Mormons. He came one day to visit me, loaded for bear in regard to my potential conversion. I fear he went away with a pretty serious flea in his ear. While I sat in a veritable fog of boredom, he told me some incredible story of how Mormonism was founded when Joseph Smith was visited by the angel, Moroni, a dismal and aptly named emissary from a better world, who instructed Brother Smith to dig under a tree at which place he found a bunch of dreary tablets prohibiting damned near everything. When I made it clear that I found the whole tale ill-constructed and lacking in both suspense and depth, Bill went away sadly shaking his head. He carried himself with that sad air of those who long, at bottom, for martyrdom. But he sensed in me a certain proclivity for metaphysical speculation and he frequently renewed his attack in spite of my irreverence. "Heard anything from the angel Moroni lately?" I would demand whenever I saw him, and he would advise me in return about the uselessness of casting pearls before swine. I did not, indeed could not have got to know Bill well, but there was an appealing quality of strangeness about him which stemmed from his having coupled himself and his family to a religion completely non-indigenous to the region. Later on, he would put his place up at auction and move to Utah.

He had a younger brother, Clyde, who lived with his parents on the lovely estate which backed on my farm; he was an odd, lonely youth who would raise one arm in greeting as he rode by in his jeep. In time, my dealings with young Clyde would become profoundly complicated and hair-raising; he will be a major character in this account in fact. For the moment, however, we were unacquainted with each other beyond a friendly wave.

With one very important exception, our other neighbors were kind, mannerly, exceedingly generous—and terribly, terribly dull. By urban standards, they were poor people; the average cash income of the families on our road could not have been much more than two thousand dollars a year. Most of them were what are known as "sundown farmers;" which is to say that they worked desultorily at some other job to augment the paltry return from their farms. Yet one could not really call them poor because their standards were so widely divergent from those of the prosperous nation in which they lived. As far as most of them were concerned, the world stopped twenty-five miles in any direction from their farms; a trip to Roanoke, the nearest metropolis, was something to be treasured for months if not years.

The exception among our neighbors has since died. His name was Fred Cline and he was one of the first people to call upon us after we took up residence upon the farm. From the first, some Southern sensibility about class made him adopt a certain formality of address which he clung to throughout our years of friendship and interdependence. He impressed his own particular brand of gamesmanship and individuality by addressing me as "Mister Cherry." I called him Fred always, and would have been delighted if he had reciprocated, but he preferred that formal variation upon my real name. There was never the slightest doubt that the variation was a perfectly conscious, if minor, ploy which gave him some degree of satisfaction.

I would like to present Fred as having been a rural primitive pure of heart and free from greed and avarice but I believe he would be the first to break out laughing if it came to his attention. Although he was extremely cagey about his lack of ability to read and write, I am certain that his efforts in that direction did not go much beyond being able to sign his name. His age, when I first met him, was somewhere between fifty-five and sixty. Even then, he was subject to bouts of what he called "wind" and shortness of breath. From having observed my father prior to his first heart attack, I was extremely suspicious that Fred Cline was an incipient candidate for a coronary occlusion, but in spite of threats, warnings and cajolery, I could never convince him that he should curtail his activities or even see a doctor. He was not a tall man but he was solidly built and inclined toward overweight. Strong as a bull and a tireless worker when the task was to his liking, he was the sort of man who would have been a godsend to an infantry platoon in time of war.

He and his wife, a beautiful, weatherbeaten woman whom Andrew Wyeth would long to paint, lived alone on a small farm which marched with mine for a short distance. Their manner of life could not have been much different from that of the forebears from whom their land had been inherited. They kept some chickens and a milk cow or two which were always milked by Mrs. Cline. The staple of their diet was home-cured and canned pork; each year, Fred would raise and slaughter a few hogs, hanging the carcasses to cool from the bough of the same tree his ancestors had, and scraping bristles from hides with the same old tools. They owned an aging team of horses which Fred used to plow the ground for his annual crop of potatoes—but he had no automobile. Though later on they acquired one, they owned no television set when we first met. In fine weather, Fred spent the days tramping his own fields and those of his neighbors; he had that common burning primitive desire to be in the know about everything that was happening in and around his bailiwick. (Once, when Dorothy and I were building a stretch of new fence, we were amused each morning when we went to our work to find Fred's footprints by each new fence post where he had stood in order to wiggle each post in judgment of the strength and durability of the job we were doing; when I kidded him about his nocturnal inspections of our work, he blandly denied the whole thing.)

In a way, Fred Cline was a hangover from that cultural past of the hill country about which certain novelists long to wax sentimental: hunting and fishing and making white whiskey, and spending the nights sociably by a fire with other men while they listened to their hounds cry as they put up a fox. But, sad to say, these things which I had expected to find still an integral part of the life of the area no longer existed. To some extent, of course, the change resulted from such diversions as television; who, after all, wants to sit by a fire listening to foxhounds when he can watch "Gunsmoke?" But more than that, it was somehow a loss of heart on the part of our neighbors towards their backwoods past—they were slowly being corrupted by the encroachments of a complex society, but the complexities of the society brought with them no balancing factor, no alleviation of sophistication. The second-hand cars they bought were doomed to end as rusty ruins in their farmyards and be replaced by other second-hand cars which would become still more rusty ruins. They were people on the verge of extinction. The encroachment of complexity did not produce a desire for more and better but instead a lack of real desire for anything. Oh, there were exceptions, of course; men who were trying to work their land in a modern manner and thinking about the education of their children. But the majority were in the first stages of a state of apathy.

Far from being one of nature's nobleman, Fred Cline did not share the essential apathy of most of our neighbors. He was interested in himself and he was interested in other people. Much of this interest was of the good old-fashioned back-fence snoop variety, but there was also a certain depth to the man. His pleasure in the animal life of the woods, for example, was profound and genuine. He had been a great hunter in his life but in all the time I knew him, the only occasions on which I saw him handle a firearm was when he took down his rifle to slaughter his hogs. Just how he had come to his decision to hunt and kill no more was difficult to fathom, but I am certain his was a conscious, intellectual position. An occasional casual anecdote would sometimes throw light on the cruelty of his nature as a boy and as a young man. Once he told me how he had deliberately thrown gasoline on a dog and set him afire. Another time, he described how, as a young man, he and his friends would spend whole nights with their dogs, attempting—sometimes successfully—to harass a deer into running off a cliff. But his manner of reference to such incidents was not prideful—nor was it unduly regretful. It was as if he were saying: I did those things and they were not good things but I thought about them and now I don't do them any more.

In the matter of religion also did Fred differ from our other neighbors. They were, to a family, strong fundamentalist Bible pounders possessed by a powerful and constant sense of being watched by a jealous and angry God. It takes a certain amount of bravery for a primitive man to deny the mores of the tribe and I never saw Fred or his wife go near a church in the time I knew them. Nor was he at all given to the commonly encountered sanctimonious references to the Deity. Once again, this seemed on his part to be a conscious decision which had been arrived at by thought. And any attempt to draw him out on such matters brought forth only a sly and rather mischievous grin which seemed to say: I've thought about all that and decided that it's none of my business. Primitive and unlettered though he was, Fred Cline was nevertheless a fundamentally intellectual man and I think this was the basis of my great liking for him. Once, later on, when we were working on some job together, he became very shifty in the way he did whenever he was about to risk himself by enquiring about some weighty matter. We were good friends by then and I let him hem and haw, knowing he would come to the point sooner or later. His question, when it came, was a beauty. It was just after he and his wife had finally acquired a TV set, a major milestone which had brought the world into the kitchen of their farmhouse with a vengeance. "Mr. Cherry," he said, "you know when they shoot them fellers on the TV?"

"Yes," I said.

"Well, my wife and them say that when they shoot them fellers, they really dead."

"Oh, for God's sake, Fred," I said, "you know better than that."

He grinned and said, "Yes, I do, Mr. Cherry, but they bound and determined to believe it."

We both burst out laughing then and I said, "Listen, Fred, you tell them that that thing is just a big box full of wires."

"All right," he said, laughing.

"And I'll tell you what: someday I'll go up and get on the damned thing and when I do, the first thing I'll do is wink at you."

Eventually I did precisely that. And, when I next saw Fred, I said, "Did you see me wink at you?"

"Mr. Cherry," he said happily, "I shore did."

Before I went to live in the hills of Virginia, I would not have believed it possible to find people in the twentieth century living in the United States of America who were so completely divorced from the economic and political currents of the times. Awareness of the two things, of course, goes hand in hand and the fundamental economic position of the hill people on their small, unproductive farms serves to keep them in ignorance of why and how they are governed. This is compounded by an almost conscious policy on the part of the

Government of Virginia to provide as few avenues of enlightenment as possible. During the years we lived in Virginia, the state was governed in a bewilderingly autocratic manner by Senator Harry Byrd and, since his death, I cannot see that things have changed much. The Governorship of the state is handed contemptuously around by the Byrd machine among a small group of tried and true aristocrats who are, psychologically, not very far this side of believing in the divine right of kings. And, no matter how much or how often these men protest the purity of their paternalistic intentions, the net result of those intentions is that the few grow more rich and powerful at the expense of the many. When the late Harry Byrd went to his grave in such a fog of eulogy, one could not help marveling at the ability of the Virginian virus to penetrate even the non-Virginian mind. For Virginia is a virus and the deadly game played throughout the nation of assigning purity to anything Virginian serves to lend dignity to methods and means of protecting and promulgating class consciousness which are essentially tawdry.

In the tidewater, in Richmond or in Charlottesville (which becomes ever more increasingly a haven for wealthy, politically right-minded outlanders), the quaint charade played by the governing class of the state may provide a certain amount of creaky charm. In the hill country, it provides only poverty, ignorance and despair. Hillbilly western Virginia and patrician Virginia make an awkward pair.

However, these views which I now hold so strongly were not born overnight. For the present, my wife and I were satisfied. The beauty of our surroundings, the demands of the future, and the strange and new sociological pickings of our new life served to command both our interest and our concentration. But we did long for kindred companionship. Ask then, and ye shall receive. And wonder throughout your life whether you should have asked in the first place.

One night the telephone rang. It was O'Hara. We had, of course, been in correspondence while he and Kate had been in Scotland. O'Hara had written that they were planning to return to the States but I had not known exactly when. Now, it seemed, they were back; I quizzed O'Hara about his plans but he was vague. In the course of our telephone conversation that night, it became clear that O'Hara wanted to pay us a visit on the farm. Both Dorothy and I were delighted; we were both ready for a respite from our social isolation. It was arranged that I should meet his train in Wytheville a couple of days later. Only O'Hara was coming; Kate and her two children would remain in their temporary accommodations near New York. There seemed no reason to inquire too deeply into O'Hara's strong desire to visit our farm. We were, after all, the oldest and closest of friends and it was not unexpected that O'Hara should wish to have a look at the try we were making which seemed so far out of character.

He arrived in due course. Both Dorothy and I were extremely interested to see what effect, if any, marriage to the woman with whom he had been preoccupied most of his life had had upon him. Although he seemed much the same at first sight, I soon began to realize that he was under great strain. I knew O'Hara as well as any man can know another and a sure sign on his part of tremendous inner turmoil was the maintenance of an almost supernatural calm. As he sat in a chair, I could very nearly measure his interior heat by the degree of willfully superimposed relaxation he managed to enforce upon his body. One of the major sources of my bemusement with O'Hara throughout the years of our friendship had been the extent of pure willfulness in his control of himself. I knew the tenuousness of that control because, on at least two occasions, I had seen it crack and heard about a few more; there was always a very definite element of danger present at such moments.

Early in his visit to the farm that winter, I realized that O'Hara's interior torment had achieved a degree of heat which even I had not before encountered. The basic signs were unmistakable; his calm was that of a Mandarin. However, he had further embroidered his blanket of spurious calm with an act of willfulness both grotesque and appealing to my sense of humor. He had—not to put too fine a point upon it—made a conscious policy decision about farting.

I confess at the outset to being hopelessly juvenile about the social contratemps afforded by an unauthorized and involuntary public fart; the anger, fear and confusion which result fill me with fierce glee.

The first time such an occurrence took place, we were seated talking by the fire in our now re-modelled living room.

O'Hara, unquestionably the best talker I have ever listened to, is in speech as precise as he is in his mind and, tends to punctuate his thoughts with aphorisms which are both funny and sustaining. As usual, I was listening spellbound when a loud fart rent the air. Feeling that he had perhaps made a simple mistake, I congratulated him in Italian, saying, "*Auguri.*" He ignored my congratulations and continued with his discourse, one leg draped negligently over the arm of his chair, his hand resting calmly on the back. I realized immediately that I was being presented with the fruits of a policy decision. I was expected to ignore this phenomenom as I might were the same thing to happen during a Papal audience. Soon, the same thing happened again. In spite of my determination to play the game, a muscle began to twitch near my mouth. The third time, I began to laugh, as did Dorothy, who was also present in the room. O'Hara looked at us pityingly for an instant and then continued with his discourse.

In my wildest dreams, it had not occurred to me that the real purpose of O'Hara's visit to the farm was to case Wytheville and its environs with an eye towards moving Kate and her children there to settle. Even though I laugh rather hollowly now as I write these words, it seemed far too much to hope that our hill-billy social desert could attract the permanent presence of the family to whom, by both shared experience and mutual predilection, Dorothy and I were closer than any other in the world. Yet, as it turned out, this was precisely what was on O'Hara's mind. I know now whence stemmed the motivation of O'Hara's desire to settle in Wytheville. He was, for the moment, without an idea of his own and so it seemed to him the better part of wisdom to shelter behind that of someone else. A human and understandable position certainly but O'Hara had strong temptations and abilities to go beyond the human in pursuit of what he believed to be his own survival.

During that first visit, O'Hara did not immediately declare his interest in settling his family in Wytheville. Like Dracula, he had some ingrained need to be invited into the sphere of his future operations. When he suggested that I take him around to see the real estate agent who had sold me my farm, it dawned on me that his interest might be more than idle curiosity. And, at that point, he was still waiting to be influenced by circumstance. Circumstance immediately played for him like a performing seal; the real estate agent just happened to have a genuinely charming house for rent for a nominal sum in an attractive part of Wytheville. Faced with the advent of genuine possibility, O'Hara asked me rather quizzically if Dorothy and I really wanted them to move into our bailiwick. The quizzical business passed me by; I was delighted and so was Dorothy, and we said so.

I heard the far off warning bell once again, however, during his visit; and once again, I ignored it. A grotesque and gloomy incident took place. It seemed hilarious at the time. Alas, it contained much portent for the future.

Earlier in this chapter, I commented briefly upon some of the sociological peculiarities of the region. Saving it until now, I purposely ignored making comment upon Virginian mores as they are concerned with drink. Like most things in Virginia, drinking is a pastime which is made as uncomfortable as possible for the lower classes. Not to say that by American standards drink is not plentiful and cheap. Because it is; it is, in fact, trustworthily axiomatic to say that the less evolved the government of a Christian community, the cheaper the booze and vice versa. To begin with, in Virginia, hard liquor is dispensed only from state-owned stores by clerks in clinical grey jackets. The entire transaction is a cross between a visit to a bank and a visit to the outpatient department of a hospital. Never, during my many visits to our local such establishment, did I encounter a single person who thought of himself as a member of the ruling classes. To such a person, standing in line in the state-owned liquor store would be considered demeaning beyond description—the houseboy or some town loafer is sent on such errands by proud tradition. The fine old Bourbon which these emissaries bring home to the gentry is soaked up constantly, heartily and in comfort. The poor devils in overalls, so déclassée as to be buying for themselves, do so with a woebegone air of guilt and the hangdog look of men compelled by tradition to drink up alleyways, behind barns, and in automobiles.

The plight of him who seeks the solace and companionship of his neighborhood saloon is even grimmer. No hard liquor is served for consumption on the premises anywhere in the entire misbegotten State of Virginia except rich men's clubs.

Three point two beer can be obtained for on the spot consumption in the warmth of certain specified gas stations. In every town, there are one or two dank and gloomy establishments where unwashed louts and losers sit drinking beer in an atmosphere of despair. It goes without saying that the same "gentleman" who, embarrased, at least, at being caught in the line at the liquor store, would very nearly prefer death than be seen in such an establishment as I describe. The proprietor of such an establishment would be made just as nervous by the presence of the "gentleman."

One day during O'Hara's visit, he and I went into such an establishment to while away an hour drinking beer. Up till that point, I had stuck pretty close to my farm and was largely unfamiliar with the modus operandi of Virginia custom. But it did not take much time or very sharp eyes that day to see that our presence in the saloon made both proprietor and customers extremely nervous. Our manner of speaking and our clothes were different from those of the other people in the bar, but it was not these things which eventually caused the contratemps. It was, purely and simply, the traditional situation of the officer's presence causing unrest in the enlisted man's saloon.

After drinking beer and talking for approximately an hour, we fell into casual conversation with some men at a nearby table—the sort of talk which is common to saloons from zanzibar to Nome, Alaska. I cannot now remember of what we spoke but certainly it was of trivial matters. The men were polite but mystified by our manner of speech and, I now realize, probably did not even understand our banter. As tends to happen when men of differing level of intelligence and experience drink together and hold concourse, puzzlement at us on the part of these men turned into discomfiture and discomfiture turned into a mild anger. One of them finally quit the saloon muttering something like, "I sware, I cain't understand a thing you fellers are sayin." The proprietor of the place watched this intercourse nervously throughout. He had been unhappy with our presence since we entered and I now know that this unhappiness stemmed from his sure and certain knowledge that the class barriers of Virginia were being contravened. Our presence was even worse for him than would have been, say, the presence of a local lawyer and doctor; even in the highly unlikely eventuality that such a thing could ever happen, the proprietor at least would have known who the doctor and lawyer were and would simply sit it out uncomfortably until they left. But we were an unknown quantity and he owed us no allegiance. When O'Hara motioned for our glasses to be refilled, the saloon proprietor did a stupid thing, but one which, in the light of my subsequent experience in Virginia, is understandable: he refused to serve us.

We, of course, demanded, why. Muttering something about our having used bad language (with which the air in the place was blue), he backed away shiftily and demanded that we vacate the premises. We refused and asked again that we be served. Again, he refused and said that, if we did not leave, he would call a cop. We advised him to call the cop, he did so, and a few moments later, a policeman entered the place; in colloquy with the proprietor, the cop glanced nervously at our table a time or two. Clearly, he found our presence in the bar as inexplicable as did the proprietor. Finally, the cop hitched up his gun belt with a sigh and approached our table. "I'm afraid I'm going to have to ask you gentlemen to leave," he said. He was polite and unsure of himself. By that time, we were not entirely sober but still far from drunk. We were, in fact, puzzled and angered by the entire situation.

Explaining that in our view, absolutely nothing had happened to warrant the presence of the constabulary, we told him that we were not prepared to leave and, indeed, wanted more beer to drink. Resistance toughened the policeman; he was adamant: we must leave. I am firmly convinced to this day that his position, like that of the proprietor, stemmed from a lifelong exposure to the good old Virginian principle that a mixing of social classes can only result in trouble for all.

As his resistance toughened so did ours; we refused to leave. He allowed as how, if we did not leave, he would have to put us under arrest. We said go ahead, and he did so. With all three of us feeling rather foolish, we left the bar and climbed into his police car. The strangest thing of all was that the entire occurrence took place in an atmosphere of the most extreme southern courtesy. We chattered together in friendly fashion on the way to the police station.

There was never any question of being thrown into a cell.

We would achieve that distinction in time, but today we were "gentlemen" and, accordingly, were treated with that mixture of suspicion and respect which such a chimerical position receives in the Old Dominion.

In truth, it was rather funny. The police clearly did not want us there any more than we wanted to be there. This became even more apparent when they questioned us and found out that I owned a farm to the west of town and that O'Hara was my guest. The combination of being a "gentleman" and owning land is, in Virginia, a potent one; Virginian social values take all that is bad from the English and leave all that is good behind. Having ascertained these fundamental facts about us, the police withdrew worriedly to another room. O'Hara remarked that it was very nearly an incredible situation and, indeed, it was so incredible that we both began to laugh. This caused an even more worried penetration of heads whose eyes examined us with sadness and lack of comprehension. It suddenly dawned on me how I could get us out of the situation gracefully. I explained this to O'Hara and he said, for God's sake go ahead. The joke was wearing thin.

About two weeks before the president of the bank where we did our business had introduced me to a young lawyer named Bean. He was a likeable young fellow about my own age. More important to our present predicament, I had also had no trouble in spotting him for a pre-eminent product of the local squirearchy. We had chatted together for about fifteen minutes that day at the bank and Lawyer Bean made it plain during our chat that he tended to consider me as an entirely logical, if eccentric, recruit to local upper-class circles. I didn't much care about that but I had liked Lawyer Bean immediately, and I would like to say here and now that throughout my years in Wytheville, he was an unfailingly loyal, courteous and helpful friend to me even though, in time, he must have come to regard me and my friends as some sort of terrible time bomb waiting to go off in the local body politic. At any rate, I was fairly certain that a telephone call to Lawyer Bean would get us out of our present predicament with alacrity and I was right.

The degree of alacrity and the change of attitude on the part of the police towards their two unclassifiable prisoners took both O'Hara and me by surprise. I called one of the cops in and asked him if I could make a telephone call. He was perfectly amenable and wanted to know whom I intended to call. When I mentioned Lawyer Bean's name, the cop's face relaxed in relief; his interior warning system had been right; we were well connected. Then the look of relief changed to one of worry; perhaps we were *too* well-connected. To make a long story short, I telephoned Lawyer Bean and explained that we had run afoul of the Neanderthal local social structure and asked for succor. He was greatly amused by the whole thing, spoke a few words to the police, and we were released immediately with many smiles and handshakes all around.

The incident was closed but a small nagging sense of worry persisted. The fact was that the social customs *were* Neanderthal. They had been born in meanness and persisted through poverty of spirit. It seemed logical to suppose that I might run afoul of them again.

A few days later, O'Hara completed the formalities attendant upon renting the house he had chosen and took the train back east to collect Kate and the children. I viewed their arrival with nothing but a feeling of soaring happiness about the future. For, not daring to allow the light to fall upon a dream so romantic, the truth is that I harbored in my heart a hope that my farm could be for me and my friends a nucleus and a gathering point from which we could go forward. And, even now, I cannot apologize for this; it was an honorable dream.

My generation had not then taken power; they waited in the wings, gathering their resources. It was then 1955 and that generation would begin to assume the reins of power around 1960. My faith was total that my hands and those of my friends would be among those which would hold those reins. I ponder now frequently the reasons this has not turned out to be true. In New York—as I scribbled furiously away at my novel on the farm, the stars of my generation which would make up the final galaxy were gathering and circling, growling and biting and snapping at the prizes which still lay on the toastmaster's table. My friends and I published our books, and our plays were produced, but the sheen of stardom did not settle upon us. There is little self pity in the words I write; one should not argue with what happens but spend the same energy in trying to understand it. In truth, I know only one thing about all of this: the stars of my generation were never ambivalent about their desire for that stardom. They studied the priorities attendant upon their quest for preeminence and they obeyed them. As one of the most famous of the galaxy said: "A boy has got to hustle". And that fine collection of murderous assailants, jet-set pederasts, silver-spoon-born politicians, and lyrical talents who rule the roost have, in the words of the old-time St. Louis prostitutes, hustled their fats with a vengeance. The pursuit of success in a society of bewilderingly compounded complexity is a matter of rigid adherence to properly constituted priorities. It seems almost comic to me, now, that I did not understand this, that I did not understand that seven years on a Virginia hill farm constitute no priority to any but a deluded mind. Yet delusions are a variable constant. They determine your choice of the life you get—and the life you get is the life you must lead. It seems poignant to me now; poignant, and perhaps a little stupid, that I could have ever dreamed of a little Athens in the hills of Virginia to which people would come and from which people would go refreshed to make their contributions. But it does not seem wrong.

CHAPTER VIII

Throughout the following months, the manuscript of my novel grew and I had much hope of it. More and more, in fact, did I come to view the project as the heaviest artillery available in the family arsenal of survival. Generally speaking, it is of course a serious mistake to assign excessive hope to any creative project. Humanly speaking, it is very nearly impossible to refrain from doing so. Even now, as I write this and bear the psychic scars of several duckings in the quicksand of public fancy, I doubt that I shall ever be able to control the vibrant hope which grows before a publication date, the opening of a play or the release of a film upon which I have worked. No stern self administered lecture about childishness and lack of professionalism seems to mitigate against this tendency. The moral, I suppose, is that everyone who attempts to contrive a work of the imagination is at bottom some kind of actor who not only wants a damned good supper in return for his song but a pat on the head for his performance as well.

1955 was, in fact—until some rather gloomy events which would mark its closing—a happy year. The remodelling of our house continued steadily. Slowly, the downstairs was finished and the upstairs taken in hand. We changed the layout of the upstairs, framing in new partitions to allow for a bathroom and extra closets. I continued to marvel at the quantity of mouse guano which we had removed from the walls of the house. It was my neighbor, Fred Cline, who finally gave me the bad news about my mouse guano. Idly chatting with him one day as we stood near a wheelbarrow load of this substance, I said that it struck me as remarkable that a few mice could manufacture that many calling cards even with decades to work on the job. Fred began to laugh and then notified me of the truth succinctly. "Mister Cherry," he said, "that ain't mouse shit, that's bat shit."

I blanched, hoping against hope that he was wrong and knowing that he wasn't. Fred asked for a flashlight and we went upstairs to have a look. Most of the ceilings had not yet been replaced on the upstairs rooms and Fred had no trouble in proving his point. We climbed up a stepladder and Fred shined the light up into the darkness of the attic rafters. Hanging in clusters, and so well-camouflaged that I had not until then noticed them, were more bats than I would have believed existed in the world. It is impossible to know how many there were but without question, the number could not have been less than a thousand. Deep in the grip of panic, I asked Fred what we were going to do. He counseled calm, saying, "Hell, Mister Cherry, them bats ain't gonna bother you none; they been livin' in that attic for twenty or thirty years and they ain't bothered nobody yet."

I could not share his equanimity. As far as I was concerned, a bat was too far behind the evolutionary game for tolerance. A proud member of a race which had fought its way up from primeval ooze, I considered a bat a miniature pterodactyl which had about as much right to be alive in my house as a dinosaur. Furthermore, I reacted according to the instructions of every old wives' tale concerning bats; the fact that I am bald, for example, failed completely to still the birth of immediate fear that one would get in my hair.

Dorothy was of course as discouraged as I by the discovery of our resident hoard of bats. However, Fred Cline's counsel concerning them turned out to be essentially accurate. For the moment, at any rate, the bats showed as little inclination to have anything to do with us as we did to have anything to do with them. The weather was still cold and bats are hibernatory mammals who do not venture forth on their nocturnal expeditions when the temperature is below a certain point. We decided to bide our time. On my part, it was a wholly ostrich-like decision; I was terrified of the things.

Early that spring, my brother Earl arrived for a prolonged stay with us at the farm. It was one of several such prolonged stays he would make with us during the years. If I sound a bit wry when I say he tended to arrive with the good weather and

114

depart with the bad, it is only the truth and frankly struck me as rather sensible on his part; it was not, after all, his farm. But it was properly a haven for him and a place to retire to when he would tire of Florida or California or Europe. And, when with us on the farm, he was always a help, pitching in with whatever task was at hand, whether house-remodelling or work in the fields.

Up till now, I have little to say about my brother except that I have always been and always will be deeply fond of him. Before coming to us at the farm this time, he had been for some months on the West Coast where he has since told me, he had for the first time received an inkling of insight into his alcoholism and had started to think about entering AA. Eventually he would do just that. But, at the time of which I write, only he had begun to suspect that he was among those many human beings for whom drink is a categoric disaster. Fond of drink then as I am now, I was aware that there was such a sickness as alcoholism, but it had not yet occurred to me that such close friends as my brother and Darroch would fall prey to it.

It was shortly after my brother's arrival that spring when the incident took place which finally led to a decisive plan of action regarding our attic full of bats. My mother also was spending a few days with us, having driven up from North Carolina. By that time, the remodelling of the house was approximately two-thirds done. The ceilings and walls had been replaced except for one patch above the small room upstairs which we planned to turn into a bathroom. There I had purposely left a section of the ceiling open to allow passage through the attic of any electrical wiring we might want to do. Even though it was clearly possible for the bats to invade the house proper by descending through this piece of open ceiling, Fred Cline's counsel concerning the live-and-let-live nature of the beasts had proven accurate enough so that my mind was more or less at rest.

By that time, our living room was completed and had become the central point of orientation for our leisure time. We were proud of this room; the possibility which it had revealed only dimly at first sight had now been realized. Utilizing the space occupied by an old stove flue, we had installed a new chimney and an open fireplace which worked beautifully and supplied pleasant and adequate heat for the room. To alleviate the gloom of the room, we had let a line of windows into the outside wall which faced the creek so that the water moving by about fifty feet below the house provided both cheerful sight and sound. In the recesses on each side of the fireplace, I had built bookshelves and cabinets. These and the rest of the woodwork were painted white and the walls a soft grey. All in all, it was an attractive room.

It was in this room that we sat tranquilly that evening in early spring. We were grouped around the fire; my brother, Dorothy and I reading, and my mother's knitting needles clicking away quietly. The bat entered the room silently and may indeed have circled the room once or twice before a flicker of movement caught my eye. So deep was my panic when it dawned on me that a bat was actually upon us that I feared I might somehow communicate that panic to the bat, causing it to attack. Speaking as quietly as I could, I said, "There's a bat in the room."

In one swift motion, my mother disappeared beneath a lap robe which had been covering her knees; from this frail refuge, she continued to offer muffled and indecipherable advice. The bat continued to circle the room as Dorothy, my brother and I discussed the situation. We carefully refrained from looking either at each other or the bat, keeping track of its progress out of the corners of our eyes in the manner with which one observes a person on the street who is indulging in dangerously eccentric behavior. Both hirsute and non-hirsute members of the company sat tensely expecting momentary savage attack upon his or her pate. Sotto voce, we exchanged conspiritorial advice about the bat's whereabouts; eyeballs rolling wildly, bodies held in motionless tension, the air was full of such whispers as: "Watch out, he's heading your way," "Oh, my God, I felt him go by," "Careful, careful." Unremitting but meaningless sounds of terror issued steadily from beneath my mother's blanket. Communicating in this manner, we decided on a rough plan of action which would grant us respite. Sooner or later, we decided, the bat would fly back into the hall; at which moment my brother, being nearest to the door, was delegated to leap up and slam the door, shutting the bat into the hall. Several times the bat approached the door and Earl tensed himself for his task but each time the bat wheeled and re-entered the living room. Finally, the bat disappeared into the hall long enough for my brother to close the barricade. My mother re-appeared from beneath her blanket and we all sat pale and trembling as we allowed the sweat to dry on our foreheads.

Unfortunately, while our position had improved immeasurably, the problem was far from solved. We held the living room but the bat was in undisputed possession of the hall. My own feeling (shared, I believe by my brother) was: the hell with it; let's just spend the night here in the living room and sort it all out in the morning. Alas, the distaff were now casting in our direction those glances of supplication and contempt employed by the female of the species during moments of peril or inconvenience. After exchanging one despairing glance, my brother and I knew we were expected to dispatch the bat. Being four years younger than he, I felt it only fair that he should take the leading role. He could not quite see the logic of this but, grumbling, he finally armed himself with the fireplace broom and took up a stance by the door.

"Now, listen," he said, "you open the door quickly and then we'll both duck out into the hall after the bat while you shut the door so he can't get past us back into the living room."

I could not see the sense in this. "After all, Earl, there's only one broom and you've got it. There's really no point in both of us going out there."

His demurer was succinct and profane; the sum of its meaning being: either both of us go or none of us goes. He was too obdurate to recognize the injustice of this so I agreed, chalking up several black marks against him for lack of generosity.

Breathing hard and burning furious quantities of adrenalin, we arrayed ourselves before the door preparing for our sortie into the bat's territory. It was agreed that on a given signal I would throw open the door and we would charge furiously into the hall, Earl wielding the broom and I providing what still seemed to me to be supernumerary and largely extraneous moral support. The furious charge did not materialize. I gave the signal and we both poked our noses into the hall like timid moles, each of us trying with subtle nudges to push the other into a position of precedence. The bat was hovering indecisively around a lighting fixture at the far end of the hall. We edged towards the beast, Earl raising his broom to a striking position. It seemed that the issue was about to be decisively joined when the bat suddenly decided to take offensive action and darted straight for us. Any pretext of being my brother's keeper vanished immediately; I panicked completely.

I had always been aware of a certain element of *sauve qui peut* in my character but my actions now were disgraceful. As the bat flew towards us, we went into full retreat. Not having been in the lead during the charge, I had a head start in the ensuing retreat. In four gazelle-like leaps, I reached the living room door, bounded through, and slammed it shut in my brother's face, leaving him in the hall with the bat. Through the closed door, I heard the frantic swish of the broom being wielded accompanied by small whimpering cries of rage. Finally gaining a moment of respite in his battle with the bat, Earl began pounding on the door for admittance and shouting imprecations. By then I had faced the inherent depravity in what I had done; but I still wanted nothing to do with the bat. In response to Earl's profane demands for sanctuary, I inquired softly through the closed door as to the bat's whereabouts. Understandably, this question drove my poor brother to new heights of berserk rage and he shouted, "It's down at the other end of the hall you son-of-a-bitch, will you open up this Goddamned door?"

"Are you sure?" I asked, keeping the door firmly closed.

I was answered only by incoherent snufflings of rage and fear. It began to occur to me that I was now in greater danger from my brother than I was from the bat. I opened the door to find the reddest, angriest face I have ever seen inches from my own. Its mouth opened and vehemently pronounced judgment: "You shit. You unutterable shit." He came through the door like Sam Huff, pausing only to make sure the door was firmly closed against the bat before starting for me to wreak vengeance. In the way of women during moments of slapstick male crisis, Dorothy and my mother were by this time reeling with laughter to the extent of being forced to clutch furniture for physical support. At that point, the humour of the situation overtook my brother and me simultaneously and his charge was interrupted by a fit of laughter. We both collapsed helplessly. Eventually, we recovered enough to venture forth again and after several more hilarious false starts, we managed to dispatch the bat. I have never enjoyed an evening more.

Fun and games apart, it was now clear that something had to be done about the bats. A few days later, I summoned the local representative of a nation-wide firm of exterminators. Full of jaunty assurance and an air of I'll-handle-everything when he arrivèd, his spirit broke when he shone his flashlight into our attic. Clearly, the job of exterminating our bats was a contract he did not want. I gave him a drink of whiskey to bolster his spirit and made vague threatening references to the honor of the firm whose franchise he held. Finally he agreed reluctantly to take on the job.

It was to be a full-scale attack. We would have to vacate the house for the day while he pumped the attic full of cyanide gas. Nothing, he assured me, could remain alive in the attic after this treatment had been administered.

The day arrived and packing up child, dog and all living, breathing things, we departed for an outing in the mountains. Early that morning, the exterminator had moved in with many lethal looking pieces of apparatus and wearing a look of grim determination. He assured me that we would be batless by mid-afternoon. When I asked what would become of the bats, he got rather shifty and said that the cyanide would drive them from the house and that they would then fly around erratically for a while and finally die lonely—and to my mind deserving—deaths in the surrounding woods. What about the ones that don't escape the house to die outside, I asked him? He replied that there might be a few such but that they would definitely be stone cold dead and harmless and would present no problem. His final remark struck me as rather ominous.

"All you have to do," he said, "is get yourself a bucket and pick up the few dead bats you'll find in the attic."

My feelings about bats were strong enough to include a lack of desire to have truck with their corpses. I suggested to the exterminator that he include this service as part of the deal

119

but he demured looking, I thought, even shiftier than before. We left on our day's outing, happy in the knowledge that our bats' hours were now numbered.

We returned at about four o'clock, the hour that the house would be free from contamination. The exterminator had of course departed by then. A slight and not wholly unpleasant smell of the cyanide remained in the house. I was loathe to investigate the attic and so postponed that task until the next day. By then, I knew the opening through which the bats had gained ingress and egress to the attic, a louvered ventilation point under the peak of the roof facing the creek. Idly, I wandered outside to have a look at it. Something crunched under my foot. I lept back in revulsion, realizing it was a bat. Further investigation revealed the ground on that side of the house to be covered with dead bats. By that time, I had given the miserable beasts so much thought that a mild clinical interest had been built up. By that time also, I had read enough about them to know that my revulsion was not ill-founded. About the only good thing that can be said about bats is that they apparently consume vast numbers of night-flying insects. For the rest, they harbor every conceivable sort of parasite and are proven carriers of rabies. So virulent in fact is their toxicity in this respect that various animals tethered for a period of time in a bat-infested cave became infected with rabies, the supposition being that this had happened through exposure to the bats' falling urine and excrement.

Now I picked one of the bat corpses up gingerly and held it, wings outstretched, to examine it. I felt reasonably safe, presuming that the Great Divide now existed between us. Suddenly, the beast let out a chilling and most unmoribund squeak. I dropped it immediately and it fluttered weakly upon the ground. Although not yet dead, it was clearly *in extremis.* I felt emboldened to pick it up again by the wings and examine it. The reasons for the bat's legendary association with evil were immediately apparent. Its tiny head was a strange combination of vulpine, simian and human. Clearly a predator, its little jaws worked open and shut to reveal rows of sharp, miniscule teeth. The fact that the bat was still alive made me decide even more firmly to give the attic a wide berth until the cyanide and its after-effects had had full opportunity to do its work. And sure enough, as I watched the

120

louvered ventilation square that evening, an occasional bat emerged and fluttered weakly away into the dusk.

A day or so later, I donned thick gloves and climbed into the attic with my bucket. It took me most of the day to clear the attic of their corpses. Fred Cline told me they would be back, saying, "Hell, Mister Cherry, they bound to be a few didn't get killed and they been livin' in that attic so long they'll come back." Fortunately, he was proven wrong. We never again were troubled with bats. The battle had been won.

That Spring, we took another tiny trembling step toward expanding the self-supporting aspects of our farm. We bought about fifty white Leghorn chicks and installed them in the old chicken house up behind the house near the privy. Following the instructions in one of the many trustworthy Government pamphlets, I rigged up a sort of incubator heated by light bulbs, within which the chicks huddled during the cold hours. We lost a few, but in the beginning they seemed to thrive mightily. Like all young things (except bats) they were at first appealing. Later on, when they were half grown I came to detest them as filthy and disease-prone birds. We lost about a third of the chickens to a common disease called coccidiosis but the rest throve. It was not too long before the roosters went to work and we were gathering enough eggs beyond our own requirements to take the excess to market.

Our chicken flock was composed of about half roosters, rapacious birds whose treatment of our little daughter, Linda deepened my dislike of them. Poor Linda, I have often wondered whether her indubitably strong character may not have had its birth in her continuing war with the roosters. She was old enough to walk by then and tottered around the house and outside it with only moderate supervision. She was particularly proud and fond of her expeditions to the outdoor privy, the route to which lay through the territory of the chickens. I don't know whether the roosters thought she was some strange brand of hen or what, but they were prone to attack her in force as she made her journey. Most of the time, someone was close enough to rescue her but many times I was too far to get there in time and it was touching to watch from a distance her determination not to be bested by the roosters.

She was a fearless little thing and she would continue on her way, bawling furiously, arms wrapped around her head to protect herself from the furious pecking roosters. Later on, whenever I had to face the odious task of decapitating a rooster for the pot, it helped alleviate the unpleasantness as I swung the axe to think that I was paying off an old score for Linda.

By that time, the O'Hara's were installed in their house in Wytheville. Their presence provided a profound and positive difference in our life. It is a deeply ingrained human need to warm one's hands at the social fire and we had felt its lack keenly. Now we dined frequently back and forth at each other's houses and the opportunity to laugh and talk with old friends after our long period of isolation was balm to our spirits and minds. I cannot now recall whether Kate was yet pregnant with the first of three children she and O'Hara would have together but, if not, her pegnancy was incipient. Kate's two daughters by her previous marriages were pleasant, likeable girls who came frequently to the farm and delighted in playing with Linda. They were vastly different children. The eldest, the child of Kate's first marriage, was both more physically sturdy and of a more prosaic turn of mind than her half sister, Jane. The elder was about twelve at the time and Jane nine or ten. Jane was not the name with which the child had been christened but one which O'Hara had given her shortly after he and Kate had been married. I gave it only passing thought at the time but it is now clear that O'Hara's insistence on changing the child's name was an indication of the depth of his strange preoccupation with Darroch, her real father. Both we and the O'Hara's carried on a sporadic correspondence with Darroch, then in New York involved with the pre-publication rites of his first novel which was soon to be brought out by Random House. Darroch had announced his desire and intention to visit us all in Wytheville—and would do so after the close of the year.

Even then, I now realize, O'Hara must have given birth to the train of thought which would later result in actions which would seem inexplicable for so many years. There was a hint of this in a remark he made to me one day. He used the phrase "Gordian knot," saying that some day, somehow this Gordian knot which held us all together would have to be cut.

122

When I asked him what he meant, he said, "We're all too preoccupied with each other and people have got other people's kids and it can't work." After saying that, he was loath to say more and quickly changed the subject.

I must now make reference to a human being who would exercise a certain bizarre influence upon events of the next few years. I will call him, Roger. I only met him in the flesh once in my life when he paid a brief visit to the O'Haras during that fall of 1955. A St. Louisan like the rest of us, he had been dealt an exceedingly difficult and grotesque hand by life from the beginning, having been born to wealth and as a cerebral palsetic. Due to loving and extremely intelligent care as a child, his condition (which, fortunately, was never as extreme as that unlucky affliction can be) had been contained to a remarkable degree. Therefore, in spite of his cerebral palsy, his physical presence when I finally met him was much less of a shock to me than I had imagined it would be. Through training and will, he had achieved a remarkable degree of mastery over his errant body. One knew immediately that *something* was wrong with him physically, but unless one had been forewarned of his condition it would have been difficult to know exactly whence it stemmed. He moved slowly and spoke in the same manner; the net effect being that of a rather pompous and rigidly controlled drunk. Roger was a man of character and a distinctly unprosaic turn of mind. He did not come into control of his money until he had reached his thirties; prior to that time, he earned his living working, among other things, as a factory hand. When he finally did inherit, he had come to the philosophically-based decision that he would search for situations which he could influence by giving away portions of his money.

Older than the rest of us by a good bit, he had swum into our ken by way of Kate, with whom he became friendly during the years she had lived in St. Louis while the rest of us were living abroad. Roger traveled a good bit and he became acquainted with the others, Darroch and my brother Earl when they had been living in London during the spring and summer of 1953. Kate had suggested that Roger look them up there.

Roger's motives in handing around his money were exceedingly difficult to pinpoint. However, I am convinced they

123

had nothing to do with philanthropy in the traditional sense; nor were they vicious in any sense covered by the dictionary definition of that word. I believe that he sought through the offbeat dispensation of his money a dimension of action rather than sensation. I do not believe that Roger had any conscious vision of the dimension of action he sought; if he met a human being who interested him and that human being wanted something, Roger would see to it that he got it simply because he sensed that desire granted to an unprosaic personality would tend to have interesting results. Such an Aladdin's Lamp approach to life can of course be terribly dangerous.

Whatever interest Roger had in any of us was directly proportionate to the closeness of his direct or indirect relationship with Kate. The fact that Darroch had been married to and so long associated with Kate made him the obvious initial candidate for Roger's attention. When Roger met O'Hara, my brother, and Darroch in London, it was Darroch who got the first chance to rub the lamp. Just why Darroch wanted it I will never really understand, but what he asked the genie for was a terribly exotic automobile which he found for sale on Great Portland Street. It was called a Bentley Speed Six and I don't suppose there are more than ten of the things still running in the world. Darroch showed it to Roger and Roger bought it for him on the spot, paying also the cost of its transportation to the U.S.A.

When word of this reached me, a slight whisper of "where's mine" immediately began in my head. In the heads of Earl and O'Hara, who were on the spot in London, there was nothing slight about the whisper at all; it was, in fact, deafening. O'Hara, immediately recognized Aladdin as being far too important in the long run to be wasted on short term, frivolous requests. Even then, O'Hara must have been thinking of returning to St. Louis to have a go at marrying Kate. It is possible that as a good psychologist, O'Hara knew that the successful accomplishment of such a move would immediately place him in the forefront of Roger's consciousness and that his hand, if properly and slowly played, could result in Aladdin providing much more than booze and exotic automobiles.

By the fall of 1955, money was beginning to grow dangerously short for Dorothy and me; the improvement of our house and land had used almost all we had and our few, largely symbolic ventures in the direction of actual farming had reduced our expenditures a bit but did little that made any real difference to bring in income. At that time, I had approximately one hundred thousand words down on paper of the novel on which I had been working. I wrote to Hiram Haydn at Random House asking if he would be willing to have a look with the idea of an advance kept in mind. He replied that he would, but warned me that it would take him some time to get around to it. Accordingly, I bundled up a copy of the manuscript, made my hexes and crosses over the package and sent it off to New York.

The O'Haras also were sailing quite close to the wind financially. O'Hara was working at his writing but he had so far published nothing and his hopes of financial succor from that direction were even more precarious than my own. Fortunately, Kate had a small private income which paid for the bread and beans. But there wasn't much left over afterwards. Presumably, O'Hara decided that the time had arrived to throw Roger into the game, for he invited him to come to Wytheville that fall for a short visit. It was on that occasion that I had my sole encounter with Roger. Left to his own devices, I am inclined to think O'Hara would have preferred not to trot Roger out for public consumption. Alas, he did not have much choice. Roger had heard much of Dorothy and me and he knew that we were close friends of both O'Hara and Kate and that, indeed, they had moved to Wytheville because we had settled there. Undoubtedly O'Hara faced the fact that it would seem extremely strange to a man as preoccupied with other human beings as Roger if he were to keep us under wraps during Roger's visit. In any case, our brief meeting with Roger was an uneventful one and I think O'Hara was relieved that no particular feeling of rapport developed on either side. Exactly what went on between Roger and O'Hara during that visit I have no way of knowing but subsequent events indicated that opening negotiations took place towards some sort of financial relationship between the two men, which would increase in scope and complexity during the next year or so.

Sometime after Roger's visit to Wytheville that fall, a sudden minor disaster took place which pushed me to the edge of a financial precipice. It was the sort of accident which seems vaguely comic when viewed with sufficient perspective over a period of time but it struck me as tragic at the time. It must have happened immediately before Christmas because my mother had arrived to spend that holiday with us. She and Dorothy were away at the time doing some shopping in Wytheville. They had taken Linda with them, thank God, for had the baby been with me, tragedy rather than tragicomedy would have almost certainly been the result.

It was a bitterly cold day; so cold in fact that our creek was frozen solid. I had gone in my beloved wooden station wagon to collect some bales of hay for the cow from a nearby farm. Returning with the hay, I had to dismount from the car to open the gate to the farm and then after having driven through the gate, dismount again in order to return and shut the gate. The ground just inside the gate was fairly level and I had got into the habit of doing a very stupid thing: neglecting to set the hand brake when I left the car with its engine running to go back to shut the gate. This day, I finished closing the gate and started back towards the wagon only to realize with horror that it had begun to move. The drive leading on down to the old barn ran more or less gently along a track levelled out of the side of a steep hill. So steep, in fact, that the ground fell away to the left of the track at an angle of about 45 degrees for about 150 feet until it reached the creek bed. When I saw the wagon begin to move, I ran to it as fast as I could but, by the time I got the door open, the car's wheels had turned downhill towards the creek and it had assumed enough momentum that I had no chance of stopping it. Accordingly, I had to stand helpless, my jaw wide with horror as I watched my beloved station wagon which was also the sole family means of transportation, plunge down the hill picking up speed every instant until it hit the frozen creek, bounded up into the air and annhilated itself against a large oak tree on the far bank of the creek.

After the first few moments of shock and trembling had worn off, I could only think of one thing: getting the disastrously broken vehicle out of the creek bed. I felt both ashamed and foolish at having been so unbelievably stupid as to have destroyed the car through pure, thoughtless lack of precaution. I telephoned a wrecker service and a half hour later they came and winched the car back up the hill. There was no question of having it repaired; it was a total wreck. Its value as scrap just about paid for the wrecker service and that was that.

An hour or so later, Dorothy and my mother returned from their shopping in the town. They were inclined to take a much lighter view of what had happened than I did. Their attitude was: no one was hurt, no flesh was torn; it was only wood and metal which were destroyed so why worry about it? I attempted to adopt the same reasonable attitude but I was too angry with myself to have much success with it because I had already begun to worry about how I was going to replace the vehicle. Life on the farm was clearly impossible without one.

I immediately began looking around for something and found an International pick-up truck for sale for five hundred dollars. For some time, we had felt the need for a truck of some sort keenly. The many small and large hauling tasks which arose even on a farm as small and amateurish as ours made such a vehicle something of a necessity; until then, the station wagon had just barely served to fulfill such duties. However the price of the pick-up truck was five hundred dollars and it was five hundred dollars we simply did not have at the time. I could always approach my mother, of course, but I did not want to do so; while I had no qualms about bracing her for capital sums for actual investment in the farm, it did not seem fair to be running to her in a case like this. Then I thought of Roger and began to wonder if I might not rub Aladdin's lamp also. And in all honesty, I must admit that I was interested in what O'Hara's reaction to such a move might be.

Deciding to sound O'Hara out about the feasibility of such a course, I dropped by to see him and told him what was on my mind. He reacted to my intentions with both scorn and a certain amount of nervousness which struck me as arising primarily from the fact that he considered Roger to be *his* pigeon and feared any possible confounding of his plans by having a second set of hands in the till. Human nature being what it is, the more O'Hara objected to my putting the bite on Roger, the more determined I became to do exactly that. O'Hara's position was rather delicate because he could not

127

actually come right out and say he did not want me to summon up the genie without displaying his colors as those of a true dog in the manger. We parted sourly after O'Hara, much against his will, had given me Roger's address, muttering about "me-too republicans," a phrase much in vogue during those Eisenhower years.

I wrote to Roger explaining that I had sustained a disaster in the automotive department and asking him if he would lend me five hundred dollars to buy a pick-up truck on the understanding that I would pay him back *when* and *as* I might be able to do so. Almost by return mail, I received a check for five hundred dollars accompanied by the following note. I quote it now because this loan of five hundred dollars was destined to become a football used for a good deal of play during the next few years. The letter was postmarked from a town in California.

Dear John,

My man in St. Louis came through like the good and true Mason he is; consequently, here is the five hundred. I hope it is in time to plug the hole in the dike. You can repay me as and when you are able—don't stew about it.

Best,

Roger.

Faced with a *fait accompli,* O'Hara's sourness disappeared. I did not then know that there would be much backlash from this transaction. Matters returned to an even keel; the transportation crisis was solved. As the year drew to a close, Dorothy and I continued to putter with our house as I awaited news of my novel with ever-growing tension.

Unfortunately, 1955 did not expire without one more gloomy incident: a second and more serious brush with the law occurred; one which involved O'Hara, my brother and myself and for which we had no one but ourselves to blame.

It began, as most silly incidents do, in high spirits. O'Hara and Kate dropped by the farm late one Saturday afternoon to pay an idle social call. Drink was taken and an invitation subsequently tendered for them to remain for dinner. Kate

128

refused, saying that she had to return to fix supper for her children but O'Hara elected to remain. Although women tend to become a bit rancorous at even such a minor defection from the hearth, I do not believe that explains Kate's vituperation in regard to what happened later on that evening.

It began and continued as a cheerful enough evening among old friends. Drink was taken before, during and after dinner and by midnight when Earl and I left to drive O'Hara back to town, we were far from sober. The route to town which I chose that night led past the local country club, a fact which, when coupled with misfortune, led to our downfall. About a quarter of a mile past the country club one of my tires blew out. On inspection, the spare proved to be flat. The country club was the closest feasible place from which to phone for assistance, and the three of us walked back down the road to see if we could use the country club telephone. It turned out that the weekly Saturday night dance was in full swing. Clad in muddy Barker boots and rough work clothing, none of us was exactly properly turned out for a festive occasion. The first person I saw after we entered the club was Bean, the local lawyer, seated at a table by the dance floor with his wife and some friends. Lawyer Bean invited us to join his party and we sat down and began to make inroads on his bourbon. The degree of intoxication among the invited guests was entirely commensurate with that of the uninvited. For quite a long time, events proceeded smoothly and, indeed, I was enjoying myself hugely, dancing with various of the ladies who seemed to find the invasion of new blood a welcome departure from what must have been a fairly ritual Saturday evening. To this day, I am not certain exactly who or what sparked the explosion. All I know is that I was seated talking with Lawyer Bean when I became aware that an altercation had developed on the far side of the dance floor. Upon investigation, I found O'Hara and my brother surrounded by a ring of angry hillbilly nobs who had clearly taken exception to something that had been said or done. Insults of increasing heat were being exchanged by both sides and there was no question that on the verbal level the locals were far outclassed, a fact which did nothing to diminish their growing fury. In retrospect, it is clear to me that we were in considerable danger. Very few of the men in that room were entirely sober and peacemakers were in short supply. And hill-country southerners, when aroused, are among the most irascible of men. Verbal provocation inevitably led to physical provocation and blows were struck. Like most fights where the personnel is intoxicated, little real damage was done. Or to be more accurate, there was not enough time for damage to be sustained before the police arrived, summoned by some intelligent member of the company. For whomever did so, I retain warm feelings; we were arrogant and outnumbered and that is a bad combination. I feel certain that had the police not arrived when they did, we would have been beaten to a pulp. At one time, in the Medinah at Rabat, I witnessed a scene of mob violence and the red-eyed, jeering crowd of men who surrounded us as we were led off by the police that night was uncomfortably reminiscent of it. The pokey seemed at that moment, eminently preferable.

And so, off to the pokey we went; trip number two for O'Hara and me; number one for Earl. This time it was full-fig pokey—cells, warrants for our arrest and all the rest of it. I have the warrant before me now. The charge reads: "Crashing a private party while drinking." It was hardly the sort of charge which leads to a life sentence; nevertheless, it was depressing. So depressing was it for me, in fact, that my psychological defense was to assume that we were being put upon. Because of this and because I knew it was going to be necessary to have a bond signed by a property owner in order to secure our release, I put up a perfectly god awful fuss, yelling and swearing and dragging my tin cup across the bars like a character from "The Last Mile". The police evidently enjoyed this hugely; they allowed me to rant on until nearly four in the morning before finally letting me telephone Dorothy. I explained to her what happened and that she would have to come down to the jail and sign our bond before we could be released. She said she would be along as soon as she could arrange to have our truck picked up and the tire repaired.

Dorothy showed up at about eight-thirty the next morning. By that time, we were all sober and thoroughly ashamed of ourselves. Later on, Dorothy told me she had found the assembled policemen laughing themselves sick over their prisoners when she arrived. I am exceedingly glad they felt this way because some of the things I had spent the night yelling at them were not of the friendliest. Indeed, I am sure, my actions would have got me a fine fat lip in a big-city tank. Strangely enough, Dorothy also seemed to find the whole situation rather comic. I recall that she brought Linda to my cell door and held her up so the child could see me through the barred window, saying, "There you are now, you can see your Daddy in jail." Linda cooed and waved away at me happily. It was certainly not a situation covered by Dr. Spock.

After signing the bond, Dorothy came back to the cell with the turnkey while he prepared to let us out. Then, Dorothy reported a strange order she had received from Kate regarding O'Hara. Looking straight at him, Dorothy said, "Kate told me to leave you in." Our immediate reaction was to break out laughing. Then, I turned to look at O'Hara and saw that this had hit him as a very serious piece of news. His face was a study in consternation. Dorothy then said it had never occurred to her to pay any attention to Kate's strange request,and that she had signed the bond for all three of us and we were free to go.

There was one more curious scene that morning after we left the jail. We drove O'Hara back to his house and took him up on the offer of a cup of coffee when we got there. When we walked into his living room, Kate was sitting in a chair knitting. As O'Hara walked into the room she looked straight at him with an expression of the most ferocious contempt I have ever seen on the face of a human being, and said one word: "Trash." His face went white and he turned and left the room without saying a word. Kate's anger and contempt, it seemed, were directed solely at O'Hara. To the rest of us, she could not have been more cheerful and set about preparing breakfast for us immediately.

The charges were of course dropped. But it was a bad ending to 1955; it had gone out like a lion, a rather sick lion.

CHAPTER IX

The letter from Hiram Haydn rejecting my work in progress arrived sometime after the first of the year. I realize now that my hope that the novel would bail out the boat financially was far greater than any essential belief I had in the work itself. I was disappointed but at the same time curiously relieved; there was no further need to play charades or indulge false hopes that my pen could simultaneously save our bacon and install my name among the luminaries. I was rather in the position of a painter dressed in a smock, floppy bow tie and all the rest of it, who suddenly decides to throw his velvet beret in the corner and paint a picture.

Unfortunately, there was nothing quite that dramatic about the change; several weeks had to be spent reviling Haydn and explaining to my wife his total inability to tell his ass from his elbow. Curiously enough, at the same time I was bitter about the novel's rejection, I tended to accept it. Some professional instinct warned me that to use as ground upon which to stand and fight a work in which one has less than total faith is tantamount to disaster. To stand firmly behind work in which one has implicit belief is another matter entirely—even when total bleakness of possibility looms ahead. Any artist worth a damn must back his real bets even though he comes to grief in the process. So, though I continued to act the role of a wronged author and to bemoan to my wife the stupidity of editors and publishers in general, my critical faculties were hard at work accepting the premises behind the rejection to the point where I could relegate the manuscript to a drawer rather than waste time by indulging in the fantasy necessary if I were to put the bundle back in the mail to another publisher.

The more or less successful navigation of those strange straits bordered by spleen and paranoia through which all rejected authors pass, had the rather happy effect of leading me towards my first fully professional act of authorship. After about a month of fruitless stewing and worry about money, I began to fiddle idly with the beginnings of a thriller rather along the lines of Eric Ambler, a writer whom I wholeheartedly admire. As I fiddled, two things became clear quite soon: I was enjoying myself a great deal and the story was not half bad. As luck or a sensible guiding hand from the subconscious would have it, I had chosen a *genre* which admits neither pomposity of intention nor execution. Even my capacity for self delusion was not up to the task of turning a sixty-thousand word thriller into the great American novel bearing a golden burden of kudos, fame and fortune. Therefore, I assigned no roles of financial or spiritual salvation to my tale and, as a result, had a damned good time. It took me exactly one month and a half to write. There was only one draft and very few corrections. I am rather proud of the fact that when the story eventually did find a publisher (under the title: *The Loring Affair*), it was printed from that first draft manuscript without even being re-typed. The book's publication was far enough in the future so that even the meager financial return it eventually brought in, would have had no effect upon our immediate financial bind. Still, I had done a good, professional job and it helped wipe out the sour, self-deluded taste left over from the bad, unprofessional job with which I had occupied my hopes during most of the past year. Art has many roles and not the least of them is its effect upon the psychic health of the artist.

Darroch finally paid us a visit that winter. Although he actually stayed with us, he spent a good deal of time with O'Hara and Kate, it being his paramount desire to see as much of his daughter, Jane, as possible. The child seemed almost desperately happy to have her real father around even for the limited time of his visit. Without question, Darroch was fond of his daughter but there was never any question of having her live with him permanently. The life of a hard-drinking, heavy-womanizing, hugely peripatetic bachelor is not exactly designed to include a child. Darroch was seeing at that time a great deal of a woman he would later marry but, for the nonce, there was no great pressure upon him to marry, and Darroch was not one to wish his few remaining golden years to be encumbered with a wife.

Darroch reported to me an extremely curious proposition made to him by O'Hara at one point during his visit. So curious was it, in fact, that I found it difficult to credit until it was later confirmed by O'Hara himself. What he had done was to offer Darroch a rather large sum of money if he would marry the girl of whom he was currently seeing so much. Not the least strange thing to me about this peculiar gambit was that O'Hara had the wherewithal to make such an offer to Darroch. About a month previously, O'Hara's fortunes had improved suddenly and rather dramatically. New and expensive clothing had begun to appear in his wardrobe and he had undertaken several mysterious trips to New York and St. Louis. O'Hara's financial situation and mine had been more or less completely open books to one another since childhood, but now he had become extremely close-mouthed about the source of his recent bonanza. My immediate suspicion was that he had come to some sort of financial understanding with Roger—and I am inclined to believe now that such was the case. However, the money could have also come from one of Kate's collateral family connections. Although she was far from well off herself, she was a titular rich girl and possessed many wealthy relatives and it is possible that one may have popped off, leaving her a legacy. At any rate, whatever the source, O'Hara had become very flush indeed.

Why had O'Hara made such a curious offer to Darroch? Dorothy and I puzzled long over that question. The most obvious answer appeared to be that O'Hara feared the possibility that Darroch might some day induce Kate to return to him, leaving O'Hara high and dry. But if such was O'Hara's reasoning, I believe he was mistaken. Some fascination with Darroch may have remained with Kate but it had become purely negative fascination. The love and trust she had formerly entertained for Darroch had been changed, by the chemistry of desertion and betrayal, into scorn and contempt.

The factor at the root of O'Hara's offer of money to Darroch if he would marry again was, I believe, the child, Jane. By that time O'Hara was well aware that Jane was a child of considerable character who was not prepared to transfer to him the allegiance she felt for her real father. The presence in his house of another man's child who was obdurately loyal to her real father and inherently suspicious of him represented to O'Hara a key tangle in the "Gordian knot" he was desirous of cutting. The easiest way of ridding himself of such a key tangle would be to rid himself of the child. Thus his attempt to entice Darroch into marriage through offering him money may possibly have stemmed from the hope that he and Kate could send the child to live with Darroch once he was married. But Darroch wasn't having any. Subsequent events would bear out the thesis that O'Hara's real desire was to rid himself of the child. What her feelings were I will never know but the fact remains that Kate would, in time, give Jane up; would, in fact, not see her daughter for twenty years. But now, I go too fast.

All in all, Darroch remained with us for about two weeks. He was always an enjoyable companion and it was a pleasant time. Darroch had that rare quality of enhancing the vision of whomever he was with, and half the pleasure in showing him the country around my farm lay in the fact that I was, in effect, seeing it with rejuvenated eyes myself. We shot his bow and arrows, walked and drove about the countryside and he helped me with a number of two-man jobs which I had been putting off until I had some help.

Two incidents occurred during his visit which entertain me in retrospect and throw a certain light upon Darroch's character. In the structure of the con man is the terrible and ever-present fear that he may be conned by an even greater con man than himself. With Darroch, this fear permeated his every action from the most complex to the most simple.

One morning, I went to get my pick-up truck only to discover that it had a flat tire. Never having changed a tire on that particular vehicle, I did not know that a peculiarity of International trucks is that the lug nuts unloosen in differing directions on each side of the truck—counter clockwise on one side, clockwise on the other. Believing that all lug nuts unloosened in a counter clockwise direction, I spent myself to no avail turning them so and of course achieved nothing but the further tightening of the nuts. Finally, I acknowledged to myself that the effort was beyond me and went in the house to ask Darroch to come out and have a go. He was in perfect condition in those days and, in perfect condition, Darroch was one of the strongest men physically I have ever encountered. Hearing my tale of woe, he put down his book and we went out to look at the truck. He picked up the lug wrench and prepared to employ pressure. But before he did so he very earnestly queried me as to whether I was absolutely certain we were turning the lug nuts in the proper direction. With the complete conviction of a man who is certain he is right, I replied that all lug nuts unloosened in a counter clockwise direction. Nodding in a satisfied way, Darroch laid hold of the wrench. Such a heave did he give it that I though the truck would come off the jack. Eyes popping, muscles straining and veins standing out, he kept this up for several seconds. He then stopped and asked again if I was sure about the direction. I replied again that I was certain. The scene was then repeated with an even greater fury of effort. As Darroch strained, a neighbor appeared over the brow of the hill, stopped his car and got out. When he saw what we were doing he began to laugh and pointed out that we were, indeed, turning the nut to make it tighter rather than looser. Wearing the stricken look of a man betrayed, Darroch dropped the wrench and turned to enter the house without a word. It took me hours to convince him that it had not been done purposely.

The other incident was of a similar nature but, alas, contained a measure of conscious mischief on my part. Like two or three other very intelligent men I have known, Darroch was addicted to the practice of reading science fiction novels. I was kidding him about this one day when he undertook to give me a long lecture about the brilliance of certain authors of science fiction. He mentioned several names as examples, none of whom was familiar to me. He seemed to be particularly impressed with the books of a science fiction writer called Theodore Sturgeon. He gave quite a long lecture on the works of Mr. Sturgeon, pointing out, among other things, that in his opinion, Mr. Sturgeon had a much clearer shot at posterity's approval than I.

I heard him out with an expression of patient, all-enduring wisdom on my face. After he had finished, I maintained a thoughtful silence for a few seconds before saying, "Well, it seems like as good a time as any to tell you that I *am* Theodore Sturgeon."

His head came up like a startled deer at that remark; his eyes assumed a look of fierce concentration. Without a word, he rose and paced back and forth across the room several times. He obviously believed the probability that I might be telling the truth was remote but still far enough within the realm of possibility to be given serious consideration. After marching up and down for a few more seconds, he announced that I could not possibly be the science fiction writer. When I admitted that I had been joking a gleam of distinct relief entered his eye.

After Darroch's departure, I continued to work quite hard on my thriller and as a result saw very little of O'Hara. Dorothy and Kate would get together occasionally but that was about the extent of our interfamilial dealings.

In March of that year, at just about the time I was finishing up my story, Dorothy discovered that she was pregnant again. The Doctor reckoned that the new baby would be born sometime during the following November. With one child in hand and another on the way, it was becoming graphically clear that the farm must be put on some sort of paying basis or else it would have to be given up in favor of a move to some community where I could earn a living for my family. I finished up my story and sent it off to my agent but I knew enough by then to refuse myself hope of it.

The problem facing me now was twofold and required answers to two questions. The first was mechanical and could, I knew, be answered by patient thought and investigation: was it physically possible to put the farm on a paying basis? The second question posed a terrifying psychological conundrum: Did I have the necessary confidence in myself to undertake such a course? I was by no means sure that I did but I kept my own counsel about it.

I knew enough about farming by then to be certain that the farm, as it stood, was not capable of being turned into a going concern financially. The only type of farm which would be capable of returning us a good living was a Grade A dairy farm. A Grade A dairy farm which was not large enough to carry a milking herd of at least thirty cows and young stock in approximately the same number was patently not feasible. I had read enough and consulted with enough dairy farmers in the vicinity to be sure of that. To carry that much stock, our farm would have to be expanded to at least twice its present size. The other things which would be needed to turn the place into a Grade A dairy farm, I did not for the moment, let myself think about at all. Unless the extra land could be acquired they would have only an academic interest.

Rightly or wrongly, I had always considered the natural direction of future expansion of the farm to be in a southwesterly direction. The only piece of land I knew definitely to be for sale joined our place at its southwestern extremity. This was a piece of about 75 acres which belonged to a man called Homer who lived in Wytheville. There were no buildings of any sort on the land and the fences were not in terribly good shape. Homer kept a few scrub cattle on his land which were largely left to fend for themselves. He would put in an appearance once or twice a week during the cold months and scatter a meager amount of hay for them. When we had first moved to the farm, I had been warned obliquely that Homer was not a particularly pleasant man and the warning had turned out to be accurate. He subsequently tried to start an altercation with me over a border fence which was allowing his cattle to forage on my land, but I patched up the fence and the dispute faded away. This was rather surprising as hillbillies dearly love a squabble about a line fence and tend to carry one over to the next generation if possible. I had always had a sneaking suspicion that Homer had cooled the line fence argument between us because he was anxious to get rid of his land and figured that, someday, I would present myself as the logical cndidate for its purchase.

Ideally, the land should have been bought cheap. As I have said, there were no buildings of any sort upon it, poor fences and it bordered on no road, egress and ingress being gained by virtue of an easement through another neighbor's property. However, when I inquired casually of Homer what kind of a price he might expect for the land, I knew I was in for trouble when he replied that he was not really interested in selling the land at all. It was known throughout the neighborhood that he had been trying to sell his land for years; now he evidently figured that I was thinking of expanding my farm and there being no other land available to me, he would be able to stick me with an unrealistic price. Then, as I went my daily round stewing over this depressing state of affairs, Fred Cline let it drop casually one day that Bill, my Mormon neighbor was planning to move to Utah permanently and that he was going to put up his farm at auction. The news that Bill's place was available interested me mightily. Added to what we already owned, it would make a farm of about 165 acres which was a reasonable size for the dairy venture I was contemplating. It was then March; Bill's auction was scheduled to take place in early May. The time had come to decide whether or not I really wanted to become a fully professional farmer.

In all honesty, I must confess that it was a decision I never really made. I decided to become a professional farmer but I did not decide that I *wanted* to become one. From my way of looking at the situation, it did not really seem to me that I had any choice. I had come this far in the direction of farming because I had considered the farm only as an adjunct of a successful literary career. But in coming that far, I had also changed myself in many ways, some of them too subtle to evaluate. What little progress that had been made in the new life I had chosen was paying me back in the true coin of my desires: growth and change.

Put more simply, I had been using time rather than killing it and allowing it to use me. If I were to back away from farming at the present point, the time I had used would be rendered meaningless and I would be back in the same old desert of fear for my family which had nearly driven me around the bend in Rome. If I were to go on to expand my farm, on the other hand, the chances were that I could support my family and at the same time by continuing the process of using time, I might arrive at or contrive a juncture of circumstance which would make me once again a legitimate candidate for choice. It was clear to me that I was not then such a candidate; I was involved in a process, nothing more. Yet it was a process tinged with consciousness and that consciousness was as much a part of the causalty as any of the other stimuli of heredity or environment. In being a farmer, I was scared of many things: that I might not succeed, of the animals themselves, of the physical labor and, most of all, of the boredom which certainly lay ahead of me. But I also felt a hard, fierce joy that I had taken a hand in what was happening to me; that I was not and never would be Pavlov's miserable dog.

After thinking it over for a week or so, I discussed the situation with Dorothy who was just as aware as I that we were caught on the horns of the old American dilemma regarding business affairs. Having no tradition of peasantry, this country cannot really accept the illusion of changelessness. Expand or perish is the unspoken rule. Even down there in the hills of southwestern Virginia, the attrition arising from that rule was taking a heavy toll. And why should it not? I have known small hill farmers with a machinery inventory of twenty-five thousand dollars and no bathrooms in their houses.

But it was the fact that change came so slowly to the hills, that made our chances at successful expansion just barely operable. Along the entire ten or twelve-mile length of our road, there was not one single Grade A dairy farm. Milk was sold by all of our neighbors but it was the casual excess milk from their family cattle. Each morning, an unrefrigerated truck picked this milk up, a can here, half a can there, and delivered it to a cheese factory twenty miles away. Such milk, called Grade C, cannot by law be sold for direct consumption but only as the raw material for the manufacture of cheese. The price paid for such milk is of course a pittance compared to the price paid for milk produced under the stringent conditions required under law for direct consumption. The rub is that a considerable investment in buildings and machinery is required in order to meet those requirements.

In our case, the primary question upon which all others depended was, could we get the extra land? After talking it over, we decided that, contingent upon our ability to get the extra land, we would go ahead and plan the creation of a Grade A dairy set-up.

The news that my neighbor Bill's land would be coming on the market had one very important negative effect. When I had believed that Luther's land to the southwest of mine was, in effect, the only land available to me, I had been preparing to make the same mistake as the proverbial gambler who plays on the crooked wheel because it is the only one in town.

The manifold advantages of Bill's land made it clear just how woeful the deficiencies of the other had been. If we owned Bill's land, we would have a farm bisected by the creek, a fact of inestimable advantage for the proper flow of cattle to the water which they require. Luther's land to the southwest, conversely, would have been useless forever as pasture because of its being without water. There were many, many other factors which made Bill's land favorable: we would take over a rather charming house complete with all the amenities thus leaving our present house free to shelter the hand we would surely need within a year or two; there was ample timber available on Bill's place which could be milled to put up the new buildings we would need; the topography of Bill's place would enable us to place our dairy barn close to the road and thus preclude the enormous expense of building access roads sturdy enough to take the daily traffic of heavy milk-hauling trucks. These were just a few of the advantages which immediately occurred to us. So vastly preferable in fact was Bill's farm to Luther's that our eventual decision was to give up the idea of expansion if Bill's farm proved to be beyond our reach.

It seemed to me that from Bill's standpoint and certainly from mine, the sensible plan would be to forestall the auction. Accordingly, I went to him with what I believed to be a fair offer. But he was determined to have his auction and he refused. In retrospect, I have always had a sneaking feeling of gladness that he did refuse. In the long run, the price the farm brought at auction was not significantly different than the one I had offered and there was the fun of buying it that way. It did not, alas, seem like much fun at the time because it meant a wait of over a month before we could find out what was going to happen to us. However, it was time badly needed. I, who had never attempted an organizational effort on any sort of major scale in my life, was now faced with the serious consideration of just what the priorities would be in setting up a Grade A dairy farm and how I would go about setting them in motion.

At this point, it will probably seem a rather odd time to describe a barroom. However, it is necessary; the place which, with my tongue firmly planted in my cheek, I now describe as my "pub" became my office, my haven and my observation post for discovering the means of solving the various problems with which I would eventually be faced. It will be remembered that, in the glorious state of Old Virginia, there are no bars; only gas stations which sell beer. The gas station which I refer to as my pub and in which I fought, argued, listened, learned and taught throughout my years in Virginia was a place which possessed a curiously perverse sort of Southern gothic appeal. An idea of what I mean can be gathered by the fact that the name of its owner and operator was, so help me God, Lucifer Wrenchum, a man who, not unreasonably, considering the fact that his entire life had been lived within the confines of a Faulkner novel, was a walking laboratory for anyone interested in the Snopes-type soul. Wrenchum's, as it was commonly called, was physically rather like a stage setting for one of those plays which take place in a roadside cafe. A certain note of individuality greeted a visitor to Wrenchum's the moment he walked in the door. Above the small bar which faced the door was a large facsimile of the front page of a newspaper whose glaring headline read simply: "Lucifer Wrenchum, World's Biggest Bullshipper." In a sort of frieze below this strange artifact were a row of jagged-edged plaques posing various maddeningly cogent and wholly unanswerable American questions. One which remains in my memory as an ever-present thorn of the time asked simply: "If you're so smart, why ain't you rich?" Lucifer Wrenchum's mind had an appealing and terrifyingly tawdry complexity. Not for him, wall decorations such as: "If you cain't put your (here a drawing of a heart) in America then get your (here a drawing of a horse's ass) out". No, Wrenchum's advices and admonishments were never prosaic; they contained paradox and a certain rude poetry.

Besides the basic salt and flour staples of a small country store, Wrenchum's wares ran a strange gamut. No salesman of any novelty, no matter how hopeless, had ever failed to make a sale in Wrenchum's. The place was literally awash in punch boards, squirrel tales to adorn car radiators, plastic baby shoes to hang from rear vision mirrors and artifacts of varying but gentle pornographic content.

The bar was the undisputed center of the action at Wrenchum's. Behind it, Lucifer Wrenchum stood dispensing 3.2 beer. Anyone who was hungry could apply for a 10 cent fried pie (known as a frahed pah), a hot, pickled sausage of throat-burning strength, or a hard-boiled egg. If he were acquainted with the customer, Lucifer Wrenchum would also provide a drink of bootleg whiskey or, if needed, a French letter.

Besides the bar behind which Wrenchum stood, the place had two other departments: One was, in effect, a second-hand store; Wrenchum was a man totally addicted to trading. I have seen poor farmers come into Wrenchum's carrying everything from a broken banjo to a set of the Encyclopedia Britannica. The prices Wrenchum paid were modest but he always made a deal. The final area in Wrenchum's was one which provided the overtone of violence and grotesquerie which one can never escape in southern hill country. A passionate gun trader and collector, one whole wall of his place was taken up by an enormous rack of rifles and shotguns. Amidst this bizarre and contrapuntal collection of objects, it was my wont to sit and drink and ponder or to exchange ideas and pleasantries with Lucifer Wrenchum or other present company.

Lucifer himself was a man psychologically ruled and tortured by a need for the baroque. If one has ever wondered about the sort of mind behind one of those roadside enterprises which sells pink plastic Flamingoes designed to bring beauty to the lawns of the trusting, one would have an indication of such in the texture of Wrenchum's mind. But only an indication; Wrenchum was no clod. He adored metaphysical speculation, of the sort which made most of his clientele as nervous as your Uncle Hart Crane. At that particular period, William Blake's Nobodaddy was fighting a losing battle for survival within the purlieus of my mind and Wrenchum soon found he could depend upon me for remarks shocking to the religious sensibilities of hillbillies less evolved than himself. Wrenchum also had an abiding faith in my erudition. "Jown", he would frequently say, mangling my Christian name in a way I cannot reproduce, "some a them wuhds you use, ah cain't even find in the dictionary." Above the Mason-Dixon line, his sense of place and distance was shaky. Once, some years ago, the telephone rang one evening at my house on eastern Long Island.

"Jown, that you?" said a well-remembered voice, "This Lucifer Wrenchum talkin'."

144

"Why hello, Lucifer. Where are you?"

"Ahm heah in New Yawk City, Jown. Wonduhed iff'n you care to come out for a drink this evenin'."

I explained that I was 120 miles away. After chatting for a while, I hung up with regret. It would have been edifying to have spent an evening on the tiles in New York City with Lucifer Wrenchum.

I saw Lucifer once just three or four years ago. Driving through Wytheville, I had stopped in to see my friend, Lawyer Bean. Lucifer's name came up and Lawyer Bean smiled the deeply satisfied smile of a southerner for whom some formal expression of life has turned out as he had expected. He gave me directions to Lucifer's new place of business and insisted that I stop by and see what he was up to. It pleased me as it had Lawyer Bean to find that Lucifer was the proprietor of the biggest pink plastic Flamingo emporium I have ever seen. But the real Wrenchum touch lay in a crudely lettered sign leaning against a row of fake ducks of diminishing size. It read: "Two day old bread—a nickel a loaf."

It was one night towards the end of March while I was waiting for Bill's auction to take place that Lucifer Wrenchum's gas station paid me its richest dividend by bringing Tiptree into my life. I am as certain as I am of anything in this life that our farm could never have been brought to flower without him.

Although the idea would come to Tiptree as a distinct and disquieting surprise, he was, for me, some kind of father almost from the first moment I met him. Let me say at the outset that I find the entire idea of nature's nobleman, the purity of the simple and the so-called natural man to be arrant cock. The best man is, I believe, the man who garners to himself the most available experience with the greatest joy and leaves that behind which he cannot have or handle with the least bitterness. The man who denies himself experience will tend to deny experience to his children and vice versa. The ignorant man is not the uneducated man; he is the man who refuses to be conscious of the fact that he is uneducated. The reason I took Tiptree into my head as a sort of father almost from the first moment I met him was that I was aware there was in him a fundamental generosity in regard to experience. By which I mean simply that he was a teacher. The best man can no more help being a force for enlightenment than the worst man can help being a force for obfuscation. The profound amount I did not know about the course of action I was contemplating matched the profound fear I felt in the face of my ignorance. I needed a teacher and let us not forget that a teacher is someone who understands both the subject being taught and the morale of the pupil who is attempting to learn. In Tiptree, I was fortunate to find someone who filled the bill.

Knowing nothing about him, I nevertheless liked him from the first moment we struck up a conversation that night at Wrenchum's. He was dressed in the worn blue bib overalls, denim jacket and heavy work shoes of a farmer. It was, I later discovered, the proper costume for him; it gave his very real physical distinction full play. He was a tall and naturally lean man; Lincolnesque is the term that springs immediately to mind. It is apt, too, as his features had that same attractive asymmetry as did Lincoln's. Tiptree's nose was particularly memorable, a great aquiline beak which dominated his face. His eyes twinkled with unmistakable intelligence. There was nothing whatever of the oracle about him; nor was he diffident. Before he and I spoke to each other, I had been watching him make small talk with Wrenchum's wife, Callie. He had a natural ease with her, the ease of a man who genuinely likes and is liked by women. I am old enough now to know that there is no greater indication of a fundamental generosity in regard to experience than the wholly natural attitude of a man towards a woman.

Tiptree and I got along together well from the first exchange of small talk that evening. The hill people I have known tend mainly to fall into two categories: worthy and dreadfully dull, hard working Bible pounders or outsiders like Fred Cline who are sometimes likeable but frequently untrustworthy, each, beneath a veneer of false humility, secretly believing that he is the smartest man in the world. Tiptree fell into no such easily classifiable vein. The obvious and primary human faults such as hypocrisy and cant were missing from his makeup and there was a very real modesty in his manner, the modesty of a man who knows what he knows very well and is perfectly prepared to admit what he does not know. I was interested in him from the start but, during the

146

course of a long evening which ended up rather drunkenly at my house, I found out three things about Tiptree which made my interest in him strong and personal: He had two sons who were undergraduates at Virginia Polytechnic Institute, he was a Grade A dairy farmer with a small herd of twenty cows milking and, last but by no means least, he was a skilled carpenter who undertook occasional building contracts.

When I learned these things, I came clean with him about my intention to buy Bill's place and set up in the Grade A dairy business. I also came clean about my inexperience and all my fears concerning the project. He gave me a great deal of encouragement that night and he also gave me the benefit of a good deal of knowledge which he'd had to learn the hard way. For example, he admitted that his dairy farm was too small; a twenty-cow herd just could not bring in enough money to handle things like the two boys at VPI. Tiptree was wholly in agreement that the thirty-cow herd I contemplated was economically viable. But he emphasized strongly that they must be thirty *good* cows and that I must strive constantly to improve the herd through breeding and replacement. By the time we parted at about three o'clock in the morning, he had agreed, contingent upon my purchase of Bill's farm, to undertake the construction of whatever buildings I would need. I went to bed that night feeling that I had met my first evolutionary hillbilly. For, by then, I was certain that four out of five families in our section would, sooner or later, have to travel the hard road which led up through the midwestern cracker ghettoes where one or two generations would be sacrificed to the gods of economic assimilation.

I woke up the next morning and reflected that there must, indeed, be a number of different ways of doing things other than mine. I got drunk in a gas station, met a total stranger whom I had invited back to my house and with whom I had sat in wine until the small hours pouring out my heart. Furthermore, I had reached a tentative agreement with him to build barns on a farm that I did not even own. And I had done that without any knowledge other than his own protestations that he was a skilled carpenter. To top it all off, I felt just fine about the entire evening and the entire arrangement. I remarked breezily to Dorothy that I had found the man over at Wrenchum's who would build our barns and brought him home to drink some more and that he was a hell of a good guy. She replied that that was nice and scrambled me up some eggs for breakfast.

Later on in the day, my spirits were somewhat dampened. Encountering Fred Cline in one of my back pastures, I let it fall that I had met a splendid fellow named Tiptree the night before. Fred Cline's face grew very long at this news and he said, "Tiptree's a turrible man, Mister Cherry. Ah've known Tiptree all mah life and he's a turrible man."

"What the hell are you talking about, Fred?"

"Tiptree'd steal the pennies off'n a dead man's eyes, Mister Cherry. Don't have nothing to do with him whatever you do."

I began to quiz him, asking for chapter and verse. Did he actually know of any specific case in which Tiptree had acted dishonestly? Well, no, he didn't. But he'd heard things. But when I tried to find out what the things were that he'd heard, he grew vague. In the end, nothing was accomplished except that my peace of mind had been seriously disturbed. Fred and I parted, both rather miffed with each other. As a parting shot, he said, "Mister Cherry, you know that boy who delivers your paper every mornin'?"

"Yes," I said sourly.

"Well, you just take a close look at him tomorrow mornin!"

"What the hell is that supposed to mean," I shouted after him. But by then he was out of earshot.

For the rest of the day and throughout the night, I worried about what Fred had told me. Had I, perhaps, fallen into the hands of a crook? Was I such a poor judge of men? Was it, after all, wise to choose one's contractor in a drinking gas station while three sheets to the wind? Finally, I slept fitfully.

Curious as to what Fred had been mumbling about, I made it a point to be on hand the next morning when the paper was delivered. I had never looked very closely at the young man who delivered it. He had struck me as a pleasantly spoken young fellow of about eighteen and that was that. This morning, I looked at him very closely indeed and almost dropped the paper as a result. The resemblance to my new friend Tiptree was far too close to be coincidental. The boy did not just look *like* Tiptree, he was his spitting image. After the boy had gone, I pondered. Rather old womanishly, I found myself taking a high moral tone about having a cocksman contractor. Then I began to laugh at myself and I began to wonder if perhaps there had not been hanky panky between Tiptree and Fred Cline's wife during some bygone springtime.

The auction was scheduled for May 5. During the remaining weeks before it, I made some inquiries about Tiptree. It was rather worrying that the answers I received in one or two cases were on the dubious side. However, the good testimonials were so glowing that they wiped the bad ones out. I clung to my determination to hire him as a contractor and enjoy him as a friend.

CHAPTER X

As we waited for the all-important date of Bill's auction that spring, a curious, seemingly almost pointlessly cruel and malicious incident was engendered by my friend, O'Hara. Some months earlier, in response to his stepdaughter, Jane's importuning, he had procured a dog for the child. This animal whose name now escapes me had turned out badly. It was not mean but simply feckless, given to chewing things up and senseless barking or howling. Since the O'Hara's already possessed an aging Labrador Retriever of massive dignity, the presence of Jane's mixed-up mongrel was undoubtably a bit of an overload. O'Hara's solution to the disposal of the beast was redolently and secretly Machiavellian to the point that neither Dorothy nor I could quite fathom the benefits he intended to accrue from it.

What he did was to crate the animal up and send it by prepaid air express to Darroch's mother in St. Louis. O'Hara did this with neither permission from the lady or warning to her. Jane's grandmother was understandably both upset and confused. She did not want the dog, had no facilities for caring for it, and therefore was forced to take steps towards its disposal.

When O'Hara told me about these maneuvers, he did so in the high good humour of someone who feels he has accomplished a genuinely clever coup. Kate also appeared to feel that an essentially brilliant joke of some sort had been played. When they recounted their prank to Dorothy and me, we both had the sudden, uncomfortable feeling that we were listening to people who were not entirely sane. Fortunately there was no grave question of cruelty to the child involved. The dog was such an impossible pet that even Jane's predict-

151

ably prejudiced view as the beast's owner could not envision his permanent tenure. But exactly why O'Hara had chosen to badger an aging and harmless widow with a malicious, apparently senseless prank was mysterious to say the least.

The child, who could not have been much more than ten at the time, was equally confused. Her watchfulness towards O'Hara became even more steely than it had been before and she confided to Dorothy that "she did not like his jokes." It occurred to me that O'Hara might be deliberately fostering a breach between himself and the child, but as yet I could see no credible reason for such a pointless and foolish act.

In any event, O'Hara's vagaries could not be allowed to occupy my mind for long. The few weeks before Bill's auction rapidly shortened to days and there were many plans to make regarding the future and many councils of war to hold devising the means to make the success of those plans possible.

My mother, heroine of the exchequer as always, agreed to advance the funds necessary for the expansion of the farm. In conference, she, Dorothy and I settled upon the sum of $10,000 as the top amount we would pay for Bill's place. I had high hopes that it might go for less. The one thing that could drive the price higher was the very eventuality that Bill was hoping for: that it would be bought by some townie who had plenty of money and wanted it solely for recreational purposes and for its beauty.

And so, May 5, the day of the auction finally arrived. Auspiciously enough, it was a lovely day, warm and balmy with the early Appalachian spring. By that time Dorothy and I were old hands at attending auctions but our bids had never been offered on anything of greater magnitude than hand tools, plows or the occasional piece of furniture. As I write now, I have before me a copy of the handbill which advertised the sale. It is a euphoric and wholly American document. Headed by advice of a free wristwatch to be given away to some lucky visitor, it goes on to advise of sale by absolute auction of Bill's farm of 75 acres located on the "Glade" road 7 miles West of Wytheville, Va. The list of personal property for sale is preceded by the words: "Mr. Retired Man This Is It!" The bill concludes with notice that lunch will be served by the ladies of Mt. Pleasant PTA.

When the bidding got to $10,000 that morning, I was fairly certain that I had lost my chance to buy the place. And the bidding got to that figure ominously fast. Indeed, it turned out that the very thing Bill had been hoping for had happened: someone was after the place to use as a recreational place in the country. Whoever the gentleman was, he must have placed approximately the same ceiling on his price as I had on mine for, at ten thousand, the bidding slowed practically to a halt. At that point, I received nudges from both my wife and my mother to continue past the limit we had set ourselves and I did so. By fits and starts, my opponent and I got to the point where the last bid had been $10,000. from me. After a very long pause, he made it $10,550. With absolutely no hope at all that I could drive him out but feeling that I would have one more, almost wholly symbolic try, it made it $10,555. I'll be damned if the five dollar increase didn't turn the trick. We were now the owners of a farm totaling 165 acres and, while we were a long way still from being in the Grade A dairy business, we now had the requisite land to do so.

It was then early May. My intention was to be well enough set up by fall to begin milking nine or ten cows and be able to apply for Grade A status. There was no guarantee whatsover that one's application would be acted upon favorably but the probability was that the permit would be granted if the proper requirements had been met. To do so was going to necessitate a prodigious amount of work between now and our proposed date to begin marketing milk. With pencil and paper, in my head and with requests for advice up and down the country, I had been working on the planning aspect of the problem for the past two months. Therefore I had a fairly sound and specific idea of what I wanted to do and how I wanted to do it.

There are two essential methods of dealing with milk cattle. The most traditional way is to house them throughout the winter in what is called a stanchion barn. Most dairy farmers today believe that this is an inefficient system. In this system, the cows are kept imprisoned with their necks in stanchions before, during and after milking. The only two positive points of such a system are these: denied contact with each other, the cows tend to escape minor injuries of the udder which lead to a disease called mastitus, which is nasty, wasteful of milk and expensive to cure. The other positive aspect of the stanchion barn system is simply that the cows have more warmth if kept inside during the cold months.

On the discredit side, the list of points against the stanchion barn system is practically endless. The most important of them are connected with labour. The cow eats, voids and is milked in the same place, which means that everything, milking machines, cleaning up equipment and feed, must be brought to the cow. I think most dairy farmers would agree also that the stanchion system creates a low state of physical well-being among cattle. Finally, the stanchion system is murderously expensive to install. In fact, I think it is safe to say that farms which cling to the stanchion system do so only because their solidly built, cement-floored barns were built by an earlier generation. The expense of building such a barn today would be prodigious and the rewards dubious.

The system which I had settled upon utilized an L-shaped structure called a milking parlour. The cows wait for entry to the parlour in a narrow runway which assures that they remain in single file and do not quarrel about precedence and pecking order and thereby injure themselves. Inside the parlour, a single operator stands in a pit some three feet below the level on which the cows will enter. Facing him are three stalls made of steel rails with a swinging gate at the rear and at the front of each, which the operator can control from his pit by levers. By a system of ropes and pulleys, he can also open and close the entrance and exit doors to the parlour as he pleases. Assuming that an operator is fully set up to begin milking his cows, this is the procedure: A milking machine is hooked up, ready to go in each stall and the cows moo and anxiously await entry in their runway. The operator simply opens the rear half of the gate of the stall furthest to his right, making it impossible for the first cow entering to go anywhere but into that stall. He then hauls the door open with his ropes and pulleys, the cow enters and proceeds to the stall at which point the operator swings shut the gate which imprisons the cow in a space comfortable but too narrow to permit much movement by the cow. The operator then proceeds to do precisely the same thing until all three stalls are occupied. As he finishes milking each cow, he removes the milking machine, opens the front half of the steel gate and allows the cow free passage to the barnyard by opening the exit door with the system of ropes and pulleys. He then proceeds to allow a new cow to fill the vacated stall, and repeats the process. The constant flow of cattle through the parlour allows the operator to minister to the herd without moving more than a few steps left or right.

The small room in the center of the long stroke of the L is a feed room where the ground corn and protein supplements are kept. Between one and five pounds of this feed is given to each cow during milking, the amount depending upon her capacity to produce. The gift of this grain also serves to preoccupy the cow and settle her down for milking. The room in which the feed is kept also contains the hot water heater necessary to provide for the proper washing of the milking equipment.

The particular milking system which I had decided to install was called Surge and is manufactured by the Ford Motor Company. I doubt that it differs seriously in principle or performance from any other. Mine was a marvellously simple and efficient machine whose heart was a vacuum pump located above two stainless steel sinks in the room which forms the serif of the L. In the center of this room was a huge stainless steel tank which received the fresh milk through a Pyrex tube and immediately began the process of cooling it to 45 degrees. This tube ran from the tank through the feed room into the milking parlour proper where it followed the same L-shape as the building.

From it descended a connection at each milking stall to which was attached a milking machine. When these were attached to the cows, the vacuum pump would cause a pulsating motion which drew the milk up into the glass tube, along it through the feed room, and finally deposited it in the huge stainless steel tank. The milk, therefore, was literally never carried or even handled.

When the milking was finished, the milking machines were hung on a rack in the two stainless steel sinks and the same vacuum pump automatically washed and sterilized the entire system by driving hot water, detergent and, finally, rinse water back and forth through the pipes.

In addition to its primary purpose, incidentally, the milking parlour is also ideally conceived for the subsidiary care of milk cattle: medical treatment, artificial insemination and preventive sprays against pests and parasites.

The other factor in caring for milk cattle is their feeding. A good milk cow consumes roughly three tons of coarse feed during a winter. Rather than feed cattle solely on hay which would also require a fantastic amount of storage space, most farmers feed both hay and corn silage in a ratio of two tons of silage to one ton of alfalfa hay. Even at that ratio, it meant that I would need a barn capable of holding at least 30 tons of alfalfa hay if I were to have the herd of thirty milking cows to which I aspired. Roughly one thousand bales of hay would be required. Accordingly, my intention was to build a 60 by 60 foot hay storage barn in conjunction with what are called "loafing sheds". Because the hay stored in it would rest upon the ground and not on the floor of a loft, the structure need support no other weight than its own. The cattle would have free access to the loafing sheds on either side of the central hay storage section. What manure they deposited in those loafing sheds could be covered with straw then cleaned out each spring with a tractor loader and spread upon the pastures. I had been told by many farmers who used the loafing shed system for feeding their cattle that the cattle would elect to remain outside the barn when not actually feeding except in the coldest of weather. This turned out to be perfectly accurate.

I called my friend, Tiptree, the night after the auction which was a Saturday. He agreed to come over the next day to take a walk around the new place with me and discuss my plans. When he arrived, we went over the plans for the big barn and the dairy barn. He made several very valuable suggestions about their placement which took into account problems of drainage I had not accounted for.

After we had finished our discussion of the proposed construction, Tiptree and I took a walk through the timbered portion of the farm. He confirmed what I had thought to be true: There was more than enough first-class timber to mill from my own trees all the lumber for the two barns and to pay for the milling by trading a like amount of milled lumber to the contractor who undertook the job. I asked Tiptree if he could recommend anyone who would take on the timber cutting but he could not. Furthermore, he warned me that the men who did that sort of work were a tricky lot and to be careful in my dealings with them. Never was better advice given; the chicanery of the man I eventually hired to cut and mill the timber led finally to the only law suit I have ever been involved in my life. Curiously enough, the law suit would lead indirectly to a grotesque and definitive confrontation between O'Hara and me a year later.

As we walked around the farm that day looking at the timber, I knew Tiptree was figuring his price to build the two barns and I was holding my breath. I wanted the barns completed and ready for operation by fall. Finally, hemming and hawing, Tiptree allowed as how if he could wait to start the job until his two sons were finished with their semester at VPI and available to help him, he could do the job for $1900. Even then, it was an unbelievably low price. Today it seems like a joke. With the timber coming off my own land, I was going to be out of pocket only the cost of cinder block, hardware and roofing materials. And, as it turned out, the total cost of my milking parlour, the machinery inside it and the 60 by 60 hay feeding and storage barn came to less than $12,000. Tiptree and I shook hands on the deal which was fulfilled by him to the last jot and tittle. Once, long afterward when he stopped by my house and we were having a drink, I confessed that I had been a bit apprehensive as to whether or not I might get screwed. Tiptree smiled his lazy smile and said, "Hell, Jawn, you cain't screw a friend."

Past experience had taught me to have considerable faith in Luther, the friendly livestock dealer from whom I had bought Vacca, the sheep and the two doomed pigs. Accordingly, I now went to see him and advised him of my plans for setting up a dairy farm. Everything I had read and everything I had been told had convinced me of the wisdom of buying only the finest stock I could possibly afford. I wanted young heifers due to come fresh in the early fall with their first calves and I wanted them to be from the same farm. For the simple reason that a going farm keeps its finest heifers and sells only the culls, this was a trickier proposition than it might appear. However, from time to time, successful dairy farms would be sold at auction and Luther specialized in buying cattle at such sales. By giving him plenty of warning, I knew that he would have time to find me something good. These would, after all, be the nucleus of the future. It was my intention to do all the future breeding through artificial insemination; the sires of the future calf crop would be literally the finest money could buy and the furthest I could extend to now in terms of quality among the heifers would pay huge dividends at a future date. Too many times had I seen dairy farms in the neighborhood which were turning in a mediocre to poor showing because of indifferent cattle bred to just any old bull of the same breed in order to keep them on the production line.

As far as the specific breed, I had very little real choice. Since butterfat had ceased some years before to be a factor in the price paid for milk, the high-butter fat, low-volume breeds such as Jerseys and Guernseys were not really practicable. The majority of the higher-volume breeds such as Ayrshires and Brown Swiss were too scarce in the locality to work and the have-your-cake-and-eat-it plan of milking Shorthorns to sell both milk and beef I am convinced always comes to a bad end. Which left Holstein-Freisians as the logical candidates. By that time, Vacca had been bred (artificially, of course) and it was time to turn her dry. So, to get my feet wet, I bought a recently-fresh young Holstein cow for family use, planning to incorporate her into the herd in the fall. That cow's name escapes me now but I remember that the same feeling of rapport and mutual warmth that I obtained with Vacca was quite definitely not present. After milking little old Vacca, crawling under this beast was like sitting under the dome of St. Peter's. She was a most undocile cow which was probably just as well; she prepared me for some of the wild Indians I would later own. Dairy cattle, let me add, are frequently less peaceful than their bovine image suggests.

The search for suitable cattle now having been laid on and Tiptree having agreed to take in hand the building of the barns, the number one priority automatically became the cutting and milling of timber for the barns. In June, Tiptree would be ready to begin and the lumber must be ready and available. Timbermen prepared to take on such a task as mine proved to be in fairly short supply. However, I did finally locate a man called Ralph who showed interest in the job. I would like to be able to say that I was aware of Ralph's penchant for crookedness from the first but I cannot. He was a nondescript little fellow who made no great impression upon me one way or the other. He owned the proper equipment and had the knowledge to do the job and that was that. He came, looked over the situation and said that he would be willing to take on the job. He also offered me an astonishingly· large amount of cash for a cluster of five or six big poplar trees standing at the top of one of the pastures. It was that which decided me and we made a deal on the spot. He was to bring his saw mill equipment in and set it up on the spot; he would then cut and mill the so many thousand board feet required by Tiptree for the barns and a like amount which would be trucked away and sold in payment for the labor involved.

To give Ralph, the sawmill man some credit, he was a hardworking little devil. But he never did actually bring his mill to my land, a fact which gave him the opportunity of robbing me. When he explained that the job was really too small to warrant setting up the mill, I complied in his request that he be allowed to truck the cut logs away to his place and return with the milled lumber. The only trouble was that, having no way of checking into the number of board feet which could be milled from a given log, I was pretty well at his mercy. It is my considered conviction that Ralph was taking twice as much as he was returning but this suspicion neither dawned nor became certainty for some time. The reassuring fact was that the timber for the barns now began to accumulate slowly but surely. It was mighty lumber, great oaken six-by-sixes and two-by-eights of a length and grade one would be hard put to find in a lumberyard.

We had long since decided that we would change our place of residence to Bill's house on the new farm. It was a smaller house than our present one; indeed the three tiny upstairs bedrooms were little more than cells. I expropriated one for an office of sorts, one was apportioned to Linda (then coming up on her third birthday) and the third would be available for the new baby due in the fall. However, we could not make the move immediately; there were the formalities of closing the transaction to be gotten through and Bill and his wife needed time to get organized for their hegira to the promised land of Utah. I must say in passing that the prospect of removing to the heartland of his religion had done wonders for Bill's spirits. Normally tending towards the lugubrious, he now moved about in an absolute cloud of exaltation. In retrospect, I find his high spirits at leaving the locality very easy to understand. There is little inspiration for the indigenous among the southern mountains. This is why there is a grudging respect behind my sallies at Bill; he needed to go and he was psychologically wily enough to hook up with a religion which would give him the impetus to go.

At any rate, we planned our change of houses sometime during the late spring or early summer. With the timber for the barns accumulating satisfactorily and the livestock dealer on the lookout for good cattle, the time had now come to give thought to the farmer's ever-present cross: fencing. Looking ahead to this day, we had spent many fine days during the preceding winter and early spring in cutting and splitting Locust trees into proper lengths for fence posts. Fence posts are a staple need of any farmer; hardly a week will go by without the need for patching fence arising.

In the rough plan which I had conceived for managing my future dairy herd, only one stretch of entirely new fence was immediately imperative. For the rest, matters could be handled by patching and making do. Roughly, the distance to be fenced was about 1000 feet. With this fence in place, I could devote the land to the west to growing alfalfa and have no problems in keeping the cattle out of it.

As I look back now over the years we spent farming, my mind always goes straight to those weeks during the spring of 1965 that Dorothy and I spent building our stretch of fence. Like a happy child returning home to love and care, my mind returns to that time assured of benefice. The best of any project is its creative aspect, the doing of it. The day would come when our farm would produce enough milk to supply a small town but there would be less satisfaction—for me, at any rate—in that than in the memory of those lovely spring days. Whenever I feel the need to recapture happiness, I go back to that time. But I do not do so often; the clear view afforded by hindsight of the degree of hope in happiness is too sad.

As fence builders, Dorothy and I were a reasonably efficient if somewhat comical pair. Trio, I suppose I should

160

say because Linda, then at that splendid age of two and a half, tagged along happily enough. Dorothy was by then manifestly and magnificently pregnant. We evolved a system to take full advantage of her girth. Otis, a very generous neighbor, had lent us a posthole digger which fitted onto my Ford tractor and hooked up to its power take-off. Thus the truly back-breaking portion of fence building, the digging of the holes by hand, was by-passed. We soon found that we could make Otis's digger work a great deal better if Dorothy stood on top of it as it bored its way into the ground. So, following the straight lines laid out by a string, we would dig our holes one by one. After each was dug, Dorothy and Linda would sit playing nearby whild I cleaned the bottom of the hole and then set the post and tamped it firm with the new earth. We did not hurry; we would break our day with long picnic lunches and, if the spirit moved us to stop altogether, we did so.

My feed problems for the next winter would be tricky. The seven acre field immediately behind the Kegley house, I planned on plowing and putting into corn then and now. This corn, picked in the fall would give me a certain amount of supplementary feed for the nine or ten cows I expected to have on the line by fall. There was a sound corn crib on the Kegley place in which the corn could be stored and removed bit by bit to be ground and mixed with protein supplement at the local mill. For the rest, I knew I was going to be stuck with buying a certain amount of hay to get me through that first winter. The alfalfa which I planned to sow in August would, of course, provide no usable yield until the following spring. I could cut a certain amount of low grade hay from my unused pastures during the coming summer but there would not be enough nor would it be of high enough quality to see the cows through the winter. However, the purchase of hay for the relatively few cattle with which I was beginning was economically feasible for that first winter. If hay is bought when it is being made, the price is relatively low. It is when one seeks to buy hay during the winter that one finds the price has risen dramatically. By the summer after the one on which we were then embarking, I figured we could be reasonably self sufficient as far as feed went. By then, our planned fifteen acres of alfalfa should yield three or four cuttings during the summer and I would have a trench silo dug which could be filled with chopped corn silage.

It was, frankly, an exciting time. While we waited for Tiptree to begin building the two barns, we had our fence to build and our corn to plant. Later on in the summer, the ground would have to be plowed and prepared for putting in the alfalfa. My brother had written me that he would be arriving for the summer and the prospect of his help with the various tasks was a welcome one.

By the end of spring, Bill and his wife and children had vacated the new house and departed for their new life in the west. Bit by bit, we moved our belongings across the creek to the new house but we were in no great hurry to take up formal residence. The fencing, plowing and planting which made up the greatest part of the work for which I was directly responsible still took place on the Kegley side of the farm and I still had to milk our current family cow twice a day on that side. Not to mention our kitchen garden on that side from which Dorothy was extracting an astonishing amount of provender for both canning and direct consumption.

As the summer began, Tiptree's two sons returned from VPI and the three of them began work on the two new barns. The calm competence with which Tiptree set to work could not have been more reassuring. By then, the lumbering operation (with its attendant thievery) was reaching an end. Tiptree began with the Milking parlour which was mainly a masonry project, being constructed almost entirely of cinder block and needing only a minimum of timber for rafters, roof-sheathing, plates etc. At the day's end, he would occasionally stop over for a drink with me and we would talk over the progress of the barns and various other matters. It was during one such talk that he explained to me the system whereby he and his sons cooperated in order that the burden of their college education could be handled. To this day, their *modus operandi* strikes me as having been conceived and carried out with truly Lincolnesque simplicity. Tiptree provided the basic cash for their tuition and they, of course, worked while going to school in order to take up the slack. Each fall and winter term, he sent the boys off to school loaded down with the edible portions of a home-killed and cured hog which they would use as the nucleus of their physical subsist-

162

ence till the end of term, cooking and eating their way through the preserved hog meat in their rented accommodations. There was a basic love and rapport between the various members of Tiptree's family that I have encountered rarely in my life. His sons never lost sight of what a vast physical and psychological reach it was for a backwoods farmer to try for a college education for his progeny. And the last thing Tiptree expected from them was undue gratitude. As builders, the three of them worked together smoothly and efficiently; neither of the sons was as skilled as his father at construction work but they were both good rough carpenters and tireless workers. During the month of June, the milking parlour slowly began to take shape. Although, it was the smallest of the two buildings, it was also by far the most complicated, needing drains and much masonry work which the hay feeding barn would not.

As the summer wore on and work on our project continued to bear fruit, Dorothy and I saw less and less of O'Hara and Kate. Once or twice, it crossed my mind that this might be happening as a result of some conscious design on O'Hara's part but I dismissed the idea as wholly preposterous. He was, after all, my oldest and closest friend. It did not make much sense that he would brutally decide to end a friendship of such duration.

Then, one day during the summer, I had a curious encounter with O'Hara on the street in Wytheville which made me begin to wonder again if my suspicions were entirely imaginary. Walking along the street in town that day, I caught sight of O'Hara approaching in the distance. At the best of times, he was inclined to be a vastly preoccupied man and this day he appeared to be in a blue study, marching along looking from neither right to left. While he was still more than a block away, I thought I saw him glance up briefly and take notice of my approach. But he immediately resumed his look of concentration and continued on towards me unseeing. I was not absolutely certain he had seen me but I had a sudden and strong suspicion that he not only had taken notice of my approach but that he was going to pretend deliberately that he had not. This struck me as such a preposterous possibility that I decided to act as if I had not seen him until the precise moment of our passing each other; at which time, if he had not greeted me, I was going to brace him and ask him what the hell he thought he was about. As we drew abreast, he continued to stare straight ahead and said nothing. Finally, at the last moment, I said, "What in the world is this?" He looked up then, of course, and we exchanged greetings. Jokingly, I asked him if he was trying to give me the cut direct? He laughed but I seemed to sense a certain false heartiness in his laughter and, what was a much rarer thing as far as O'Hara was concerned, a definite loss of composure. Once we began talking, he could not have been more pleasant and, as I recall, we went into a restaurant and had a cup of coffee together. At parting, my suspicions were laid at rest and I felt slightly paranoid at having had them in the first place. Later on, I recounted the incident to Dorothy and she pooh-poohed my fears, saying that he had probably been simply lost in thought. However, a nagging sense of worry and wonder persisted. Certainly, the concourse between our two families persisted in becoming more sparse that summer. However, it was easy to ascribe this to our preoccupation with the magnitude of turning our farm into a paying proposition and, once again, I dismissed the whole business from my mind.

Early that summer of 1956, Luther, the livestock dealer telephoned to say that he had a line on nine Holstein heifers due to come fresh with their first calves during late summer. I went with him to look at the cattle and was suitably impressed. I should mention that by now I was beginning to develop a certain "feel" for cattle. During the preceding months, I had not only spent a great deal of time reading everything I could get my hands on about the management of a dairy farm, I had also ranged far and wide talking to various progressive dairy farmers and trying to assimilate as much knowledge as possible. As a result, when I went with Luther to look at his nine Holstein heifers, I had a pretty good idea of the sort of cattle I was looking for. These, while far from cheap, struck me as being an ideal group of heifers to form the nucleus of my future herd. They were large heifers and had clearly been allowed to gain their maximum growth before being bred. Furthermore, they came from a dairy farm where records had been kept on the cattle from which they stemmed and the records of milk production on that farm were impressive. In buying heifers which have not yet thrown their first calves, one is able to judge conformation much less satisfactorily than in the case of cows which have had calves previously. The udder of a first calf heifer has not yet taken shape for one thing and the proper shape and placement of a cow's udder is of great importance as a clue to her future ability to produce. Then too, first calf heifers are still ungainly and long-legged; they have not yet assumed that wedge-shaped, rather bony conformation which is the indication of a good, high-producing cow. Perhaps, most important of all was the fact that Luther, the livestock dealer felt strongly that these were potentially valuable cattle and definitely worth purchasing. By then, we had had a number of dealings and he had never let me down. I also took Tiptree along to have a look at the heifers and he too was strongly impressed and advised their purchase.

The single thing that worried me the most about the cattle was that some sort of mistake might have been made in the records kept of when they had been bred and that they would begin having their calves before the milking parlour was completed. I could imagine no more terrifying prospect than suddenly finding myself stuck with nine wild and unbroken Holstein heifers in need of twice-a-day milking and no facilities for dealing with them. However, Tiptree set my mind at rest; the milking parlour was far enough along in its construction by then for him to be able to assure me that it would be completely operative well before the heifers began coming fresh. Accordingly, I unlimbered my check book and a few days later, the heifers were delivered and installed on the new side of the farm. Having been ungrazed throughout the spring, the pastures were lush and they foraged happily. As always, Tiptree had given me a wise piece of advice: to spend a portion of each day walking around them and among them so that they would become accustomed to my presence. I did so and I have no doubt that it helped; but I viewed the coming day when I would have to break them to the dairy barn with grave misgivings. They were big strong animals and wild as March hares. I would be an awful liar if I said I was not frightened to death of the prospect of dealing with them at close quarters.

The balance of the summer passed in dealing with the various tasks which had to be done: the new fence was finished and the various pieces of old fence patched up adequately; the corn crop needed to be cultivated several times and the pastures had to be mowed before the weeds went to seed. In August, my brother and I began the plowing for the alfalfa crop. I would usually work on it in the mornings and he would replace me in the afternoons. It was rough ground we were plowing which had not been worked for many years. And the sowing of alfalfa is a tricky business; unless the ground is well-plowed and worked over and over with disk and harrow until the earth is finely pulverized, the chances are that the stand of alfalfa obtained will be poor. In late August, the ground was finally in good shape and I hired a neighbor who owned a seed drill to put in the alfalfa. After it was in, I borrowed a machine known as a cultipacker and went over it, packing the earth down in grooves so that it would have the maximum chance to retain moisture. After that, there was nothing to do about the alfalfa except await the following spring; we would not really know until then whether or not we had achieved a satisfactory stand. Which was no small question; the success of our feeding program depending to a great extent upon the yield of our alfalfa.

Around the first of September, we finally completed our move to the new house, leaving my brother in sole possession of the Kegley place. In time, I would install a hired hand and his family in the old house but we would never live there again. My brother would be going south before long but he planned to remain to lend his moral and physical support until our cattle had begun calving and our dairy barn was actually in operation.

Although a great deal smaller than the old one, the new house was an unqualified joy. It had been so long since we had enjoyed such fundamental American rights as central heating and truly operative plumbing that we had to get used to them all over again. No matter how honorable a position the two-hole outdoor privy may enjoy in song and story, as far as I am concerned, nothing became ours like its abandonment. The new house was not without charm; it sat back from the road on a slight rise facing down the hill towards the creek, a view of which was afforded by a large picture window in the living room. Besides a long living room with a dining alcove at one end, the house had on the ground floor a modern kitchen, bath and large master bedroom. The house was an old one and its fundamental construction was that of a log cabin, albeit thoroughly modernized with whitewashed cement filling in the chinks between the logs. At the rear, the house looked out at the pastures which rose gently behind it and towards the nearby barnyard. From the back door, it was a walk of about sixty yards to the new milking parlour. In addition to the new hay feeding barn which was still only half done, there was an old, rather tumbledown log barn which I planned to use as a calving barn and whose loft contained whatever hay we had managed to accumulate.

As August drew to a close, the finishing touches were put on the milking parlour and the machinery was installed. I was keeping one eye on that process and one wary eye on the nine new heifers. It was, of course, impossible to tell exactly when they would begin dropping their calves but it was an event which was obviously imminent. By that time, Vacca had dropped her second calf so that I actually had two cows to milk already. On Tiptree's advice, I started penning the heifers and the other two cows up in the holding pen at least once a day and putting them through the milking stalls in a series of dry runs. As a little incentive, I would give each a scoopful of supplemental feed in order to implant the idea in their heads that pleasure of a sort awaited them within that mysterious building. As soon as the machinery was installed, and I had been well rehearsed in its use by the manufacturer's representative, I used it on Vacca and the other Holstein cow already in milk so that I could become accustomed to its operation and the new heifers could become more or less accustomed to the noise of the vacuum pump and the pulsating hiss of the milkers. The behavior of the heifers during the dry runs through the milking parlor boded nothing but disaster for the day when they would actually have to be broken to the milking machines. They were a wild-eyed, unruly lot at best who tended to shy at the slightest movement as well as to hang back and refuse entry to the milking stalls. Occasionally, one would panic completely and attempt to turn around in the narrow passageway and, several times, the situation got so far out of hand that I had to drive a cow down through the operator's pit in order to get the traffic pattern under control.

167

Thank God for those two weeks of dry runs with the heifers and actual practice with trustworthy old Vacca. For when the heifers actually began to drop their calves, it was sheer pandemonium. By then, I was keeping a very close eye on the cattle indeed, walking to the pasture three and four times a day to see if there had been any developments. The first sign of trouble was one morning when I counted the cattle and discovered I was two short. It turned out, of course, that the first two heifers to calve had not only done so but they had broken out of the pasture to have their calves in a dense wooded area bordering the creek.

Obeying iron-bound atavistic laws of self-preservation, a calving cow will hide her calf and then purposely try to lead you away from the place where she has hidden it. It took my brother, Fred Cline and me most of the day to find the two calves and carry them back to the calving barn. Once we had the calves, their mothers had no choice but to follow, trumpeting with mighty bellows their protest against such kidnapping. We then penned the mothers up with their calves for forty eight hours; the calves needed the colestrum for that period and the cows' milk was, of course, unusable until the period of colestrum production had passed. After forty-eight hours, we separated the cows from their calves for good and prepared to break them to the milking equipment. I must admit that throughout the years I was a dairy farmer I never managed to become completely inurred to the process of separating cow from new-born calf. The tiny calf would stand wobbly-legged within the calving barn and bleat with longing while its forlorn mother bellowed her heartbreak and frustration in reply. If neither sight nor contact was allowed to pass between the two, most cows would resign themselves to the loss within twenty-four to forty-eight hours, but I have known many who continued their keening for a week. Usually, however, the combination of being milked twice daily plus the special feed they enjoyed at each milking made them settle down quite rapidly.

Undoubtedly through the aegis of Fred Cline, word had spread up and down the road that day when we put our first two unbroken heifers through the milking parlor. I do not think there was any particular malice among the spectators that day; they simply knew there was a damned good show going on and they were determined to enjoy it to the full. Between myself, my brother and the cows, we certainly saw to it that they got their money's worth. The cows balked, jumped, kicked and generally carried on to the point where I ceased to believe they could ever be broken. At one point, I remember taking a kick on my bad knee from one of those Holsteins that, had I not been standing at the outer edge of her kicking radius, would have lamed me for life. However, one way or another, we got through it.

It always comes as something of a surprise how quickly a completely new routine can become second nature. By the middle of October, all of the new heifers had dropped their calves and we had a grand total of eleven cows on the milking line. By then, my brother had gone and I found that I could handle the cows fairly well by myself. Parenthentically, I should say at this point that my wife very wisely and deliberately steered clear of having anything to do with milking cows throughout our time on the farm. In time, she mastered the intricacies of hooking up the milking machines but that was it as far as she was concerned. By mid-October, the routine was clearly established; I would rise about five thirty in the morning, fix myself some breakfast and then walk down to the dairy barn and hook up the milking machines, prepare the feed cart and generally get the barn ready to function. Then I would walk to the top of the pastures to collect the cattle and drive them down to the holding pen in the barnyard. I was both amused and a little touched at the change which had come over my lovable little Jersey cow, Vacca, as a result of herd life. Before the addition of the new cattle, Vacca had become almost as friendly as a pet dog and had loved to stand placidly chewing her cud while I scratched her ears. But now all that had changed. Poor Vacca was literally about half the size of her monstrous new sisters but she had evidently decided to maintain her place in the pecking order through a combination of pugnacity and experience. She let me know in no uncertain terms that the days of love and ear scratching were over; clearly she felt such indignities would lower her status among the other cattle. Occasionally, when I got her by herself, a little ear scratching would take place but it was plain that she wanted it to be our secret.

We were fortunate in having nothing more than minor and

ordinary complications among the nine new calvings. One or two cows failed to "clean off" properly which means that the placenta was not thoroughly ejected, a situation which, if not properly handled can lead to infection and subsequent difficulty in breeding the cow. In correcting this situation, I made the acquaintance of Jim, a young veterinarian newly set up in practice in the neighborhood who would prove to be a good friend and a mainstay in time of trouble for the future.

We were granted Grade A status almost immediately after our cows began coming fresh. This meant that almost from the beginning we had a small but tangible monthly income from the milk. A diary farmer in Virginia at that time was paid two prices for his milk: $5.65 a hundred pounds (fifty quarts) for an amount which was known as one's "base" and about two thirds that amount for any excess milk produced over and above the base. The base was established on the basis of the previous year's production. In the case of beginners like myself, an arbitrary base was assigned pending the establishment of a true base following the first full year's production. As I recall, our net monthly check that first winter came to about $300. Far from riches, certainly, but I knew this would increase substantially with the addition of more cattle and the establishment of an annually larger base.

Particularly fortunate that fall was our luck in the matter of the gender of the calves dropped by the new cows. More than half the calves obtained were heifers, a fact of great importance to the future growth of our herd as they would be kept, raised, eventually bred and added to the milking herd. The bull calves were kept only to an age of about two months and then sold at the local livestock market as milk-fed veal.

Once I had returned from the pastures with the cattle and shut them up in the holding pen, I was ready to begin the milking. In the main, the cows soon settled down to the routine nicely although I do not remember a time during the years I milked cows when there were not one or two bad hats who had to be contained with anti-kicking devices to keep them from kicking the milking machine loose from their udders.

Within a month after beginning to milk the cows mechanically, I was adept enough so that the entire process, from getting the barn set up to hosing it down when finished, did not take much more than an hour and a half. It took me perhaps another half hour to feed the calves on milk substitute which they drank from buckets equipped with nipples. They objected to these violently for the first day or so but soon became accustomed to them. The technique was to hold the calves firmly and jam the nipple into their mouths, using one hand to pump the milk substitute down their throats. They would reject it at first and, as they spewed it back, it was rather a messy business; but, invariably, the moment would come when they would accept the nipple as substitute teat and begin gulping heartily.

Luckily enough, we had a prolonged Indian summer that fall and as our pastures were undergrazed to begin with, it was not necessary to feed the cattle heavily on hay until fall was well along. The cows spent all their time on the pastures and their twice-daily milking and the twice-daily feeding of the calves were the only categorically demanding tasks which had to be fulfilled that fall. The balance of the day was spent puttering with the many small jobs which always need to be done around a farm.

The next stellar event on our agenda was, of côurse, the arrival of the new baby, due sometime in November. Dorothy was calm about the whole business and the doctor had assured us that there was no apparent reason to be worried. Still, one is never entirely at ease until the child has been officially checked in as having all ten fingers and toes and certified as hitting on all six cylinders. All of which, I proclaim with thanks to chance or Providence, eventually turned out to be so.

In the preceding pages, I have intimated an awareness that a hairline crack had appeared in my lifelong relationship with O'Hara. Now, at the end of a fine season during which I had been able to preoccupy myself with apparent reality for the first time since the war, the crack became a discernible fissure, which would broaden in time to a gaping chasm, forever unbridgeable. The calculated and subtle cruelty of the incident which outlined the future may appear as small on this page as it still looms large within my mind; but it struck straight to the heart of my most cherished area of illusion: the essential value and eventual prevailance of myself in conjunction with my friends. Therefore, I make no more of it than I must.

It is late afternoon of a splendid day in late October, prosa-

171

ically enough, my favorite season. Its exquisite beauty and pervasive melancholy are, for once, balanced by a sense of accomplishment within me which is small but very real.

I have hooked up the machinery in the dairy barn and Dorothy, Linda and I have walked to the top of the farm to drive the cattle down for the evening milking. We do not hurry; there is no need. Indeed, there is amongst the three of us an unspoken sense of need to prolong the moment. Even the dog behaves for once with a measure of sanity; she has declared a rare and temporary truce with the cattle. The dog is eminently unsuited to farm life and constantly puzzled. Only a few days before, she accompanied me to the thickets below by the creek as I mended a piece of fence. Finished with the task, we were returning through the underbrush when a fox jumped up so closely beneath the dog's muzzle that even the dog's epic ineptitude as a hunter did not prevent her from grabbing the fox by the throat. As usual, the dog's interior confusion triumphed; she had known turbaned Moor and the swish of Roman clerical gown but this was clearly beyond her ken. She turned to me for a ruling and in doing so relinquished the fox. The fox, dazed by this stroke of luck, gazed at me also. We stood thus for a moment in a comic tableau of mutual astonishment and then the fox snarled softly and disappeared into the undergrowth.

As Dorothy, Linda and I walked to the top of the farm to collect the cows, I told Dorothy this story and she was amused. At the very top of the pastures, we sat for a while and watched the cattle graze, their shadows long in the low sun. Even in the relatively short time I had been dealing with them, their massive function had breached my admiration and worked its way into my blood. The best of them will produce 6,000 quarts of milk a year for perhaps ten years; they are tremendous sustainers of life. After a while now they moved together and started down the hill towards the barns. They moved sedately at first and then, spooked by something, they began to jump, run and frolic. The sudden shedding of their dignity was somehow comic and on this October afternoon, Dorothy and Linda and I began to laugh. Cows bring to mind a group of heavy-bosomed dowagers suddenly giving in to an overpowering desire to frolic in the buff. The fit passed as

172

quickly as it began and we followed along behind them as they plodded down the hill.

From the hill, we could see across the country for miles. The road leading to the farm was visible for brief stretches as it curved and wound around the hills. On this day we caught sight of the station wagon belonging to the O'Haras as it approached. It was perhaps a half-mile away and unmistakeable. Like my late-lamented cherished vehicle, it was one of the last models manufactured whose bodies were actually covered with wood panelling.

The prospect of finding O'Hara and Kate and perhaps their children waiting at the house was a pleasant one. Busy with the climax of actually putting our farm into production, we had recently foregone nearly all social intercourse. Now, although we did not speak of it, both Dorothy and I were terribly pleased that our friends would be waiting at the bottom of the hill. It had been a good day and now it would be a perfect one. Dorothy mentioned that there was a roast in the freezer which she could cook and I was relieved to remember there was a sufficiency of booze in the house. We both felt strongly that it would be a memorably pleasant evening. Dorothy and Kate could pour drinks and begin the preparation of dinner while O'Hara (who had never seen my dairy barn in operation) could accompany me to the barn while I did the evening milking.

Dorothy helped me drive the cows into the holding pen and I closed the gate on them before walking with her to the house to greet the O'Haras. Even though we could not actually see their car from the holding pen, it never occurred to us that they would not be at the house waiting for us. But as we rounded the barn to gain a clear view of the house, their car was nowhere in sight. Then Dorothy and I walked to the back door of the house and stood looking down at a wicker basket which had been left on the doorsill. We recognized the wicker basket as one which belonged to us and which had been left at the O'Haras' house. Then, as we stood looking down at the basket, the meaning of the collection of objects within it slowly began to dawn upon us.

All the detritus of our deeply interwoven interfamilial relationship had been carfully and pointedly assembled. It was all there down to the last jot and tittle: the borrowed books, the child's toy casually left behind, the sweater borrowed to keep off a sudden, unseasonable chill, the necktie removed during a game of chess on a hot night. It was all there; nothing was missing.

The message was clear and unmistakeable. There would, in time, be a more formal ending, a strange Walpurgisnacht during which few techniques of grotesquerie would be left un-utilized to encompass all the inherent regrets and remorse which accompany a deliberately and cruelly sundered friendship. To this day I cannot say with absolute certainty why it was sundered; nor can I believe with absolute conviction that there was need for it.

CHAPTER XI

Our second daughter arrived safely on November 16 of that year 1956, and was duly named—if not christened—Sylvia, after our old friend Sylvia Pennebaker. Shortly after her birth, the cold weather began and the desultory rhythms of a farm in winter took charge. I rose early to milk my eleven cows and returned again to the task at half past four of the evening. In the hours between, I occupied myself with literary efforts but such beginnings as I made that winter were poorly organized and ineffectual. The clarity of vision and organizational grasp so essential to pulling off any literary project were simply not present and I believe this was due to the concentrated expenditure of precisely that sort of energy during the preceding six months. For the first time in many years, I was wholly bereft of that extraordinary fusion of imaginative clarity and formal discipline which makes the practice of any art as exquisitely rewarding and pleasurable as it is painful and frightening. Unfortunately—or, perhaps, fortunately—the temporary inability to deal with the formal aspects of writing did not abate the psychic energy which is art's well-spring. Rarely during my life in fact have I felt that psychic energy bubbling inside me as strongly as it did that winter. My solution to its containment was the artist's classic combination of drink and talk.

Dorothy's and my friendship with O'Hara and Kate being, at best, in limbo and, at worst, in ruins, we now found ourselves more or less isolated from any meaningful social contact. We had no real desire to be included in the social rituals of middle-class Wytheville and even if we had, the foolishness of my past behavior made the possibility of such inclusion problematical. My very real fondness for Lawyer Bean per-

175

sisted—and from time to time we would be invited to gatherings given by him and his wife but that was about the end of it. For the rest, we were left to subsist upon our own resources.

In Dorothy's case, being the mother of a newborn child, these resources were considerably more operative than my own. Certainly the demands and rewards of rearing children are not sufficient to occupy a woman's whole being throughout her life. But equally certain is the fact that a healthy woman's preoccupation with the spiritual and sensual communion which exists between her and her newborn child is total and categoric. In a nutshell, Dorothy's psychic energy was being happily and profitably employed during that winter of 1956–57, while mine was not. Such an imbalance is traditionally a time of danger.

Now, in that winter of inaction of 1956–57, the seeds of a relationship were planted which would lead me in time to such grotesque heights of self-deception that all previous efforts in that direction would come to seem like nursery school exercises.

My "pub," Lucifer Wrenchum's gas station, was the center from which I spun an incredible web. Earlier, I mentioned briefly but with portentuous intent, a young man whom I called Clyde. From the start, even when our acquaintanceship was limited to the exchange of casual waves as he passed in his jeep, he interested me because he appeared to be one of the loneliest human beings God has ever placed upon the earth. Lonely but not at all forlorn; he emanated such a pronounced quality of tenuously contained intellectual tension, in fact, that it managed to communicate itself even through the casual waves he threw me as he passed.

Clyde was then in his late twenties and lived with his parents in a lovely house about three miles from my farm. His father was a retired local businessman, unprepossessing in all ways. His mother was more memorable, a taciturn, rather handsome woman who usually dressed in men's clothes and spent most of her time painting in oils in her studio beside their house. I always had the feeling when talking with her that she was a person who felt she had been short-changed by life in all its essentials but bore no seething grudge about the

176

transaction. She was a withdrawn woman with a certain degree of distinction, and her son, Clyde, had inherited both these qualities. I do not know what the degree was of Clyde's parents' education; he, I know, had dropped out of one of the famous southern universities after two years. There was a pronounced degree of hopelessness in the relationship between the various members of Clyde's immediate family; it was as if they had tacitly admitted that there was no real reason or need for communication amongst themselves, and except for the barest administrative dialogues, they had given it up.

From the first, it was Clyde's seemingly total lack of all means of support which fascinated me. Although he was entirely presentable and by local middle-class standards, thoroughly eligible, I never saw him with a girl. The closest thing to a friendship he enjoyed was a relationship with my neighbor, Fred Cline and his wife. Clyde ate the vast majority of his meals at the Clines' house and the handsome, weather-beaten old hill woman seemed more of a mother to Clyde than his own. It was at the Clines' one day that I first made Clyde's formal acquaintance, having encountered him in the kitchen as Mrs. Cline fed him. He was mannerly, even courtly, but so reserved and watchful that I knew forging a closer acquaintanceship with him would be a difficult and drawn-out business. In certain essential ways, I have never known a man who reminded me more of an animal than Clyde; beneath his outward calm and attractive cropped-hair cleanliness, there was the pulsating fear of a beast who trusts no one.

Financially, he had no visible means of support. The natural tendency when one encounters a person in that position is to dismiss him as one of the world's incompetents. But in that direction, my inclinations are thoroughly unnatural. The basic battle in all spiritual survival as far as I am concerned is to beat the nine-to-five rap. Therefore, my immediate reaction when faced with a person who combines a seeming freedom from regimentation with a lack of self-justificatory harangues is one of excitement and curiosity rather than contempt and dismissal.

Clyde affected a hillbilly accent to which he was not legitimately entitled as a literate, moderately well-read man. He felt, I believe, that it was good protective coloration and in truth it suited him and was a working adjunct to his essentially secretive nature. And in certain aspects of his nature, he *was* a hillbilly; the shy, ingrown backwoods people were the only human beings with whom he felt even vaguely at home. There was also a quite discernible aura of violence which surrounded him; rarely did I encounter him when he did not have on or about his person a hand gun of some description. Readers of southern gothic literature will recognize Clyde immediately; he could have walked straight out of the pages of any William Faulkner story. And yet I must confess at the outset that in spite of the fact that I believe I am the only human being to whom Clyde ever gave his entire confidence, I cannot say with conviction that I know the truth about him even to this day. The following story is a case in point.

It was told to me by Fred Cline who was an imaginative man and not above invention when he wished to embroider a given person's legend. And Fred Cline found Clyde eminently legendworthy; it was the sense of violence within Clyde that Fred Cline found so fascinating. I cannot say with accuracy that I know this story to be true. But it checks out psychologically and I believe it.

According to Fred Cline, he accompanied Clyde one day on a trip to Roanoke on some mysterious errand. It was a summer day and they made the trip in Clyde's aging, topless Jeep. En route, they were passed by a carload of teenagers who were apparently mischief-prone and well tanked up on beer. The teenagers had evidently been picnicking and they had a basket containing a substantial amount of litter. As they passed Clyde's Jeep, one of them up-ended the basket of litter and dumped it over Clyde and Fred Cline. Without an instant's delay between concept and execution, Clyde calmly picked up a forty-five caliber automatic pistol which was, as always, within reach and fired the weapon through the engine of the teenagers' automobile. This story made my hair stand on end but it pleased Fred Cline no end. He would chortle with glee when he told it and say, "Mister Cherry, them boys' faces turned dead white and that ole engine jus' coughed and fell apart, you shoulda been theah". I thank providence that I was not. One thing is certain: if the story is true, there is somewhere in Virginia a group of ex-teenagers who presently counsel their children with inordinate firmness against acts of malicious mischief.

Take Outsider, outlaw, puritan, free-thinker and rigid ascetic who neither smoked nor drank and whose body contained not a single ounce of superfluous flesh and add to it a nature both secretive and devious, mix and stir with attitudes of total disdain for society and humanity, and fundamental contempt for nearly every human being he had encountered in his life, fold in a depth of animalistic fear to bind all the other ingredients together and serve topped with an intellect as hard as a chisel: you will have Clyde. Is it any wonder that it became almost habit with me to wonder about his whereabouts when I read in the newspaper of any successful bank robbery within a hundred miles. Yet these things and other knowledge of Clyde came slowly.

Like a timid animal, he made his first tenuous overtures to me that winter. His Jeep began to pass more frequently. The casual wave was replaced by a short chat between us as he sat in his Jeep with the engine running. Finally, he began to halt, dismount and chat a little longer. Clearly, he had me so much on his mind that he was nervous and, like a wild animal, perpetually poised for flight.

Urged on by unused energy, I went more and more frequently to Wrenchum's in the evenings to drink. The actor in me required some sort of stage and Wrenchum's was the nearest thing to one available. I was deep that winter in Schopenhauer and Nietzsche and the ideas of those two formidable maniacs tend to produce a dangerously euphoric glow. However, intellectual excitement engenders its own climate of receptivity and the gaunt, taciturn backwoodsmen who made up Wrenchum's clientele seemed to take pleasure in the spate of largely incomprehensible and poorly digested ideas which came pouring out of Farmer Sherry night after night. Wrenchum himself was in seventh heaven; being usually on the edge of a dangerous precipice of boredom, he was correspondingly ready to grapple with ideas and abstractions large and small. I could not help reflecting as I held forth in Wrenchum's gas station that the scene was uncomfortably

179

close to the sort of play written by the late Maxwell Anderson during the thirties. Or, for that matter by Inge, during the fifties.

Clyde soon realized that I could be found there most evenings and, more and more often, he began to turn up at Wrenchum's also. Within a very short time, it became apparent that he was as athirst for a certain kind of morally serious idea-prone intercourse, as I. In those early days, as we worked our way slowly towards friendship, getting Clyde to open up was a job for a truly expert psychological safecracker. Never have I encountered a more closed human being. Only the fact that we shared certain basic similarities of outlook made the growth of our association possible. Like me, he had a deep and abiding distrust of society and the causes associated with society. Unlike me, this had led him to a belief that life was a battlefield on which one was primarily concerned with doing in the other fellow. He had no generic interest in people and he found my hopelessly hooked position in this respect almost impossible to understand. We shared a passionate interest in money but Clyde's interest was limited to the techniques of its amassment rather than its possible meaning or use. The only genuine interest I ever saw him display in actual individual human beings, living or dead, during the early days of our friendship, was in men who had displayed extraordinary acumen and vigor in putting together great fortunes. He was extremely well-versed in the minutiae of the lives of men like Morgan, Frick et al. Whenever, he spoke of these gentlemen and their various coups and setbacks, he came alive as at no other time. Several times, I jokingly suggested that he had the makings of a tycoon but at each mention of this he would change the subject. With my fundamental premise of those years—namely, that the world was an eternal hodge-podge—he was in total agreement. My corollary conviction of the possibility of growth with the individual minds and spirits of the race, he found totally strange at first but he was curiously, almost hungrily receptive to it. I knew nothing then of the actual facts of his life and protest again that I know very little more in terms of actual truth now. But I was aware as I talked with Clyde that winter that I had encountered a genuinely strange man who, in some way, was ready to face the fact that the loneliness and secrecy of his life was leading him up a dead-end street.

In those early days, he seldom visited our house. Thus Dorothy had far less direct exposure to him than I. Nevertheless, her few brief conversations with Clyde and my reports to her of our discussions together brought her interest in him to the same pitch as mine. His attitude towards Dorothy was advertently simple but psychologically complex. It was an attitude I have frequently encountered in fundamentally crippled men. He simply did not consider any woman as a fellow human being and, instead, accorded her a recognition based solely upon her associations. Thus, as my wife, Dorothy was treated with unfailing courtesy and respect but, as an individual human being, she had little if no existence whatsoever in Clyde's cosmos. Later on, this changed as he became a familiar of the house and I think he gave Dorothy a considerable amount of thought; but only as an adjunct to me. That I must be in some measure as much an adjunct to her as she was to me was a concept beyond his reach. He was not misogynistic; in fact, at bottom, I believe he longed for some kind of relationship with a woman. But in the light of all the things which happened later on between us and the loneliness of his essential nature, I am inclined to believe his mistrust of other human beings has been compounded so as to preclude such an event.

In a materialistic sense, Clyde had fewer needs than anyone I have ever encountered. Food, drink, trappings of style and all the other things with which most of us preoccupy ourselves were supremely unimportant to him. His abiding need for proximity to firearms was clearly an obvious commentary upon the duality of fear and hunger for power which ruled his being. He had also one other curious passion: fire engines. Initially, this struck me as being comically jejune; later on, it would become a prime factor in our relationship. But early on it seemed to have no more importance than any other Tom Swift-type hi-jinks. The depth of his feeling for fire engines, however, could be measured by the fact that he, who had nothing but disdain for all social organizations, was a proud and dedicated member of the local volunteer fire-fighting unit.

In the beginnings of our friendship and for a year after its fruition, my attitudes towards him and my motives regarding him were totally without tinge of any self interest beyond the normal sense of gratification involved in the relationship of teacher to pupil. There is no question in my mind that a near-mortal hunger for intellectual companionship was assuaged for him by our concourse. When a book would come up as, for example, "Thus Spake Zarathustra Tharathustra," I would invariably find that he would seek the book out and read it. Continuing to use that work as an example, this is not such an easy thing to do. There is truth in Nietzsche's warning that the book had been written in blood and must be read in blood; to my mind, there is no more dangerous mixture of lifegiving wheat and poisonous chaff between covers and only a hard, morally serious, self-conscious mind can extract the sustenance by distinguishing between the two. Many times, I watched Clyde perform this feat and it never failed to impress me; his mind was wholly unburdened by the flab of utopian preoccupation. He was not fooled by the shibboleths of the age; he understood and did not depart from the stern standard implicit in the dictum: "Man is the measure of all things". Long before I encountered Clyde, he had smelt the possibilities of synthesis between consciousness and experience. And he had formulated an ingrained need to judge himself and his actions according to his performance in regard to those possibilities.

And now, I shall leave him for a time and at the same time ask, if I may, that the reader consider him as someone who had become part of the fabric of our lives. So that, as I speak of other matters, he may perhaps be imagined as present in the day to day conduct of our lives, speaking to me of my affairs and, more frequently as time goes by, of his. And tending more and more to use the pronoun, we in reference to both.

As winter wore on into the spring that year, the date of my lawsuit against the timber cutter and sawmill man crept up. A preliminary hearing was held in the chambers of a Judge in an attempt on the part of the defendant to prove that my suit was not justified. I confess I found the entire business highly enjoyable. I was accompanied by Lawyer Bean as my attorney while the defendant was represented by one of those legal figures of fun so beloved in rural southern districts complete with long locks, florid speech and an IQ of about 10. This monstrous advocate placed me on the stand in an attempt to discredit my accusations by using the basic technique of showing me as a foreigner and non-hillbilly suspect in all my contentions because I did not really understand the mores of the locality. The lawyer was barely literate and given to the embellishment of his questions with complicated Biblical allusions of whose meaning he had an infirm mastery. I had about as much trouble with him as Goose Tatum would with a member of the Junior Varsity and both Lawyer Bean and I had a fine time. The Judge gave the opposition short shrift and the case was scheduled to come to trial about a month later.

The few times I had encountered O'Hara during the winter had proven that his decision to sever our friendship had been firmly and consciously taken. Even in a town as small as Wytheville paths need not cross except through coincidence. O'Hara and I passed each other occasionally but always on opposite sides of the street. The single occasion on which we did come face to face, we went no further than a momentary exchange of small talk. It was as if we each tacitly acknowledged the end of our friendship but at the same time awaited the proper moment for some ritual celebration of its passing.

Therefore, I was not terribly surprised to find O'Hara seated in the forefront of the courtroom spectators on the day my lawsuit came to trial. In no sense could my lawsuit be described as anything other than piddling; this in itself convinced me that O'Hara's presence there that day indicated that his depth of preoccupation with our breach was at least as grave as my own.

In the finest tradition of anti-climax, the case failed to come to trial. At the last possible moment, the defendant offered settlement in an amount which struck a nice balance in satisfying both honor and purse, and I accepted. The Judge ordered a recess before proceeding with the next case on the docket and the spectators filed out of the courtroom. O'Hara, however, hung back, waiting to speak to me; whether out of curiosity as to the reasons for the lawsuit's disposal or more complex motives I could not tell. We chatted for a few minutes in friendly enough fashion while I

183

explained that I had, in effect, won the legal proceedings. When O'Hara suggested that we buy a bottle of Sherry and share it in his office, it never occurred to me to refuse. He was afoot so we climbed into my car, drove to the liquor store and thence to the room he used for writing located up over a store on the main street of the town. It was then midafternoon, about half-past two.

Strangely enough, there was not an instant's edginess between us that afternoon. Nothing, after all, could mitigate the fundament of our common experience and we shared much laughter that day in remembrance of it. The first note of strangeness came as I looked at my watch and found that it was half-past four, the hour when I had to leave to get back to the farm for the evening milking. We had reached the end of the bottle of sherry by then and I rose to announce that I must leave. O'Hara scoffed at this and suggested that I forget my cows for once. I replied to the effect that those cows were the bread and butter for my family and must be dealt with according to schedule. I then suggested that he was perfectly welcome to come to the farm and that we could pick up another bottle of Sherry, drive to the farm and resume our drinking after I had finished taking care of my cows. He pretended to find this plan inconceivable and said with a disparaging smile, "What makes you think I'd go out to that Goddamned farm?" Underneath his disparagement, he so clearly wanted to accompany me to the farm that I made no reply but simply continued putting on my coat in preparation for leaving. He reached for his coat also and when I left he left with me.

We stopped at the liquor store again and bought another bottle of Sherry. At that point, there was not the slightest vestige of drunkenness in O'Hara's behavior. However, he opened the second bottle of wine as soon as we got back in the car and began to drink from it as we drove to the farm. He was clearly under a tremendous amount of strain because by the time we had completed three-quarters of the twenty-minute trip, he had managed to get outside fully half of the bottle. As we reached the farm, he was showing definite effects of drink but he was still far from advertent drunkenness.

O'Hara and I entered our house by the back door which led into the kitchen where Dorothy was preparing dinner.

Dorothy's eyes widened as she caught sight of him but the greeting they exchanged showed no particular strain on either hand. I took O'Hara into the living room where Linda was playing with the baby and settled him down with a glass for his sherry before changing into my rubber boots and setting out for the dairy barn. Later on, Dorothy told me that there was nothing overtly dramatic in his behavior after I left for the barn. She went in and joined him in a drink for a while and then returned to her tasks in the kitchen, leaving O'Hara playing with the children. She also told me that he was working very hard on the remains of the bottle of wine but that he showed no pronounced ill effects at the time she returned to the kitchen.

I was about half way through with the milking when O'Hara appeared at the dairy barn. It took only one glance to see that he was drunk and dangerous. The scene which followed was as eerie a performance as I have ever witnessed.

All three of the dairy barn stalls were occupied as O'Hara entered; one by a bad acting cow on whom I had to employ an anti-kicking device, a contraption which fitted over the cows back and clamped to the cow's hip muscles, constricting her so as to make her stand quietly. Before I could stop him, O'Hara opened the gates of two of the stalls, allowing the cows within them to tear loose from the milkers and make good their escape through the open exit door of the barn. One of them was, of course, the cow wearing the anti-kicking device. Cows are creatures with an ingrained fealty to habit; anything unusual excites them. An ordinary visitor to the barn during milking will make them nervous but the presence of this drunken madman drove them absolutely berserk. O'Hara's actions following the release of the cows were the most peculiar of all. He reached up and got both hands around the glass milk pipeline in the manner of a man about to chin himself. This was an essential and expensive component of the barn which was terribly fragile and difficult to replace at short notice. My first thought was to knock him out so that he could do no real damage. For until that point he had caused pandemonium but no actual breakage. Then, as I started for O'Hara, another force within me took control: curiosity. O'Hara's interior wires had clearly crossed, shorted and blown some sort of fuse but what was really at the bottom of it? I stopped in my tracks to watch; what followed was genuinely spooky. As I mentioned the glass pipeline was exceedingly fragile; so fragile in fact, that a small child could have broken it with one pull. Now, as O'Hara pulled on the pipeline seemingly with all his might, precisely nothing happened. The tendons in his neck and the veins in his forehead stood out with the force of his effort to break the pipe but he was unable to effect its breakage. Quite obviously, a terrible war was going on within his mind: a deep, raging desire to destroy was being balanced in some way by a desperate desire to hold that desire for destruction in check. Looking back, I don't believe it would be possible for anyone to sustain such an intensity of emotional crisis for any length of time. And, in truth, I do not believe O'Hara's attempt (or non-attempt) to break the pipe could have lasted more than thirty or forty seconds. When the crisis passed, his collapse was sudden and complete. He relinquished his grip on the glass pipeline and sank to the floor like a poleaxed steer. He was out absolutely cold. I stood staring down at him for a long moment experiencing one of the most complicated mixtures of emotions it is possible to describe: naked fear, anger, revulsion, pity and love were all boiling around in my mind together. I could not bear to touch him immediately so I went out and re-captured the two cows he had allowed to escape and put them back in the holding pen. By then, I had calmed down somewhat and I was no longer frightened of O'Hara. It seemed clear that his capacity for mischief had been totally spent. I picked him up and staggered up the road to my car where I spread him out in the back seat. The depth of his sleep was a mixture of drunkenness and the aftermath of a concentrated expenditure of psychic energy the like of which I have not encountered before or since.

After finishing my chores at the barn, I walked back to the house and told Dorothy what had taken place. She listened in disbelief but had little real comment to offer. Nor, in truth, do I now. Perhaps O'Hara's father had the right of it years ago when we were boys and he visited my father to enlist his cooperation in keeping the two of us apart. Unfortunately, I don't believe it for a minute. That O'Hara wanted to destroy my farm seems clear; that, in like measure, he wanted to avert that destruction seems equally clear. As the Sailor said long ago in Spain, I can't ride and I can't drive.

I drove O'Hara back to his house in Wytheville. When we arrived, he was still out cold. The front door was unlocked and I carried him into the drawing room. Kate was seated there, her eyes like obsidian as her knitting needles clicked away in undeviating rhythm. As I unloaded O'Hara into a chair, I said, "Well, here's your home-loving man." This perhaps unseemly jocularity failed to elicit either gleam of amusement or recognition.

The O'Hara's remained in Wytheville for perhaps another year. During that year, they engendered one or two ploys with a distinct ring of insanity which served to rigidify the breach. One, which mystifies me to this day, had to do with the money I had borrowed from Roger. I received in due course a post card from O'Hara saying that he had decided to assume my debt. This was followed by a peculiar legal document signed by O'Hara and Kate in which they formally indicated that they had paid my debt to Roger and that I now owed the same amount to them. With the grandiosity of true disconnection, O'Hara's card informed that no coercion would be brought to make me pay but that, if and when I wished to pay, I could hand over the money to Lawyer Bean. I ignored this and eventually—and I must admit, after a dereliction of many years—paid off my debt to Roger.

Also during that year, the O'Haras accomplished a much more peculiar, perhaps even tragic transaction which had nothing to do with us: the effective severance of Jane, Darroch's child by Kate, from their immediate family. She was sent on a visit to Darroch's mother, chose not to return and was eventually raised and educated by Kate's own mother and her second husband from whom O'Hara and Kate remained rigidly and bitterly estranged.

187

CHAPTER XII

With the advent of spring that year, the tempo of farming activity naturally quickened. As the pastures were well out and the need to buy winter feed now hopefully behind us forever, the time had come to augment the herd. Buying a cow here and one there, we increased the herd to about twenty-one cattle. Of course we would not actually have that many on the milking line throughout the summer since most of our original eleven cows would have to be turned dry during late summer and early autumn for the two months preparatory to their having their next calves.

In theory, a good dairy farmer aims to have as many of his cattle as possible producing during autumn and winter because it is during that period that his "base" is established. The larger the base, the larger the income, since milk produced up to the limits of the base brings a significant amount more than milk produced in excess of the base. There will always be excess during spring and early fall because the cows become more productive during those periods of maximum pasture growth. The ideal situation, for example, would be one in which a dairy farmer could breed all his cows during October or November so that they would be in full production throughout the "base building" months, and dry during July, August or early September preparatory to calving again in the fall and returning to full production for the next "base building" period. It goes without saying, however, that the ideal is extremely difficult to arrange. And the difficulty is greatly compounded if, as in our case, one is following a policy of doing all of one's breeding by artificial insemination to the end of bettering the herd.

The benefits of artificial insemination are as unquestionable

189

as its difficulties are numerous. Understandably, nature prefers her own methods of procedure and a cow in heat turned in with a bull has an immeasurably better chance of conceiving than a cow bred artificially. I rather imagine that in the days since I was a farmer the artificial breeding techniques have improved somewhat, but at that time the difficulties were tacitly acknowledged by the fact that the price of breeding a cow artificially included three attempts. If, for example, as happened to me many times, the process does not succeed until the third attempt, it means that the cow is three months behind the desired schedule and will be wastefully standing dry during the "base building" months when one most needs her in production.

It can readily be seen that the beef cattle breeder has a far easier road to hoe in respect to breeding than has the dairy farmer. The beef breeder wants his crop of calves to arrive as the pastures come out in the spring. Therefore he simply turns the bull in with his herd nine months earlier and leaves him there for a couple of months and nature arranges the rest. But with dairy cattle, one has to first keep careful watch every day so as not to miss the telltale signs of a cow's being in estrus and, even then, face the fact that the chances are that the artificial insemination will not take on the first try. And there is always the heartbreaking possibility that a high-producing cow will turn out to be impossible to breed by any means and must eventually be sent to market as meat. I mention in passing that this happened to us with one of the most promising cows we owned. Eventually we got around to keeping a bull as a backstop to our artificial insemination program, but for the first two years we depended solely on the latter.

In terms of pure, brute labour, that summer of 1957 was a tough one. Because we could not afford to buy certain complicated and expensive pieces of machinery such as a hay baler and a silage chopper, I had to arrange to have this work done by neighbors who did own such machinery. I paid for this partly with money, partly with a percentage of the hay being made on my own land, and partly by trading my own labour in getting in the crops of the farmer who helped me with mine. Thus it was a rare day that summer that I was not busy with haymaking, whether my own or that of the neighbor. In addition, of course, the cows had to be milked twice daily.

I would be a terrible liar if I did not admit that certain seeds of discontent with my lot as a farmer were being sown. Unquestionably, there is dignity in manual labour but there is also drudgery and boredom. It was not long before any psychic rewards I may have enjoyed from heaving ninety-pound bales of hay onto a wagon for eight hours were outweighted by the resulting numb fatigue. The future seemed far from idyllic and I was already casting about in my mind for a way to expand the farm's operations and lessen my own thrall to it simultaneously. In Herbert, the farmer with whom I traded labour and crops in return for custom work, I thought I could discern the possibilities of an answer. Like my friend Clyde, Herbert was one of that small minority among the hill people who sensed the need for keeping abreast of the times. Unlike Tiptree, alas, he was an essentially prosaic individual whom it was far easier to respect than like. He possessed in abundance all the virtues which fail to fascinate me: he was both good husbandman and good husband, kindly father and indefatigable church goer who believed every word in the Old and New Testaments was the precise and literal truth. Needless to say, he found me about as familiar as someone from Mars. Still, we got along quite well basically and during the course of the summer it began to occur to me that his farming operation and mine might be susceptible to a form of amalgamation.

Although, he wanted desperately to install a Grade A dairy operation of his own, two things stood in the way of it: capital and land. What little capital he had was tied up in his machinery inventory which he paid for by doing custom work for other farmers. To augment the little land he owned himself, he sharecropped other men's land or in some cases rented it outright. The heart of his farming operation was raising and feeding hogs on the corn he grew upon his own and other's land. Generally speaking, he was quite adept at this, keeping a number of good Hampshire sows and a good boar so that the quality of pork he raised each year was high. However, unlike the price of Grade A milk, the price of pork is subject to fluctuation and there were many years when the profit he enjoyed did not really justify the labour.

191

The rough idea I began to toy with that summer was essentially very simple: that Herbert and I might become fifty-fifty partners in a farming operation in which he would be responsible for all the actual farming and I would be responsible for the care of the cattle. The more I thought of it the more feasible it seemed. If every acre of land I owned could be made available as improved pasture, my 165 acres could in time be made capable of supporting anywhere from seventy-five to a hundred milking cows. The feed for these cows could then be grown by Herbert on land owned, rented or share-cropped by him. And the young stock for replacement could be accommodated on pasture land owned by him—land basically unsuitable for cultivation because of rock outcroppings or excessive hilliness. Were we to enter in upon such an operation together, it did not seem too much to hope for that we could, in time, divide an annual income of anywhere from twenty-five to thirty-five thousand dollars and, even more we could, through artificial insemination, eventually breed our stock up to a genuinely superlative standard of production. In time, too, there would be the possibility of changing such an organization into a purebred operation whence additional income could be derived from the sale of high-quality dairy bloodstock. But though I stewed about these matters constantly, for the while I kept my own counsel; understandably, such a proposition would represent to Herbert an earth-shaking decision which would have to be subjected to his own and the Lord's most exhaustive scrutiny. But more and more, it occurred to me that Herbert would be a perfect partner in such a try; he was an essentially fine, honest and dependable man whose present position was narrowly circumscribed by lack of both money and imagination.

Thus, as my farm took hold and showed signs of succeeding, so did my disquiet grow. Was I, after all, going to get hooked on the horns of the traditional American dilemma: belief in big, hope for bigger—and the poignant, hopeless longing for biggest? Not if I could help it, I told myself. I needed a tangential idea but it was not forthcoming. By tangential idea I mean precisely the proverbial eating and simultaneous having of the cake, the desire for which, in spite of being prohibited by damned near all our song and story, is still the driving wheel of the evolutionary appetite.

In that realm of simultaneous cake consumption and possession, my young friend, Clyde made some disclosures to me that summer which provided room for some not entirely healthy thoughts. In attempting to live a life in which, no matter how ludicrous one's attempts may be at times, moral seriousness represents a paramount value, the great booby trap is of course, self-interest. Up to this point, my relationship with young Clyde had been entirely pure for the very simple reason that I had not been able to conceive of him as a possible factor in furthering my own ends. Because he was a strange, lonely, secretive man who struck a responsive chord with my perhaps excessive abhorrence for the prosaic, I made myself available to him in the sense that I imparted what little I knew or felt without reservation. In the course of that summer of 1957, he returned the favor. It was an odd story he told me. Whether or not it is true is less important than the fact that I believed it. Like Pilate, my attitude towards truth is fundamentally quizzical. I tend to believe in a man's statements more because of their poetical and psychological coherence than through fealty to blind, measurable fact. Even though I wonder now as I begin to tell it, Clyde's story made sense to me then and it makes sense to me now. But, as I listened and believed, the subtle serpent of "where's mine?" began to stir.

While very young, Clyde had taken his first few faltering steps towards achieving a form of synthesis between his passion for fire engines and his abiding interest in money. His approach was simple: he simply saved his pennies until they turned into dollars and his dollars until they had multiplied to a point where he was able to seek out a stockbroker and purchase a tiny number of shares of common stock. The company whose stock he chose to buy was, of course, one engaged in the manufacture of fire engines. It also proved to be an old, conservative and extremely solvent firm whose market had been steady and dependable and whose total number of outstanding shares of common stock was not, by contemporary standards, vast. Clyde had, since boyhood, continued to buy the stock, using the traditional technique of putting each new bit he acquired into hock in order to acquire more. This painfully slow process had, he informed me during that summer of 1957, resulted in his titular ownership of

193

an amount of stock in the company with a then current market value of approximately $120,000.00. He made no bones about the fact that the structure he had created was a complete house of cards. Whatever the margin requirements were at a given moment, he employed them to the maximum extent commensurate with the minimum standard of safety. He would occasionally suffer a setback and be forced to sell off some of his stock to meet a rise in the margin requirements, but his overall progress had followed a rising curve. The company involved was sound and the market value of the stock continued to enjoy a steady, if unspectacular, rise.

As one who, rightly or wrongly, has always had a strong desire for life to be more interesting and surprising than it tends to be in actuality, I could not have found Clyde's description of his life as a junior tycoon more pleasing. That a wiry T-shirt-clad youth who spent the days riding the backwoods roads in a battered jeep could begin buying stock in a fire engine manufacturer simply because he liked fire engines, and eventually reach the point where he entertained serious hopes for someday assuming control of the entire company, struck me as having so much poetical pizzazz that it never occurred seriously to me to disbelieve Clyde's tale. The techniques he was employing were, after all, the same old ones with which that particular game is played. In my mind, I could see no reason to assume that Clyde was any less intelligent or single-minded than, say, Louis Wolfson. In fact, for the so-called "stock raiders" such as Wolfson, Clyde had the bitterest of hate, contempt and fear. By the time our friendship began, Clyde was understandably, expertly-versed in the workings of what he had thought of for many years as "his" fire engine company. And his fear of so-called stock raiders was perfectly legitimate. The company was both solvent and sound: a combination which makes those financial predators wheel and circle for the kill. Clyde's greatest worry was that some such gentleman or group would smell blood, institute a proxy fight, take control and milk the corporate edifice dry as is so often done. Clyde's intentions or dream or whatever you want to call it was the precise opposite. Could he, in time, accomplish his design, his intention was to make the company thrive more abundantly rather than to reduce it to a

194

hollow shell. His aspirations seemed to me to be on the side of the angels.

Dorothy also was temperamentally disposed towards believing completely in Clyde's bizarre disclosures. Perhaps this stemmed in both our cases from an undue dollop of romanticism in our natures, but no matter. Certainly an insistence upon prosaic circumstances can reduce life to a prosaic level, and not the least factor in the enduring quality of our marriage has been a commonly-held, fervent belief that such a fate is worse than death.

Equally certain was the fact that Clyde's disclosure of his cards had no immediate, dramatic effect upon our lives. It simply inculcated a stronger sense of mutality. As the summer drew to a close, Clyde interested himself more and more in the workings of the farm and, more and more, he and I tended to use the word "we." "We ought to get a new tractor," he would say, or "we still need a few more cows."

We did indeed need more cows and, equally important, the feed situation was now such that we could handle them. We ended the summer with our large hay-feeding barn comfortably full of high-quality alfalfa hay. In addition, we had a trench silo dug, and filled it with fifty or sixty tons of chopped corn silage. For those completely unversed in farming lore, I suppose I should explain that a trench silo is nothing more than a giant trench scooped out of a gentle hillside by bulldozer. Ours was perhaps 20 feet wide, 100 feet long, and at its deepest point, about 15 feet deep. Into this trench load after load of freshly chopped corn stalks and ears is placed layer by layer while one tractor is driven back and forth along the top to compress the silage tightly enough so that the optimum conditions exist for healthy fermentation. When the trench is completely filled and packed, sheets of Polyethylene are placed over the top; these in turn are sealed by a heavy layer of straw. A fence is then placed around the trench to keep the cattle out. The silage within preserves itself through a process of fermentation until it is needed for feed later on in the fall. At that point, it is opened and the cows are allowed to eat their way into the trench for a certain period of time each day.

With our barn full of hay and our trench silo filled, we had

195

enough feed to increase the herd to our planned thirty cows. Unfortunately, we did not have the money to buy the eight or nine first-rate cows we needed, but I had been toying around in the back of my mind with a rather odd scheme through which I suspected that I had a fair chance of getting hold of the money.

During the course of the summer, whenever I came into the house for lunch, I found my eldest daughter watching a certain daytime quiz program on TV. Since she was just four at the time, I had no idea why this program fascinated her so much, and I would frequently watch with her for a few minutes, as much interested in her reactions as I was in what was happening on the screen. However, two things occurred to me as I watched the program: the first was simply that successful contestants on the program were walking away with anywhere from one to ten thousand dollars. The other thing that intrigued me had to do with a growing suspicion that I could take the program. It was a simple enough game in which one played against an opponent whose mistakes were equally as valuable as one's own successes. About all that was required to win, it seemed to me, was the requisite gall to get up there in the first place, a reasonably cool head, and precisely the sort of useless load of extraneous information with which I am burdened.

I mentioned idly to Dorothy that I felt I might possibly be able to tap the program. She agreed but we talked about it very little more because the difficulties in such a project were clearly insuperable at the time. It would require a trip of a week or two to New York which would mean that I would have to get someone to take care of the cows for that period. Such a jaunt would also entail expenses, and there being no guarantee of success, it would very probably turn out to be money down the drain. Finally, it was wholly out of the question in any case until the crops were in in the fall. So I put the scheme away but I did not entirely forget it. Whenever I stopped again to look at the program for a moment, the suspicion struck me with growing strength that this just might be my pigeon. It goes without saying that, in 1957, the quiz programs were unsullied by the breath of scandal; the breathtakingly cynical crookery would not come to light for a year or so more.

196

In time, of course, it had long been my intention to hire some kind of hand for the farm. Although not a pressing problem immediately, it would be an absolute necessity I knew, within the year. I had instituted no active search for such a fellow however. And so when Luther the livestock dealer informed me that fall that a feasible-seeming man had applied to him for employment, I was not at first too receptive to the idea. Luther had no job to offer the man nor did he have a house available for him to live in, a matter of crucial importance since the man had a fairly large family for whom housing was as important as employment. Our first farmhouse on the Kegley side of the farm was standing empty. Luther told me he had given this man my address and that he probably would be around to see me within a day or so.

In due course he turned up. Ned, as I shall call him, was of a distinctly unprepossessing appearance but there was a quality of gentleness about him which was appealing. He was from over the border in West Virginia and most of his life had been spent as a coal miner. He made no bones about the fact that he had hated and feared the life as a miner. He was, in fact, in some measure grateful to the economic conditions which had thrown him and many others permanently out of work. During one period of his life he had worked as a herdsman on a dairy farm so he was not without experience in handling milk cattle. As a worker his potentialities were distinctly limited. I understood him immediately in that he had accepted his lot in life and was without resentment towards it or desire to kick against the pricks. He was somewhere between forty and forty-five, unskilled, unlettered, and by virtue of such deprivations, sentenced immutably to a life of laboring for other men. I could see immediately and did not mind one bit that his basic defense against this intolerable situation was to gear down the pace of any task he undertook to the barest tolerable momentum. Having no inherent belief myself in the virtues of hard work for hard work's sake, his psychological position struck me as being the only operative one available to him. I sensed also that he liked cows and would be good at dealing with them. Knowing my hillbillies very well by then, I quizzed him at length about his personal habits; the last thing in the world I wanted about the place was someone who would take five drinks of white whiskey and turn into a tear-ass monster. He assured me that he was not subject to temptations of the flesh and this turned out to be absolutely true. His sin was sloth and, as he was clearly not responsible for it, I accepted and forgave him his sloth from the beginning. He was, in a nutshell, a man totally and definitively broken on the wheel of life; he wanted nothing more than work he did not actively fear or hate and a dwelling for his family. Those shamefully minimal gifts were within my power to bestow and we struck a bargain. It was one which I never regretted; he was, throughout the time he worked for me, loyal, dependable and slow, which was more than anyone had the right to expect paying the prevailing wages of the time and the region.

Within a week, Ned and his family were installed in the Kegley house. It bothered me somewhat that their tenancy there would almost certainly return the house in time to its former hillbilly drear. But houses are better lived in badly than not at all. Within a short time, Ned's two sons had found employment in the region and with their combined wages and the produce of the farm, they seemed happily solvent.

With Ned installed on the job and proving both dependable and responsible in dealing with the milking herd, my mind began to tinker more actively with the possibility of pulling off a successful raid on the TV quiz program. Strangely enough, what finally decided me to take the plunge was a suit of clothes.

One day that fall, I drove with my young friend, Clyde, to Roanoke on some errand or another. While walking through the business district of Roanoke, I chanced upon a tailoring shop which had the unmistakeable aura of quality and craftsmanship. As I stood looking in the window of this establishment, some long-denied aspect of dandyism gave birth to an immediate and irresistible longing for a suit. Years before, when Dorothy and I had embarked for Europe, I had been sartorially well-equipped. Time and attrition had reduced me to a sartorial nadir; a battered tweed jacket and aging grey flannel trousers were the best I could muster for festive occasions. For the rest, my habitual garments were the blue denim jacket and jeans then favored by Mr. H. Rap Brown.

Now, thus clad and unshaven, Clyde and I entered the tailor shop where we were regarded with suspicion by an aging Jewish tailor with a thick German accent. Upon being asked to show us samples of his work, he complied rather nervously. My nose had not misinformed me; he was indeed a craftsman. Without further ado, I ordered him to set to work upon a double-breasted suit of fine grey banker's flannel shaped and cut in such a way and with certain modifications which would raise it from the level of the mundane. The cost of this magnificent garment was to be one hundred and fifty dollars. Even as I ordered the damned thing, I was aware and guilty of the fact that it was an entirely unjustified and whimsical purchase. Clyde was highly amused at the entire business and listened in with great enjoyment as I gave the tailor his instructions. Leaving a deposit, we quit the shop and Clyde immediately said, "John, what in the name of heaven, you gonna do with a hundred and fifty dollar suit?" On the dubious basis that the unjustifiable must be justified, I replied that I was going to wear it up to New York to win some money on a television quiz program. Clyde received this news with a gentlemanly reticence in regard to judgment and demanded when I would be going. I replied that I would be off as soon as I had my suit.

Due to certain difficulties with the tailor, this did not occur as I wished. Magnificent craftsman though he was, he was used to catering to the taste of Roanoke businessmen. The effect I was desirous of achieving was roughly that of an Englishman in the Tattersalls enclosure at Ascot on the day of an unimportant race meeting. The tailor, however, seemed to want me to be turned out in the style of the late Sewell Avery. After a month of wrangling, some sort of compromise was reached, the effect of which was not bad at all. In possession of my suit and with all bridges behind me, I prepared to leave for New York. Both Dorothy and Clyde saw me off with the worried looks of those watching a loved one bite off more than he can chew. I myself was extremely dubious about the entire venture. However, I assumed a look of confidence as I boarded the Greyhound bus, that mode of travel having been chosen to assuage my conscience in regard to unjustified sartorial expenditure. With true Celtic schizophrenia, I was prepared to take it out of my hide in order to put it on my back.

Twelve bone-shaking hours later, I arrived in New York where I sought out one of those dingy hostelries in the West Forties in which the very air in the lobby smelled nefarious. In the safety of my six-dollar-a-day room, I hung my suit up carefully and gave thought to my plan of campaign. Now that I was here, just how the hell was I going to go about getting on the quiz program? Abandoning as too simple the obvious approach of going directly to the proprietors of the program to seek status as a contestant, I spent the day fruitlessly trying to enlist aid in my quest by calling my literary agent and various old friends and acquaintances in the advertising business. Such aid was not forthcoming and after an evening spent crawling the Third Avenue pubs, I awoke knowing that I would have to take the bull by the horns.

It turned out to be surprisingly easy. I presented myself at the office of the show's owners and producers where a full waiting room made it plain that many others were seeking the same bonanza as I. A bored receptionist gave me a form to fill out and a short, multiple-choice quiz to fill in. I did these tasks rapidly and returned the papers to the receptionist. Seemingly, the information garnered from this form and test provided clear clues as to the desirability of a given candidate because within an astonishingly short time I was shown into a palatial office and there scrutinzed by a young man with exceedingly larcenous eyes. We chatted for half an hour or so about this and that, after which he laconically informed me that I was to hold myself in readiness for a call summoning me to the wars. This, he said, would take place anywhere from four days to a week depending upon the rate of attrition among the contestants presently before the camera.

It was, in fact, actually a bit less than a week before the call came instructing me to present myself the following morning at the studio, a former theater in the Times Square area. I was there on the dot of ten clad in my suit which, by now, I had imbued with the full supernatural powers of a talisman. At the studio, I was briefed by the same young man who had interviewed me previously. He could not have been more friendly but his eyes were no less larcenous than before. After warning me that I would probably not get to do my turn that day, he spoke to me very seriously about a point which he stressed as having the utmost importance. Should one be fortunate enough to remain at bat for several days, at the close of each day's show, one would of course reply when the M.C., a great flatulent mass of glossy hair and shining teeth, demanded if it were one's intention to proceed. What the producer (which was the young man's role) now stressed with Biblical sincerity was that I must inform him of my intention to proceed or not to proceed *before* each day's show, and that my answer to the MC would be a meaningless charade. I agreed but with certain private reservations; how would such a thing, after all, benefit me? All powdered and painted like a whore, I passed two rather strained hours that morning in a waiting room off stage with two other aspirants to easy money; all three of us were nervous to a point of hysteria. But I did not get on that day. I had warned Dorothy that I probably would be on that day and, when released after the show, I telephoned her to tell her what she already knew: that I had not been on the show. There was more than a touch of hysteria on her end of the line: "Where were you?" she demanded in a voice a full octave higher than usual. "Tomorrow," I replied tersely, "I'll be on tomorrow and I'll call you after the show." She rang off, clearly under considerable strain.

I made my debut the next day about halfway through the show. Repainted and powdered, I made my entrance into the area which was white hot with lights. I had one small task to perform which I could not put off because I did not know whether I would be up there five minutes or five days. I was determined to honor my promise of a wink made to Fred Cline a couple of years earlier and the first thing I did was locate the camera with the red light lit and wink at it as hard as I could. The monstrous MC raised an eyebrow at this but went on with his mawkish introduction of me as I stood there with an idiotic grin on my face, muttering silent prayers to my suit. After that we had a brief and horrid moment of show biz hi-jinks during which I had to play straight man to the MC while he made a terrible joke upon which I had been briefed earlier. Then the game began. I shot down the defending champ and one other postulant and quit the day six hundred bucks richer. Greed now running rampant in my soul, I replied with an enthusiastic affirmative when the M.C. demanded if I would return on the morrow.

However, the truly interesting thing happened after the show. The young producer approached, his usual bland, laconic air replaced by something like genuine excitement. By a strange alchemy, and measured by a peculiar standard that I did not understand, it appeared that I had been some sort of success. Some odd note of approval which the producer watched for carefully had been granted me by the audience. He asked me to lunch and I accepted, saying that I had to call my wife first. Dorothy was very nearly incoherent with nervousness; she told me that she and Clyde and the children had watched together, interrupted by many querulous cries of "What's Daddy doing on the TV?" from Linda. With the nonchalance suitable to a new TV personality, I assured her that all would be well.

I rang off and went to lunch with the producer. To this day, I wonder how I would have reacted if I had known at what an extreme point of moral danger I stood. A year later, it would come out that this very show and its more flamboyant evening prime time big brother were the original source and worst offenders in the TV Quiz Program scandal. And I am equally certain that, from the day of that luncheon with the producer, I was being evaluated as a potential player of a rigged hand on the big time evening show owned by his firm. Nothing was ever said to me but I also never saw that producer have more than two words with another contestant, let alone take one to lunch. Then, too, his attitude underwent a subtle change; he showed me that same peculiar deference employed by a pederast out to corrupt a boy. Whether I have my suit (now, alas a victim of moths) to thank or what, I believe to this day that it was a miracle that I did not get involved in some very murky waters. And I am not all that sure of my character to say with exactitude that I would not have taken the plunge if invited. I kept my purity through chance; not the slightest odor of hanky-panky made itself felt to me until the entire sordid mess came out a year or so later.

As I recall, my tenure upon the program from start to finish lasted about a week. And I am not entirely sure that the questions were not being rigged a bit in my favor. I have no doubt whatsoever from the way I was treated that the management wanted me to keep on winning. I made some horrendous errors. One that still rankles involved the demand for

the female star of "Born Yesterday." With aplomb and without hesitation, I replied, Billie Holiday. Another infirm area
of mine was American history and I very nearly came unstuck
playing eeny meeny miney moe with a question the answer to
which was either Jackson or Johnson. But on the whole I
remained alive and prospered mightily. Each day after the
show, I spoke with Dorothy on the telephone. Both she and
Clyde, she reported, were in an advanced state of nervous
collapse and everybody along our road was staying home
from work to watch the show. The deep dichotomy she entertained towards the whole project was perfectly posed during one day's telephone call when she said, "You're doing fine
but you make so many mistakes."

All told, I was on the program about five days. At the close
of the fourth day, I was roughly $2,800.00 to the good. The
amount I needed for the purchase of new cattle was three
thousand dollars, give or take a hundred. Now the hand of
fate prepared to deal me one of those buffets that, in the end,
turn out to be a kiss. That year was one in which the nation
and New York in particular underwent a dreadful epidemic
or something called Asiatic Flu. As I awoke that morning of
my fifth day as a contestant, I knew immediately that I was a
very ill fellow indeed. I had the works: chills, burning fever,
and a general overall feeling of not caring whether school kept
or not. Nevertheless, greed is a strong goad and I arose,
stumbled into my suit and took a taxi to the studio. The
preceptors of this charade with which I had involved myself
took one look at the reeling apparition I represented and
shipped me over to the infirmary of the network presenting
the show. There, my temperature was taken and found to be
103. I was crammed full of drugs which made me even grog-
gier, and transported back to the studio where I sat in a
dream-like haze as my cosmetics were applied. The hour's
wait until the show went on the air at noon was sheer torture.
Yet oddly enough, once on stage, I came to life like the
proverbial fire horse. According to the producer's instructions, I had informed him before the show that it was my
intention to remain on the show. In fact it had not seriously
occurred to me to quit until I was shot down. About halfway
through the program that day, however, I began to ask myself what real point there was in remaining on the show

203

longer? If I triumphed on that program, I could quit about thirty-five hundred dollars to the good, which meant that I had enough money to buy my cattle and that I had had a damned good time and made my expenses to boot. If, on the other hand, I remained, I could theoretically in one losing game both be eliminated and lose a portion of my winnings. And even though I kept on winning that day, I could not kid myself that I was at my sharpest; a temperature of 103 is not exactly the happiest of circumstances in the situation I was in. So, as the last game of the show began, I decided that, win, lose or draw, I was going to resign. At the end of each show, there was a painful little ritual designed to inculcate an air of spurious excitement. As one won the game, the organist would play a few euphoric trills and the MC would flash his giant, white teeth at the audience and shout, "The winner and still champion is our farmer-novelist from Virginia, Mr. John Sherry." Then, pausing to milk the maximum effect from the moment, he would give me the full benefit of his charms and say, "And now let's find out if our winner and champion elects to stay and risk his championship tomorrow." Then, another pause and the question to which he already knew the answer: "Tell us, Mr. Sherry, do you stay and play or take your winnings of thirty-six hundred dollars and go?" Falling for some unknown reason into a British idiom, I replied, "I'll have the money." (What I was saying, of course, was that very American thing: I'll take the money and run.) The combination of the unfamiliar idiom and having received an answer contrary to his expectancy, threw the M.C. into momentary confusion and he stuttered out an affronted, "W . . . what?" Correcting my speech, I said, "I'll take the money and go, please." The M.C.'s professional aplomb reasserted itself immediately and after a brief, dagger-like glance (he was one of the show's owners), he bared the ivories at the audience again and said, "There you have it, ladies and gentlemen, our champion elects to retire undefeated like a true wise man." A few more euphoric trills from the organ and some fatuous waves to the audience and we were off the air. The M.C. turned and walked away without saying a word. The producer was standing in the wings as I came off the stage and he turned his back and pointedly ignored me. I was not having any of that; I wanted to find out where the pay-off window was. When I asked him about it, he turned and regarded me with a distinctly baleful eye before replying coldly, "I don't know anything about that part of it; the network will get in touch with you." He then turned and walked away. (In point of fact, I had to put a lawyer on the case before I finally collected a couple of months later; as anyone who has ever had dealings with the film world knows: show biz cash is very difficult to pry loose from the source.)

In any event, my meteoric career as a TV personality was over. Shivering with chills and fever, I staggered back to the flea bag to get my things, telephoned Dorothy to pick me up in Roanoke and got a plane from La Guardia which had me safe and sick in my own bed by nightfall. It was one of the few conquering hero returns I have ever made and I must say, it's not a bad sensation at all.

There were some amusing aftermaths to the adventure. Adopting the basic human attitude of, "if he can do it, why can't I," a number of friends immediately took steps to get a piece of the action. I warned each that their chances of getting on the thing were better if they represented themselves as having a regional identity. I remember with particular amusement one very urbane writer-friend passing himself off as a most unconvincing hick. My brother-in-law came all the way from the mid-west to have a go. I am sorry to report with a certain glow that to a man all returned empty-handed. Which, in view of the scandal which later emerged, was a very good thing.

We were able to pick up eight or nine very good cows in the course of the next couple of months which brought our herd to its planned strength of thirty. The monthly milk check was now averaging about a thousand dollars and, even though it all went right back out in expenses, we were living well off it in the process. There was even enough money left over from the quiz program to buy a rather nice second-hand Buick destined in time to be the instrument of an act of which I am thoroughly ashamed and remorseful.

CHAPTER XIII

During the calm of that winter of 1957–58, something important happened to me; its effects upon future actions and behavior would turn out to be much more profound than a simple mention of the occurrence implies. I say happen advisedly because it was the first time in my life that I conceived an artistic effort which was completely my own. Heretofore, my novels and short stories at best had tended to be consciously modelled upon the work of writers I admired and, at worst, full of poorly ground personal axes and general spleen venting. I had always had a sneaking desire to write a play and indeed on two occasions had attempted the task. Once, shortly after we were married and were living on 12th Street in the Village, I had completed a comedy of sorts which had been fatally marred by very nearly hysterical self indulgence in the worst sort of mixture of both the literary sins referred to above. The second attempt had been in Rome when I completed one act of a play in the manner of Mr. Tennessee Williams and then abandoned the project in awareness that stylistic and spiritual plagiarization was a game which could never provide balm for my spirit. Yet imitation of that sort is commonly accepted; indeed, it is doubtful that publishing as an industry could exist without it. The vast mass of literary effort consists of *pastiches* of other men's work, many of them done with impressive and admirable skill.

That winter, a play came out of my typewriter. It was flawed, crude and shockingly arrogant but it *was* a play. More important, it was *my* play; by some strange alchemy I still do not understand, I had finally managed to produce a synthesis in form of some of my ideas and their representation in terms of action. Crazily enough, the play came out in verse; I have never been one to skimp in loading the dice against myself. I called it *Abraham's House* and the root of its conception was an attempt to portray and present a psychological paraphrase of the Biblical Abraham using a contemporary story and contemporary characters. The Biblical germ at the heart of the play's creation remained for better or for worse my secret to the end, and died as the play died the morning after its Broadway opening night in 1964. It was by then called *ABRAHAM COCHRANE* and much tampering had gone on with it in the interim—some for the better, some for the worse. It was still essentially a pretty harsh play but then the biblical Abraham was a pretty harsh man. At any rate, I exhume this now not in the play's defense or in attempt to rationalize its failure but to show that, for the first time in my life, I had created something that winter which was my own. And, because it was my own and had meaning for me, the act of its creation became for me the beacon on which I knew I must home.

Never having been exactly a master of the world's realities to begin with, my mastery of the theatrical world's realities was inept to the point of high comedy. I tore the final page of the piece from my typewriter one day during that winter of 1957, decided it was pretty good and showed it to Dorothy, who agreed. The road ahead seemed clear; I could see no reason why a full-fig Broadway production could not be arranged immediately. Certainly, by the following fall the play would be on the boards in New York and fine fat weekly royalty checks wold arrive along with hordes of admiring and deferential journalists.

Just what should be the first step, I asked myself? Well, the answer to that seemed easy: I remembered having glanced through a story in Life Magazine a month or so previously which dealt with a man called Roger Stevens, depicting him as the preeminent theatrical producer of the hour. Seemed like the right sort of fellow for me; big, strong, monolithic-looking chap. I reached for the telephone immediately to put the poor fellow out of his suspense regarding his next theatrical production, and let him know the script was ready. Surprisingly and irritatingly, it turned out that Mr. Stevens could not come to the phone; instead, I got a cheerful girl who has since risen to be a high executive dealing with original plays for CBS. She could not have been nicer but she was also hard put to conceal her amusement at being telephoned by a farmer in Virginia who hoped that Mr. Stevens would be ready to proceed with the production of his new play in the fall. Had I ever written a play before? No, not really but I had written a couple of novels. Well, that was interesting. Whether the lady smelled a new Moliere in the provinces or whether she was simply amused by the babe in the woods she had on the other end of the phone I do not know, but she was kind enough to suggest that I send my play along to her so that she could have a look at it. I mailed off a copy immediately wondering only how long it would be before she could prepare the contracts and send them down to me.

About a week later, an envelope arrived which was about the proper size to contain contracts. It felt pleasantly fat to the touch; everything seemed to be proceeding nicely according to schedule. When I finished her surprisingly long letter, I was a bit dazed. It was simultaneously balm for my ego and the first of a series of lessons in the facts of theatrical life which continue to this day. She was honestly impressed by the work and made that clear in chapter and verse. She then went on to warn me firmly that I would never achieve a Broadway production for that play because (1.) it was in verse (2.) it was too harsh (3.) it was too sophisticated. She went on to say that an off-Broadway production might be possible but that it was barely probable. She ended up her letter with an offer whose shocking generosity I failed to recognize in my ignorance: to put me in touch with any literary agent specializing in plays I named. Audrey Wood was the only one I had ever heard of so I named Audrey Wood. My young lady was as good as her word and promptly put me in touch with Audrey Wood who took two months to let me know that, in her opinion, my talents failed to make me eligible to join her galaxy of such stars as Mr. Williams and Mr. Inge. (It is rather interesting to note parenthetically here that Darroch, whom I had used unabashedly as the physical prototype of the leading role in that play was used just as unabashedly in the same manner by Inge in his play "Man In Boots" which eventually became "Picnic"; Inge and Darroch had been barroom cronies in St. Louis when Inge was functioning as a critic for one of the St. Louis newspapers.)

Refusing to abandon faith in my play, I passed the balance of the winter trying to find someone who would interest himself in it. It was a necessary enough course and a perfectly healthy one if pursued in a spirit of calm. But pursued in the mounting climate of anger and hysteria which I was manufacturing, it is very unhealthy indeed. I believed in *Abraham's House* and continued to believe in it until it was laid to rest by the critics in 1964. Even now—as dead friends and departed lovers do—it inhabits my mind. It has become experience, to be learned from, to be encompassed.

But, until an act or a person or a possibility becomes experience, each is undertaken only in faith. And there is bad faith as well as good. I cannot claim that my faith in my play was wholly good. It tended to lead me towards a resentment of reality. It is a hard, well-nigh impossible lesson to master that a successful act of creation may bring no tangible reward other than succeeding acts of creation. But, hard though that paradoxical lesson may be, it is categoric. In my inability to learn it, I gave birth that winter to a terrible, harmful rage which would not abate for many years. I swore a mighty oath to myself and to my wife that I would see my play performed; but mighty oaths are, at best, only a way of getting up the momentum to go about things ass-backwards; they are spoken in a desire for revenge rather than function.

It was from such a tarnished spirit that an act of immediate, dramatic stupidity sprang during the spring of that year and from which other wrongful directions would be taken in due course. The first began harmlessly enough one afternoon when I stopped in to buy a sack of cement from a local merchant and erstwhile drinking companion with the improbable name of Clancy Yancey. It was towards the end of the working day, that time when, prior to hiring Ned, the discipline of caring for my cattle would have had my nose clamped to the grindstone. Therefore, though it was my rule to be with Ned for at least a part of each milking day, there was no real need for my presence. So when Clancy Yancey invited me to join him in a snort of Bourbon whiskey that day, I felt no qualms about accepting. In time, he closed up his place of business and I accompanied him to his house where, after more Bourbon, I accepted an invitation to supper. After supper and more Bourbon, Clancy Yancey invited me to accompany him upon an expedition to a small town over the mountains in West Virginia where he was going to play his banjo at a country dance scheduled for that evening.

Accordingly, we set out for the dance in my new second-hand TV quiz show Buick. Neither Mrs. Clancy Yancey nor Dorothy (whom I had consulted by telephone) had expressed interest in the outing, so we went alone.

Whatever other faults I may possess, I have never shown a predilection for advertent physical disaster. I am not accident prone, have never broken a bone and managed, luckily enough, to get through sixty-five bombing missions unscathed. Yet the fact remains that on that cold, clear, moisture-free night with no other automobiles in the immediate vicinity, I managed—as we drove across the mountains—to roll that Buick over three times and down a twenty-five foot embankment where we came to rest, God only knows how, right side up in the middle of a creek with the engine still running. How we got there, I do not know but Clancy Yancey and I were nesting companionably on the ledge beneath the rear window. Clancy spoke first; his words were a testament to both hillbilly *sang froid* and the needs of the human spirit: "Is my banjo all right?" I disengaged myself and crawled forward to shut off the ignition while he poked in the debris for his banjo which had, in fact, come through the action unscathed. Miraculously enough, neither of us had suffered a scratch. Slowly coming to our senses, we both realized that we might be in danger in the car and we made a mad scramble for exit and both managed to fall in the creek as a result. As we climbed back up to the road and surveyed the scene, we were two sober, soaked and frightened men. Just how we managed to come through the crash alive is still a mystery to me. Clancy Yancey, who in my book had a perfect right to take me apart with a tire iron, could not have been more gentlemanly about the whole thing. He just looked at the wrecked car in awe, said, "Godallmighty" and then said, "Well, these things happen." Well, they don't just happen and I knew there was going to be plenty of homework ahead but it was not the time for it then. I thumbed a ride to a phone, called the service manager at one of the auto agencies and he came with their wrecker, retrieved the ruined Buick and took us home. Because there were no other cars involved, no insurance and the police did not even show up, the wreck passed immediately into oblivion; I did not even fill out a form concerning it.

Dorothy's reaction when I limped in and told her what had happened was a cold, contemptuous rage of an intensity I had not believed her capable. I can remember few periods of hard feeling in my family that lasted more than an hour or two. This time, her anger lasted well into the afternoon of the next day. Nor did the fact that I was helpless the next day mitigate it. Every muscle in my body was so bruised and sore that I literally could not move. I have never felt such a complete and utter worthless fool in my life.

During the next few months, I stewed constantly upon the basic unrest in my mind which had been the real cause of the automobile wreck. My life, it seemed, was a *troika*—the horses which I was attempting to drive in concert being my farm, the needs of my family, and my own needs as a writer. As a *troika* driver, I obviously did not have the situation well in hand. As a writer, I could sense a period of fecundity looming ahead somewhere in the near future. Also as a writer, I was thinking now purely in terms of the playwriting with which I would be preoccupied during the next ten years. I would, in fact, eventually write another novel but it was undertaken purely as a necessary initial step in translating a dramatic idea to the screen. If I could have avoided that step by dealing directly with a film company, I would have done so, but I was warned by my agent and friends in the theatre that it would be very hard to achieve such a thing without experience or connections. But the basic element in the problem I dwelt on during that summer of 1958 was not writing; it was the farm.

As I toiled among the hay and corn that summer I was forced, in honesty, to admit to myself a rather spooky thing: the truth was that I no longer wanted the farm. There were a thousand ways to rationalize such an admission and I used all of them at one point or another. Looking back now from the vantage point of time and a tiny bit of success, my lack of desire to go on farming seems merely sensible. But at the time it filled me with guilt for a number of reasons. The most important was of course my family. At considerable financial, moral and physical expense, I had arranged a way of life

212

which provided for us a certain amount of well-being. Or at least so it seemed. Unfortunately, I myself felt distinctly unwell in the midst of all this well-being. Some of this, to be sure, was due to the profound emotional disturbance attendant upon the shattering of my lifelong friendship with O'Hara. But the major part stemmed from the fact that I could see nothing ahead for me as a farmer but endless reaches of boredom. For a man more contemplative than most, it is rather odd that my fear of boredom is so profound. The Eastern concept of a purely contemplative life seems to contain a natural affinity for poverty and despair. To each his own, of course; but, alas, for me, there must be a dimension of action. To stand upon my own land throughout the remaining years of my life watching the seasons change while I tilled the land and accepted her bounty was certainly a concept of some nobility. Surely the spirit would expand and grow under the kindly influence of nature's benefice. Or so, at any rate, I had frequently told myself. During the preceding five years as the farm grew from dream to reality, it had seemed an acceptable assumption. But now, as the actively creative part of the project was over and the cyclic aspects of its management stretched changelessly ahead, I was experiencing a distinct shrinkage of the spirit and the sphincter, a state of mind and being which is fine for the arts of war but dreadful for the arts of peace. And it was the arts of peace, specifically playwriting, which I had on my mind.

I have nothing against hicks—except when they get into high places—but I am very definitely not one myself. And in a social setting as arid as the hills of southwestern Virginia, I could see little possibility for myself and even less for my wife and daughters. But more important than that was the fact that the farm had served the purpose for which I had originally sought it. Putting aside for a moment the Calvinistic guilt which I felt at even entertaining the idea of getting rid of the farm, the truth was that I had wanted the farm as an aspect of necessity within a search for freedom. I had always believed that the decade of the Fifties which corresponded roughly with my own Thirties was a period for me of great moral possibility and grave moral danger, the key years of life among which sloth, conformity and self-indulgence lurk like assassins on a shadowy street. They were the years during which, unless dealt with and approached with circumspection, my character—frail reed that it is—could have been leaked away through drink and dishonesty. Instead, it had been contained and perhaps even strengthened. Unquestionably, my marriage had been the major weapon in the struggle; but, among the rest of the arsenal, the farm was the second biggest gun, even though the authorship of a couple of books had not been harmful. But now it was 1958. I was thirty-five and the decade had only two more years to run. The Eisenhower years seemed to have been designed by some master hand as the perfect time to cultivate one's garden; certainly not much else was happening. But even then, in 1958, one would somehow smell the impending change and excitement of the Sixties. It was then that my generation would emerge and take power and I wanted to be present and perhaps to take part in the excitement rather than go on working my hill farm so crazy in my head that I couldn't be trusted not to crash an automobile on a dry, clear night with no help from a living soul.

And so, as we made the hay for the following winter's feed, I faced the fact that I wanted to get out from under my farm and began to think about a possible plan for doing so. I saw no way it could be anything but a gradual process. I discarded immediately any question of putting the farm up for sale or auction. The chances of getting a fair price from someone who wanted to go on operating the farm as a unit were slim. And I found the idea of an auction extremely distasteful; the likelihood of all we had assembled being disassembled and sold as components was great. The best chance to achieve what I wanted seemed to me to be the idea of the partnership with Herbert that I had long considered. With Herbert's wages deducted from my share in the profits from such an arrangement, I would, in effect, be supplying a pair of hands to replace my own and I would be free to take my family and roam wherever I wished, assuming, of course, that those wishes would be compatible with whatever income we had at the moment, whether from the farm or from other sources including writing. If in time, Herbert came to find the idea of having an inactive partner oppressive, some sort of arrangement could be arrived at whereby he could buy me out. I decided to broach the scheme to Herbert.

He was surprisingly receptive to it. His face grew long as he listened and I knew he would need much time to weigh the pros and cons and pray over them, but he saw immediately that there was much to benefit him in the idea. In substance, he risked nothing but the three or four hundred dollars a year I had been paying him for custom work with his machinery and he gained a chance to be the boss man of a farming operation with the potential of very large profits when judged by the standards of the region. By the end of the summer, we were getting close to reaching a final agreement. Although I had no immediate plans for doing so, I warned him that sooner or later we would be moving on and that he would be stuck for all effective purposes, with an absentee landlord. This seemed to bother me more than it did Herbert. And, in truth, it did bother me; everything I had ever read tended to support the view that the practice of absentee landlordism is a pernicious one. Still, I was not displeased; a small chink of light had appeared in the iron door of my imprisonment by the farm. Then my young friend Clyde dropped his bombshell.

His bombshell was so massive that it did away with the chink of light in the prison door by throwing the door wide open. The requirement which Clyde's plan demanded of Dorothy and me was both simple and sublime: total faith in Clyde. Or, as some will decide immediately, total madness. Even from the present vantage point, I cannot say with any conviction that I know one or the other to be correct. Which brings me to a question for which now is as good a time as any to deal with: was Clyde a crook? The answer has a great deal to do with my friend Tiptree, the barn builder's remark, when I told him certain reports had made me apprehensive about his honesty. He smiled, if you recall, and said, "Hell, Jown, you cain't screw a friend." Generally speaking, hill people tend to a highly personalized morality. Fred Cline believed with unshakable conviction, for example, that after paying the insurance premiums on his barn for a number of years, he had the absolute moral right to burn down the barn and collect the insurance. And my young friend Clyde was, despite his superimposed culture, a hill person to the core. So the social answer to the question of his crookery is: no in the hills of Virginia and a probable yes in Bronxville, N.Y. or

215

Evanston, Illinois. My own personal answer to the question is a categoric no. I believe firmly that everything he tried to do stemmed from a deep desire to benefit me and an even deeper desire that the relationship which existed between us continue to grow and expand, to transcend the social, and eventually contain and use power. That the very relationship which he so cherished finally turned out to be the force that pushed him into over-extension and collapse is a very sad thing but I do not think it was wrong. If we are not given the grounds to examine our own identity in action, we remain faceless and unclaimed human beings. But if we make that examination, there is no guarantee that what we discover will be pleasing. Now, for reasons both selfish and philosophical, I begin to sweat at the very thought that life might ever demand of me again a choice such as the one I had to make in regard to Clyde.

His proposition was a simple one: that we give him our farm. In return for throwing in our farm, Dorothy and I would become in effect his partners in any enterprise he entered in upon, whether fire engines or cashew nuts. The specific terms of his plan were simple enough: he would provide us with a monthly income whose floor would be five hundred dollars a month and whose ceiling was theoretically limitless. Should we wish to travel, he would also provide the wherewithal to pay for the costs of transportation. For the rest, he made no bones about his intention of adding the farm to his present financial house of cards once it was legally in his possession. This did not worry me too much because I believed then that the basic technique of acquiring vast fortunes is to borrow against what one owns in order to increase one's holdings. (So basic do I believe that technique to be, in fact, that I have learned in the ensuing years to give it an extremely wide berth and indeed have never owned so much as a share of stock on margin. It is such a basic technique, that one has to have a nervous system capable of writing "Ode To a Nightingale" in the middle of a steel band in order to use it successfully.) The other reason it did not worry me much was that the farm was already mortgaged to the hilt of possibility, a fact which would provide sound checks and balances against the height, width and handsomeness of Clyde's potential dealings.

Clyde was, of course, familiar with the details of the loose partnership with Farmer Herbert which had been planned. Herbert was, by then, a factor which could not be ignored or abandoned, a fact with which Clyde was in hearty agreement. The last thing in the world he wanted was to be the working manager of a farm; he was not suited to it by virtue of either temperament or experience. Clyde's intention was to be the financial *eminence grise* of the combined operation, using his financial legerdemain to make sums of money available for the planned expansion.

Ignoring for the moment—now as I did then—the all-important factor of self-deception, Clyde's proposition was one to which I was immediately and powerfully attracted. First of all, it contained a great deal of cast your bread upon the waters, and I have always been as strongly inclined to accept the moral directions of Jesus Christ as I am disinclined to participate in ceremonies where his body is symbolically cannibalized in order to obfuscate his thought; that thought, of course, being total and absolute anathema to the bankers who occupy the front row seats at the feast. I was attracted to Clyde's plan even more because—in theory, at least—it contained a strong triangular pragmatic base in terms of: from each according to his ability to each according to his need. It presented each of us with a blank canvas to be painted upon in a style and manner of our own choosing: for Farmer Herbert, farming; for me, art; and for Clyde, money. If theory could be turned successfuly into fact, I believed then as I believe now that a large step forward would have been taken.

I listened to Clyde's proposition, told him I was interested and that I would think about it and talk it over with Dorothy. I did so and found, just as I had expected, that she was as fascinated as I. It is hard for me to imagine what it would be like to be married in the dolorous sense that institution commonly enjoins. By which, I mean the prosaic joining together of two human beings in defense against the dark who fumblingly breed in search of tenuous meaning, receive the precious gift of life and then do their best to smash it up through almost religious adherence to the rigidity of their fear. The experiment which one's life truly is, must be performed and the results accepted. In times of low spiritual tide, my wife has been wont to remark that she is a coward except in regard

217

to my intentions; to which my only answer will always be that I too am a coward except in regard to her support for those intentions. The net result of our discussion regarding Clyde's proposition was that we would give it a whirl if Farmer Herbert were amenable to accepting Clyde as his partner rather than me.

Which proved to be the case. Farmer Herbert saw immediately that nothing was essentially changed; that he still had the chance to win much and risk little. Older than I by five or six years, Herbert was terribly bemused by the fact that young Clyde could possess the wherewithal to purchase my farm. Perhaps the lie which was the kernel of the mistake I made was the omissive lie of failing to tell him that the sum needed by Clyde to buy my farm was the single dollar bill required to make the gift of my farm a legal transaction.

From my friend, Lawyer Bean, who would handle the legal details of the transaction, it was, of course, not possible to conceal such knowledge. I believed in Clyde and the fire engines and Herbert and the farm and myself and the playwriting because I *wanted* to believe in them. I knew that I could not justify that belief to Lawyer Bean even as I knew it was my bounden duty to do so. Therefore, I simply refused to attempt such a justification, watched his eyes grow wide with concern as I informed him of my intention, and then saw them narrow with sudden suspicion of my madness. He lectured me about the risk I was running according to the dictates of his legal conscience and I heard him out in the politeness based on the absolute conviction that my belief was a factor superior to his commonsense warnings. When he was finished, I instructed him to proceed with drawing up the legal documents. This he did and in due time they were executed by Clyde and me, the dollar bill changed hands and the farm, conceived in Rome as a dream and upon whose creation we had labored for the preceding five years, passed from our legal possession.

The world was now theoretically our oyster. What I conceived of as an act of faith had been performed and it seemed only right and proper that one of the immediate rewards of that act was the possession of a magic carpet which would take us anywhere. Like everything viewed from hindsight, it is now clear in retrospect that the destination we chose was

218

perfectly symbolic of the web of self-deception I had spun for myself. Did I, whose belief in his recently-completed play was so passionate, choose New York? Or London? No, not for a minute. After much excited pouring over of Atlases, we chose that world-famous theatrical capital of the Universe, the island of Barbados. But the chill of autumn was already upon us. For years we had battled those rural winters, often in primitive circumstances. The sun beckoned to us so irresistibly that we could not refuse. We'll only stay six months or so, I told Dorothy, and I could use the time profitably writing, spurred on by the undoubted inspiration which would arise amidst strange circumstances. After six months in the sun, I assured her, we would be rested and rejuvenated and ready to take on New York, armed, I hoped, with still another string to the old literary bow.

Or we could return to the farm; one of the basic points of our agreement with Clyde was that our house would always be available to us, shut up and guarded by him for us during our absence. In point of fact, we now left it to my brother who needed a place to cogitate and hibernate throughout the winter. He would also take care of Gordo, the Boxer, whose passage to Barbados was prohibited by stringent British-oriented quarantine laws.

Finally, the day of our departure arrived. We were like children before a picnic, filled with that sublime sense of expectation which precludes knowledge of the ants in the food. We were, after all, a family with an itchy foot which had not been scratched for a long time. So, it was in a spirit of excitement and impending holiday that we drove to the filling station in Wytheville where we were to meet Clyde on the morning of our departure. He would drive us to the airport at Roanoke in our Jeep station wagon of which he would then assume possession as part and parcel of the farm which we had given him.

Clyde was late and harassed of appearance when he finally appeared. No matter, there was always a slight feeling of "knock twice and ask for Joe" in any dealings with Clyde. It was one of the things which, in my dangerous but alas unchanging abhorrence for the prosaic, I found attractive. So great was my trust in the future of our plans that I had not even bothered to cash a check, it having been agreed between

Clyde and me that cash which he would provide, would be the best means of proceeding initially. I had, I think, ten dollars in my pocket, a few hundred more in my checking account which, according to agreement, would be replenished at monthly intervals. Now, there was a slight, almost imperceptible memory of a whorehouse as he proffered, and I hastily pocketed, an envelope stuffed with cash. It passed away immediately and we exuberantly took the road which would lead us to the air which would lead us to the sun and happiness.

CHAPTER XIV

I am sure that by now ample warning has been given of the fact that happiness is precisely what we did not find in Barbados. To travel in the opposite direction to that indicated by need and intention impelled by a total calculus which contains a giant error is not exactly the most efficient means of achieving happiness.

However for a time, at least, the sun, sea and trade winds served to foster its illusion. The island itself was a charming place, a splendid mixture of an overwhelmingly British veneer applied to the basic noise, colour and excitement of an island with a long history of passion and violence. We loved the busy Bridgetown streets where, almost on the first day of our arrival, what must have been the biggest black whore in the world solicited my custom in a voice hardly lowered for the benefit of Dorothy and other passers-by, using an idiom that had me gasping with laughter. A sailboat fancer since childhood, it was sheer magic for me to find Bridgetown harbour filled with old Gloucester fishermen now employed in carrying nitrate from British Guiana. So beautiful carrying full sail in the distance, it was rather sad coming close to one to find her hogged and filthy. Even though we had no business in Barbados, we did not realize it during the first month and so were able to enjoy ourselves amidst the novelty. It was certainly about as far away from a Virginia hill farm as it is possible to get and I suppose we all needed that.

While we looked for a house, we lived in a pleasant compound of small apartments which were hideously expensive. Then we found and rented a lovely big house on the St. Lawrence coast about a twenty-minute bus ride from Bridgetown. It was right smack on the beach, a huge, cool, high-ceilinged house through which the breeze from the trade winds blew incessantly. With the house came Norah, the black cook, and a colleague who did the laundry. Norah had the best natural hand with children I have ever encountered and ours adored her. Little Sylvia called her "Nort" and trailed happily around in her wake all day long.

For the first two or three weeks on the island, we made no attempt at seriousness and simply wallowed happily in the holiday atmosphere to which we were so unaccustomed. And I wallowed, I must admit, in the rum. Wonderful Barbados rum; there is no tipple quite like it in the world. I thought of rum as a harsh spirit fit only to be mixed with citrus juices but that which we encountered on Barbados was as mellow as aged Scotch. As a general rule, I am inclined to think it the better part of wisdom for Celtic Calvinists to eschew tropical islands with cheap drink until the safe seventies have been achieved. Our rum cost something like a dollar and a half a gallon and was delivered to the door much like the milk. I partook thereof. Yet it was all very healthy somehow; the sun and the sea and Norah's wonderful cooking maintained a splendid, constant glow. What we were having was a holiday. But holidays were somehow not our style; they belong properly to people who do not believe that working nine-to-five is a living death. It goes without saying that my type-writer did not leave its case. It sat on a table beside some copies of my play, *"Abraham's House,"* from which I guiltily averted my eyes as I walked past.

The day came when we were supposed to receive money from Clyde. It did not arrive but it did not immediately occur to me to be seriously worried. I ascribed his dereliction to some technical cause such as delay in the mails and put it from my mind. A week went by and still it did not come; I was no longer able to tell myself or Dorothy that I was not worried. I wrote but there was no answer. Then a letter arrived and I was relieved; everything was going to be all right after all. But the letter contained no money; explanations of grandiose plans and a rosy future, but no money.

I was beginning now to be very worried indeed and a letter from my brother did nothing to alleviate things. Even accounting for the fact that there was no particular love lost between him and Clyde, his letter described some very pecu-

222

liar goings-on. Clyde, he reported, was carrying himself like a man on the edge of a serious emotional breakdown. According to Earl, he was doing senseless things like cutting down an apple tree in the yard of our house with his chain saw. Worst of all, he had intimated to Earl that he had plans which definitely did not fit the letter or spirit of our agreement. His parents' handsome house on the creek a few miles from ours had been vacated by them a few months before when they had decided to move back into Wytheville. Now, he told Earl, he planned to give that house to us and to move Ned, the hired man, into our house. Admittedly the house which Clyde wanted to give us was better appointed and more palatial in every way than ours, but nevertheless I was appalled at the thought of Ned and his hillbilly brood living in our house.

Then, in the nick of time when nagging worry was about to turn to throbbing fear, a letter arrived from Clyde which contained both money and what seemed at first sight to be reasonable explanations for many things. The delay in sending the money, he explained, had been due to a straightening of circumstances forced by the purchase of a new tractor and some other equipment—items all, I knew, the farm needed badly. The apparently senseless act of cutting down the apple tree was explained as having been forced upon him by some serious blight which gripped the tree. The business about moving Ned and his family into our house he went into at considerable length. His parents' house had—he did not make it absolutely clear which—either been given to him or sold to him for a nominal sum. As it was unquestionably the most suitable house for us in the environs of the farm, he had decided that it should be made available to us on the same terms as our farmhouse had been: we would not legally own the house but it would be our house in that it would be available to us for as long as we lived. Moving Ned and his family into our farmhouse was justified on the ground that it would facilitate Ned's care of the cattle through greater proximity to them. All of the points in his letter were defendable from a standpoint of both generosity and function and I accepted them in the spirit in which they were offered. But the sum of money he had sent was less than that agreed upon. He promised quick delivery of the remainder, however, and I shoved what reservations I still possessed into the back of my mind on the basis of that promise.

The reservations did not remain quiescent, of course. There now began for Dorothy and me the single greatest point of strain that our marriage had undergone to date. Incessantly I delivered great long pep-talks on how everything was going to turn out exactly as planned, and Dorothy answered in kind, vehemently reaffirming her faith in my insane decision of having given away everything we possessed in the world.

When quite a young man, I read in some more or less trustworthy academic study of prison inmates that some ninety per cent of the male persons incarcerated in American prisons claimed that a woman had been the direct agent of their imprisonment. Assuming even a segment of statistical truth in such a claim, leads one to a consideration of the profound implications in such a state of affairs. Personally, it led me to an undying fascination with the mysterious role women play in life with regard to judgment. The negative aspects of those judgments do not interest me much. That ladies sat in the bleachers and turned their thumbs down on gladiators, or that there is in fact a tendency among women to castrate men psychologically, are both only facts as the cutting edge of a sword is a fact. It has always been the force behind the sword which interests me. In a play of mine, the following interchange takes place between two old ladies both nearing the end of their lives. As they contemptuously scoff at the male-fostered contemporary concept of the female's desire to castrate the male, they speak thus:

JULIA

Well, we try, I suppose. But the truth is that it's easier said than done.
(Pause)
We try because we must. But the only real joy we ever experience is in failing.

SARAH

Why is it such a well-kept secret?

Oh, I think we want it that way. Indeed, perhaps it has to be that way. The men might be too frightened otherwise. All the *real* judgments are made by women. The symbol for justice is, after all, a woman. Oh, men play at making judgments with their trials and courtrooms but it's a formality. The real dock where a man stands to be judged is a woman's heart and mind.

(She pauses, smiling)

And bed, I suppose.

That this continuing process of judgment regarding men by women takes place is something I believe implicitly. And these female judgments stem from an atavistic synthesis of intellect, emotion and sexuality so mysterious that we symbolize that mystery by placing a blindfold over the eyes of our female symbol of justice. Unfortunately, the negative aspect of these judgments tends to be both more interesting and more amenable to artistic treatment than the positive. For every fundamentally positive heroine such as Abraham's wife, Sarah, we have among our cultural heritage a veritable host of fundamentally negative female protagonists running the gamut from Messalina, through Hedda Gabler, to the heroines of Mr. Tennessee Williams. But it is the force behind the female judgment which remains more interesting to me than the fact of it being positive or negative, precisely because the force is rooted in such a mysterious combination of the animal need to breed young, the intellectual pragmatism to achieve security for their nurturing, and the moral purpose to insure their growth.

Beneath my wife's vociferous agreement with my protestations that all would be well with the outcome of my late decision to give away our farm, I now began to sense a subtle smell of the force of female judgment being mustered. Behind her hopeful but questioning eyes, there were the beginnings of the same sharp gleam the losing gladiators must have spotted in the box seats. Apart and aside from our daily ritual sessions of mutual (and growingly false) reassurance, we began to avoid each other. The degree of reproach in her attitude grew more perceptible daily.

225

To which, like all self-deceivers, I could make no answer but drink and avoidance. I clung desperately to my belief in my own actions with no more evidence than the fatuous insistence that they were mine, and so—as if by divine sanction—correct. The sand of Barbados was warm, beautiful and liberally sprinkled with rum. I continued to stick my head therein.

Unquestionably, the imaginative pace of my moral disintegration was a great deal faster than the actual circumstances. Looking back, I tend to see myself as having been poised teetering on the brink of the Pit. However, it is closer to the truth to say simply that I was a badly worried, frightened man spending each and every waking hour in a desperate attempt to avoid coming face to face with my own stupidity and, more important, taking some sort of specific action to rectify my errors. Such a state of spiritual attrition acts like sandpaper on the nervous system; one's ordinary sensitivity becomes so painfully acute that one feels as vulnerable as a newly-laid egg. As I sat late upon the barstools of Barbados, my red-faced, Scots-Irish look of impregnability hid a quaking heart as timorous as a fawn. In those circumstances, one tends to have some curious encounters.

At about three o'clock in the morning of a fine tropical day, I was sitting idly at the bar of one of the Bridgetown beach hotels listening to the strains of a steel band playing in the distance. A man entered the bar and immediately captured my imagination as he walked the length of the room towards the place where I was sitting. He reminded me a great deal of Darroch. Like Darroch, he was a big man, strong-looking and formidably self-assured. As he walked towards me, I had one of those blind flashes of insight that so frequently turn out to be bull's-eyes of accuracy; I knew suddenly and with absolute certainty that he was a professional con man. Having nothing else to do and being thoroughly bored with myself, I decided to inform him that my drink-heightened, X-ray vision had pierced his cover. As he passed, our eyes locked for a moment and I said in a casual, conversational tone, "You're on the con". He paused almost imperceptibly for a moment and then continued on past me to a table looking out over the sea. I turned back to my drink absolutely certain that something was going to happen. Sure enough, about fifteen minutes later, a waiter came over to the bar, indicated the man sitting at the table and delivered the message that the gentleman would like me to join him for a drink. I joined the man and we introduced ourselves; for present purposes, I shall call him Brad. Brad immediately asked me if I did not think I was heading for trouble sitting in a barroom in the middle of the night making preposterous remarks to total strangers. There was such a total absence of anger in his question and such a strong underlying note of curiosity that I was even more certain that my flash of insight had been correct. So I agreed with him about the possibility of trouble in such unorthodox social procedures but repeated my complete conviction that he was a confidence man. He burst out laughing and told me I was crazy. We began to talk and, from the first, I found I was enjoying myself tremendously. I do not remember the stories he told me in detail but they were all delivered with consummate artistry and they invariably reached a peak of suspense which, in one way or another had alerted every aspect of my mind open to greed or larceny. On he went, telling stories which always hinged on some great business opportunity in some part of the world where easy pickings could be had for the asking. As these various tales came to an end, I would laugh and repeat my belief that he was a confidence man. He would laugh also and tell me I was out of my mind. So we chatted on in this manner for an hour or so and had several drinks. Then suddenly, as he finished one of his stories, his eyes turned very hard indeed. He leaned back in his chair, regarded me for a long moment with a level gaze and said, "O.K., kid, what's your proposition? I won't have anything to do with guns or women." My insight had turned out to be absolutely correct, but even funnier was the fact that the only explanation he had been able to conceive for my conduct was that I was a con man also. I managed to disabuse him of that notion. We had another drink or so and parted in friendly fashion.

I saw him a number of times after that; he was, of course, a very appealing concoction for any writer. Feeling fairly certain that life would never again hand me a professional confidence man to play around with, I tried my best to find out what made him tick. In all the externals, he was ultramagnificent; his wristwatch, for example, must have cost a good deal more than any automobile I had owned. He was certainly not queer for most of the times I saw him he had a girl with him and they were always damned good-looking. I always wanted to get him to talk about his professional experiences but he very definitely shied away from that topic, remarking only that he was currently having a bit of a holiday after some sort of successful venture in Venezuela. It must have been very successful because he spent money prodigiously.

While he was loath to talk about his business, Brad was completely open about his life which, like all the rest of us, he was interested in figuring out. His story was banal enough in its essentials: he had been born in the south somewhere, a cracker kid from the wrong side of the tracks with a lot of physical attractiveness, intuitive psychological sense about people and a high degree of athletic skill. Like an old-fashioned Cosmopolitan short story, the girl in the house on the hill had fallen for him in high school, they planned to marry but her family had broken it up because of his cracker background. He had then left the town to drift here and there, living off of various shady deals and picking up the social expertise he needed.

At the same time he was likeable, Brad was a genuinely sick human being in that the fundamental weapon in his arsenal was a complete and utter refusal to accept any aspect of human possibility. His contempt for human beings was profound and unchallengeable; indeed, I believe the stirrings of a faint but real liking for me frightened him to death. Anything that worked in a human sense he wanted to stay wholly clear of; a number of times, I pressed him to come to our house for a meal and meet Dorothy and the children but he wanted nothing to do with such matters. Liking anybody would lead to a soft heart, and when you get right down to it, a soft-hearted confidence man would be about as effective as a one-armed baseball player. Because he could not allow himself to be a friend to anyone, he was not mine either; but he was phenomenologically interesting. He drifted away one day but he still flits through my mind occasionally.

Perhaps it is true that life does tend to imitate art. Barbados is the only tropical island I have ever had any truck with, but for the most part, the cast of characters on Barbados were fairly interchangeable with those in a Somerset Maugham short story. About halfway along the mile walk between our house and the hotel where I did most of my drinking lived a rather pretty blond woman who was the daughter of that fabled, standard standby of the pre-war Sunday supplements, the White Rajah of Sarawak. I would drop in on her occasionally to talk over the ups and downs of White Rajahdom. The White Rajah himself was evidently in London, ungainfully employed and blowing in the family loot on chorus girls. His daughter and I compared notes on our upbringing and it was clear to me that there was a good deal of difference between growing up on Sarawak and at 415 North Hanley Road, St. Louis, Missouri. She had a cheerful Dutch boy friend named Joop around who lost no time in presenting Dorothy offers of consolation after my departure. For the rest, Sadie Thompson and the preacher must have been around somewhere.

And depart, I did. Even mustering all my self-deceptive defenses, I could not indefinitely withhold from myself the realization that I must return and make some sort of an attempt to straighten out the muddle for which I was responsible. The gleam of imminent judgment in Dorothy's eye was growing sharper. I knew I must now try to get my farm back. But I did not want Dorothy or the children with me as I made the attempt. For I was by no means sure I would succeed and I knew that if I failed, some gigantic, irreparable crack would appear in the entire fabric of our lives.

The silent reproach emanating from the script of my play was also instrumental in making me return. My oath concerning its future was still mighty and still flawed. But it was also still the beacon on which I knew I must home.

It was a strange, sad trip. Once the decision to go back had been taken, I felt a certain measure of relief. Then too, I am one of those who feel exuberant at the start of any trip; were I setting out with Virgil for a walk around the Inferno, I suspect I would be lighthearted at the beginning.

For the first part of the journey, my seat-mate was a young British Army Doctor, returning home to be discharged after several years' service in various parts of the British West Indies. He was an ex-public schoolboy and a Londoner who felt that his years in the islands had been a bonanza from the Gods but who was more than a little apprehensive about his professional future in England. (Having since lived in England, I now understand his fears a little better. The ordinary run-of-the-mill English doctor tends to lack the *esprit de corps* of his sleek, well-paid American counterpart. The American medical profession seems to surround itself with a protective sense of its own mystery and importance. The British National Health Service not only provides care for many who would not otherwise have it but also seems to prick the balloon of self importance which one finds so often among American physicians. Once, in England, I petitioned our local doctor—who was also a social acquaintance—for medicine to induce the removal of some uncomfortable proturberances on my foot called Plantar warts which had been hacked at with knives and prayed over but had steadfastly refused to depart. The local doctor casually gave me a bottle of some kind of acid which had the look of something which might be found in the medicine cabinet of an indigent recluse. I applied it, and lo and behold, the things went away. When I gratefully praised the doctor to his wife, she said in surprise, "You mean he actually cured something like a real doctor".)

At any rate, my young traveling companion was lacking in confidence in his own abilities. On the ever-sound basis that the best way to strengthen one's low spirits is to try raising someone else's, I asked him about his past experiences and his future hopes. As the aircraft hopped from island to island, we drank gin and tonics together and discussed the state of man and the universe. I remember, at one point, kidding him that some day he might be faced with a terrible professional decision which would literally require the wielding of a knife to cut into the unknown. For some years after that, I received a Christmas card each year from him inscribed with the notation: "I haven't cut it yet".

We parted as the aircraft landed at some island where he would make a connection for Bermuda and thence to London. In view of the lugubrious purpose of my journey, it seemed somehow improper to go on drinking alone, and after the young doctor left, I sat staring out of the window at the darkening sky as the aircraft plowed on to Puerto Rico. By the time we reached that island at about ten o'clock at night, my spirits had sunk to a very low ebb indeed.

At Puerto Rico we were informed that there would be a

delay due to some malfunction in the aircraft and led to a dreary waiting room where we sat dispiritedly in that gritty-eyed condition of fatigue which travel inspires. There I had an encounter which restored to me some slight sense of balance regarding the importance of my own troubles.

I was awakened from my despairing half-doze by an employee of the airline depositing a person upon the empty chair next to my own. It was a little Puerto Rican boy not more than nine years old. From what disease or condition I do not know, but he was horribly crippled and horribly frightened. I tried to close my eyes for a moment and heard a short, soft sob. When I looked down at him, he looked back, eyes white and frightened and coursing with tears. We stared at each other for a moment and then, mustering a few words of rusty Spanish and a gesture, I asked him if he would like to sit on my lap. He nodded his head with great shyness and I gently picked him up and held him. His tears did not stop and, after a moment, I knew that I was going to begin weeping also. So to save us both embarrassment, I carried him outside the building and we walked up and down for a time, both weeping. After a while, that seemed to make us feel better and we were able to stop. In my pidgin Spanish, we tried to talk and he told me that he came from the interior of the island and was being sent to New York for treatment of his condition. We conversed thus until the employee of the airline appeared to carry him away to his flight. Shortly after that, my own flight resumed also.

CHAPTER XV

1958 was drawing to a close when I returned to Virginia from Barbados to make the attempt at getting back the farm I had so wilfully given away. I was by no means sure I could accomplish this but I was absolutely certain that if I failed to accomplish it, I had blown the whole game; that the preceding years would have been wasted in the sense that they could turn out to have been both meaningful and rich. There is, of course, nothing dishonorable about plain, good old fashioned failure; if one displays his wares for approval and to the best of his belief, they are not shoddily fashioned, one can—indeed, one must—live honorably with the accolade of their acceptance or the dolor of their rejection. The facts of either eventually become simply experience; they are incorporated into the clay of being, the totality of oneself. The only real failure is the rejection of experience—which is purely and simply the refusal to build the edifice of self. Perhaps the best existing example of a human being who wishes to reject meaning and render his own time meaningless is the junkie. Mr. William Burroughs (A St. Louisan also—I remember being taken to call upon him at his parents' large house there by my friend David Kammerer, since dead of murder) has stated this with powerful succinctness in the preface to his book, *THE NAKED LUNCH:* "Nothing ever *happens* in the junk world". Where nothing happens, no experience is possible. But there is another way of refusing experience and this was the method into whose camp I had thrust my foot: the insistence upon rigging the deck against oneself and the dishonorable failure which results from a refusal to recognize that the deck has been so rigged. Which was more or less my position on that grey winter day that my aircraft landed at Roanoke after the flight from Barbados. I wanted desperately to go on believing in my own pipe dream. And in spite of a thousand inner voices warning me of the truth, I was determined to go on playing the crooked hand I had dealt myself and—I now believe—dealt Clyde also.

My thousand inner voices were immediately joined by two tangible outer ones: those of my mother and my brother. They were waiting for me as I came through the gate at the terminal. Apart from them and clearly at odds with them, Clyde waited also. The eighty-mile drive from Roanoke to the farm had to be made with either one party or the other. Perhaps the clearest indication of the deep ambivalence which had me in its grip regarding every future decision is the fact that I—whose memory is generally good—cannot remember with any degree of conviction as to accuracy what the choice was that I made. Nor can my brother or mother. I incline to the view that I got into the car with mother and Earl. Mother stated flatly she could not remember. My brother is wholly uncertain but remarked when I recently asked him about it, "You probably went with Clyde. It would be the best bet because he was the key to everything and you were terribly concerned about him."

At any rate, whether I made the ride from Roanoke to the farm that day with Clyde, or not, I certainly spoke with him long enough at the airport to have no doubts whatsoever that he was a man under dreadful, almost unbearable strain. He had, it turned out, gone through with his plan of moving our belongings into the lovely house lately owned by his parents. His manner of doing this had left a sour taste in everyone's mouth. He had waited until my brother had driven to North Carolina to pay a visit to my mother and accomplished the move in my brother's absence. Warned by the same feeling of impending disaster that we all shared at that point, mother had chosen to return to the farm with my brother where they found the furniture jumbled and stacked in any old way in the new house, and Ned, the hired man, in possession of our former dwelling. Upon discovering this, my mother elected to remain, await my return and provide both moral support and victuals; the former, alas, being of a much higher order than the latter; in the coming months, more TV dinners would disappear down my gullet than I would have thought existed in the world. So great, however, was my fear and worry that I could not extricate us from the impossible position I had placed us that plain bread and water would have struck me as being far beyond my just desserts.

There is very little question in my mind that I arrived in the barest nick of time. I am convinced now that all of the musical chairs that Clyde was playing with the houses was being done in preparation for some sort of devious action designed to pull his chestnuts out of the fire. The most likely explanation is that he was considering the old and honorable hillbilly custom of arson. The Kegley house now stood empty and was insured for enough to provide the few thousand dollars that F. felt he needed to shore up his house of cards. But, if this was the idea with which he was flirting, it became psychologically difficult for him to carry it through once I was again physically present.

The one factor which still remained constant in the midst of the chaos and suspicion which now surrounded all of us was the farm itself. One cannot destroy a soundly constructed edifice overnight and Clyde had only been at the financial helm for about three months. And I must stress again my firm belief that Clyde had no advertent intention or desire to destroy the farm. He saw it as a single aspect (and eventually, a very minor one) of his long-range financial plans. Our financial policy regarding the farm had been the traditional one which every farmer must follow: to re-invest every bit of income from the milk except the minimal amount needed for our actual living expenses, and at the same time to be extremely chary of making commitments which would be hard to meet. Clyde had, in effect, reversed that policy in that, not only was he milking away the actual cash income from the farm to increase his problematical stock holdings, but he had also contracted to buy on time several expensive items of machinery which the present state of the farm's development could not actually justify.

Whether financial chaos precedes psychological chaos is like the proverbial question about the chicken and the egg, a difficult one to answer. Certainly, I was now faced with both.

Although there was little rancor on either side, the personal relationship between Clyde and me had been irreparably damaged. Herbert, the farmer, smelling chaos, had become disenchanted and wanted out of our arrangement for which he could not be blamed a bit. He had lost but he had risked little and was by nature inclined to be philosophical about the whole thing.

It was certainly the financial chaos which took precedence among the immediate problems to be solved. I knew that even if I could manage to do it, the process of getting Clyde to return the farm to me legally was not going to be one accomplished overnight. In the meantime, the farm continued to pump out milk, and the check continued to arrive each month. But this check came of course to Clyde and was consumed immediately in partial support of his various schemes and adventures. I say partial because it was soon very obvious that he had spread himself catastrophically thin; the farm, almost from the moment of my return, was awash with angry gentlemen flourishing duns for payment which had not been made on various pieces of equipment. Clyde turned out to be a past master at making good his escape when these gentlemen appeared. They would invariably be directed to me by some neighbor who believed that I was still the actual owner of the farm, and I would explain to them that I was not and do my best to pacify them. I was thus in the strange position of having to try my best to protect Clyde in order to avert the beginnings of a series of chain-reaction legal actions which could have very easily resulted in the total loss of the farm. The final irony was that I no longer owned the farm and the prospect that I would ever do so again seemed at that point distinctly questionable.

The long-range problem was whether or not and if and how I could get my farm back. The immediate, categoric one was money: cold hard cash to keep Dorothy and the children going on Barbados. I scraped up enough for her immediate needs and attempted to inject a suitable note of confidence regarding the future into my letter. There must have been a discernibly false ring to it for she immediately took certain steps on her own in the finest tradition of good soldiering. "White Sands"—our house on Barbados—being very large and well-staffed, Dorothy decided immediately upon going

236

into business as a boarding-house keeper. The island was by then in the midst of its high season and accommodations were at a premium. With an unerring feel for the off-beat, Dorothy chose two tenants so phantasmagorical that the children always spoke of them with giggles: a near-centenarian father and his caretaker-son, not all that much younger and totally dispirited from a lifetime of waiting around to get his hands on the cash in the face of his father's growing selfishness, contempt and tyranny. Luckily, the father's tyrannical proclivities were directed solely towards the son whose daily ration of torture was the old man's major sport and diversion. For the rest, Dorothy has always claimed they were not bad to have around, a contention about which I remain as quizzical as I am grateful.

With the breathing space thus afforded, I was able to hustle up the sums of money needed to keep us going and avert the dangerous incipient acts of foreclosure whose aura surrounded the farm. Oddly enough, it was not a wholly unhappy time. It never is when one has made a conscious attempt to face the facts of his own stupidity and undertake corrective measures. It is in flight from consciousness and reality that true unhappiness lies; I had experienced its apogee on Barbados, twice compounded by the lotus eating circumstances which I had not earned and did not need. But now, amidst the TV dinners and maternal homilies which were frequently cogent and always irritating, a sense of moral purpose began to reassert itself. Externally, the three of us in that house during that long winter must have presented a certain bizarreness of appearance—much like the characters in a play by Mr. Harold Pinter. Internally, I suspect there was a good deal more intellectual cohesion present than that puzzling artist's creations actually contain. To the specific problems concerning the farm, we applied our combined intelligence and avoided each other as best we could, conducting, in our own manner, the continuing investigation of ourselves. My brother dwelt deep in a world of complex abstractions to hold at bay the realization that his final, winning battle with drink must soon be fought. My mother, in the way of mothers, made stern effort to withhold judgment on her sons and, for the rest, remained the good audience she has always been, displaying an interest in the show, a willingness to pay high prices for seats and vibrantly positive hopes for the outcome.

For myself, I found my mind again becoming an efficient instrument of sorts after long lapse. In the midst of all that I had to do that winter, the creative urge appeared to spread its leavening solace. In an attempt to encompass all I knew and what I thought, I wrote a long essay that winter. It will never see the light of day but it has lent itself well to cannabalization throughout the years even though much fortifying flesh remains upon its carcass; and much, I must admit in honesty, went bad and had to be cut away.

To end whatever suspense remains regarding my repossession of my farm, the answer is, yes. I did get it back. It was done without coercion and I do not believe there was any real rancor borne in Clyde's mind or my own. Only sadness. It was a long, slow and difficult process persuading him that he should give it back. The primary reason he did not want to give it back was of course that such an act was an admission of failure on his part, something he longed for as little as the rest of us. But underneath all the philosophical implications, there was a deep, almost peasant hunger for the possession of land itself; for Clyde land was the ultimate value, the ultimate strength; not to farm, or use in any way but simply to own. In the face of such a primeval need, it is still something of a miracle to me that he gave it back. But more than that, it is a testament to the depth of his dedication to the idealistic meaning of the odd arrangement we had conceived. No, Clyde was not a crook.

And so the day finally came when, after many missed meetings and endless discussions frequently marked by rage on the part of all, Clyde appeared at Lawyer Bean's office and formally signed the documents which returned the farm to my ownership. After that, during the relatively short period of time remaining to us on the farm, I would see him occasionally as he passed in his jeep and we would each extend an arm to wave in greeting as we had when I had come to live on the farm six years before. But that was all.

Now, I shall jump ahead in time for a moment to reveal a barb—still lodged in my heart—which will always cause momentary pains of shame. In 1962, my old friend Pennebaker who owned a house near ours in Sag Harbor came to me with puzzlement, bearing a strange document.

Penny knew Clyde, having met him years before when Penny paid a visit to our farm during a hegira around the United States making a film for the Brussels World's Fair. Penny also had known O'Hara for many years. What he brought with him that day was a postcard written in an unknown hand postmarked New York City. It was addressed to him and bore only the numerical references to a certain chapter and verse of the Book of Isaiah. Penny told me he had looked up the reference and found that the verse said, in effect, "Intercede for me with my enemies." Penny, knowing well the weight which then still pressed upon my mind regarding my shattered friendship with O'Hara, asked me if I thought it was from him. For reasons I will tell before I close this account, I knew it was not. Furthermore, it was not O'Hara's handwriting. At first, I was as puzzled as Penny as to the postcard's origins. In time it came to me that it must have come from Clyde. I hid behind my uncertainty but the fact remains that I did nothing about it.

The farm returned to my possession sometime during March of 1959. Dorothy's lease on the house at Barbados expired at the end of March and she and the children planned to return on the first of April. The extent of my anticipatory anxiety to see them all came as no surprise to me in the case of Dorothy, but in the case of the children, it was something of a shock to find how much I had missed them and how much I longed to see them. Fatherhood has always been for me a state whose joys lie in realization rather than anticipation. I have always received the news that a child was on the way with gloom and its actual arrival with elation. Now I had come to realize during our parting that I was actually a father; that the existence of my children was as necessary to me as mine is, presumably, to them. The hook was in and has never since managed to work loose.

It was a splendid trio that came tumbling off the aircraft at Roanoke on that cold April morning. All three brown from the Barbados sun and glowing with health, they made those of us waiting at the gate seem like troglodytes. I wish that I had then owned a tape recorder and had the presence of mind to use it while their accents remained. Through association with the maids at "White Sands," the children had managed to acquire splendid Barbadian. For the next few weeks, I never tired of overhearing instructions given by six-year-old Linda to her sister such as "Don' speek dat word to me, you crazee mon?" It is better for their future, I suppose, but alas bad for my funny bone that these marvelous accents soon passed away forever.

Having the farm back in my legal possession did not solve the problem of its eventual disposition. What Mr. John Updyke calls "the great northeastern megalopolis" still beckoned imperatively. No matter how problematical it may have seemed at the time, I was certain that whatever future I had lay in that direction. But the existence of the farm as a fact of direct, personal responsibility sat athwart that road as an insurmountable obstacle.

By then, I had firmly faced the fact that as far as the farm was concerned, it was going to be impossible to have my cake and eat it. Partnerships, such as I had thought of with Herbert, were not going to work out. And clearly it would be madness to go off leaving the farm in the care of Ned, the hired man; without constant supervision, he would follow a minimal routine which would run the farm inexorably into the ground. No, the farm would have to go. But how? Whether out of simple vanity or some more noble motive I am not sure, but I did not want the farm to perish as an entity. But in order to continue as a functioning entity, the farm would have to be run by some person with a direct and heavy stake in its future.

The other thing that had become clear to me by then was that barring the sort of grand plan for expansion at which I had failed, the farm was and would remain a family farm. By which I mean that the structure of any family which took it over would have to include sons who would provide an adequate labor force and whose interest in doing their best would be conditioned by the probability of eventually inheriting the farm. Had I been the father of sons, perhaps my decision to leave it might have been too difficult to make. If so, I am glad thrice-fold that my name stops with me; I have little doubt that, in such a case, I could have turned out to be the most reprehensible sort of Eugene O'Neil-type patriarch, passing on dissatisfaction with my own lot to my sons who would wait like a pack of growling dogs for my demise.

During the months of negotiation to regain the farm, I had

given this problem a great deal of thought. In the process, I had found my mind returning again and again to a family on our road which exactly suited the farm's requirements. The father of the family Tugwell was in his mid-thirties and still in possession of that physical and psychic energy necessary to make a major move. His several sons were on the verge of emerging into young manhood. In his present status, Tugwell was a perfect example of what I have described as a sundown farmer; he owned one hundred or so acres of land on which he kept some cows and a few chickens but the major trade he followed was that of house painter. He had, in fact, painted our large hay-feeding barn a brilliant red.

While the farm was not actually in my legal possession, I could not make any specific proposition to Tugwell. Now, as spring wore on into summer, I brought the matter up with him and found him receptive to it. The essence of the arrangement I suggested was simply that I lease the farm to him for an intial period of five years with an option to buy the place at extremely advantageous terms. I would then arrange with the bank to re-finance the farm in such a way that the machinery purchase agreements entered in upon by Clyde could be paid off in full through a loan secured by a chattel mortgage on the machinery in question. Thus I would be responsible for one monthly payment to the same bank which would, in time, theoretically amortize both the chattel mortgage and the larger mortgage on the farm itself. In the deal I proposed to Tugwell, the amount he would pay me each month to maintain his lease on the farm would exactly balance the amount I must pay the bank to satisfy the mortgage payments and the taxes on the farm. Indeed, the mechanics of the process I had in mind would insure that the entire process would be automatic: Tugwell's monthly payment would go directly to the bank. Thus, I would be absolved from direct responsibility for the farm although I would still be its owner. Tugwell would then have a period of five years during which he could decide to purchase the place outright at the predetermined figure we had discussed. Furthermore, during that period of five years, he would have the opportunity to reach a pragmatically-based decision as the farm's outright purchase. Or, to be more precise, he would have ample time to conceive his own future plans for the farm and assess the farm's potentialities in terms of the income it was bringing in currently. It was, I think, an entirely equitable arrangement. I was fairly certain that if we came to an agreement on the deal, he would decide to buy the farm within the five-year lease period. And as things turned out, I am happy to report that we did reach such an agreement and that Tugwell did actually purchase the farm outright in 1962.

It is rather interesting to note here that the notification of Tugwell's intention to exercise his option to buy the farm caused in me a severe, if highly temporary, trauma. Dorothy and I were living in Sag Harbor by then, poor as church mice but happily undergoing what was for me an extremely productive period. By rights, I should have been out of my mind with delight that the farm was off my shoulders forever and that we were in possession of the first un-earmarked capital sum of money we had ever possessed. I was not. I went through a month of deep depression before I awoke to consider my blessings. Post-parturitional pains, it seems, follow all creative effort.

Because it took place at roughly the same time as the final sale of our farm, it is, perhaps, as good a time as any now to set down an occurence which passed between myself and O'Hara some years later. The underlying depression resulting from my separation from him did not and will not ever pass lightly from my spirit. There was not, for many years, a morning on which I did not awaken to a feeling of desolate loss, puzzlement and loneliness. The interchange which took place between us helped me to encompass and contain those feelings and perhaps even mitigate them. More than anything, have I wondered about the nature of friendship itself: what it actually is; what it actually means. "None other than himself, a greater knows," says William Blake, as deep a diver into those murky realms where man, nature and God meet, as ever lived. Did O'Hara and I actually wish no more from each other than the other's subservience? With the exception of that which passes between men and women, it seems true that the only deep attachments are those formed in youth. I know that the only attachments I have to other men presently are either social and business arrangements at one end of the spectrum and tutelary ones in which I learn or teach at the other. But the admixture of love I feel so profoundly in the case of women seems to have passed from beyond my grasp in regard to men. The most I feel in regard to men now is pride in those I have helped, shame for those I have hurt, respect for my equals and an irritated, despairing sense of responsibility for those who are not.

O'Hara and I—for better or worse—refused each other subservience. But, in doing so, we heightened our individual needs for pre-eminence rather than having subjected those needs to synthesis. Our failure was that we could not (or would not) labor together further in the understanding of ourselves. Thus does friendship die.

Our interchange took place over the telephone. I had been told by our mutual friend, Bill Murray, that O'Hara had returned to Wytheville and that he and Kate and their children were living there in the same house they had occupied before. I longed to ease the sore hurt of the past and I told Dorothy that I was thinking of calling O'Hara on the telephone. With that wisdom which knows wounds cannot be avoided and stands ever ready to bind them up, she counseled me to go ahead. I was nearly forty years old when I placed that call and my heart was as tremulous as that of a young girl. It was a person-to-person call in every sense of the word. I heard Kate's voice as she answered and listened to the operator's request for O'Hara. I waited while Kate went away to fetch him to the phone. Finally, his voice came over the line. There was a short pause and then he said, "What makes you think you have the right to speak to me?" A click followed as he hung up the telephone. Thus is friendship interred. There would be another meeting between us; but it would not take place for many years.

The farm's immediate future was settled by early summer of that year of 1959 and no further hindrance stood in the way of our departure for the environs of New York. I traveled to New York and with the aid of my sister-in-law found a reasonably pleasant duplex apartment located in the New Jersey suburban town of Bergenfield. The landlord wanted a year's lease which I signed and bound with the proper advances and deposits, arranging that our occupancy would begin a month hence. I returned to Wytheville and we set about the hiring of movers and the packing of our belongings.

Some weeks later, we watched the moving men lash down the last of our belongings and move off down the long winding drive by the creek. Dorothy then gave that beautiful house a final sweeping and we prepared to leave. My mother had long since returned to North Carolina. The aspirants to fame and fortune who drove out past our farm for the last time that day numbered five: Dorothy, my brother, and me, and our two daughters, Linda and Sylvia. In time, there would be a third daughter, Anne, whose name I mention now only because I would not like her to feel left out should she ever read these pages. With us also was Gordo, the Boxer, destined not to survive this penultimate uprooting.

I smile now in memory of that group of pilgrims. There was much, in truth, of the family Joad in our equipage. An old, faded blue automobile which needed coaxing every step of the way was the best we could afford. It was of that class of vehicle in a state of decomposition so advanced that holes had rusted in the floor through which the children delighted in thrusting sticks to their great pleasure and my great exasperation. On we rattled up through Virginia, Maryland and, finally, onto the New Jersey Turnpike. Had I, from another car, watched this group passing, I would have given only short shrift to their chances of survival. Never has captain lived who felt less confident of his ability to bring his ship safely to port.

And then, once rolling down the New Jersey Turnpike at our top speed of fifty, I began to take heart. I noticed that the cars tended to go by us in groups and that, within those groups, they seemed to fight for precedence, endangering themselves and others. Smiling at myself but with a certain seriousness of belief to which I still adhere, I formulated a dictum for the future: Go your own speed, I told myself, stay out of groups. It is certainly a good dictum for travelers on super-highways, and perhaps not a bad one for life. I can claim, I fear, to have obeyed it only moderately well.

So ends this story of a defensive action. As in all defensive actions, blood had been shed and soldiers had fallen. But it was over now and, for better of for worse, the offensive action was about to begin. All that had taken place, as everything does which takes place this side of the grave, had now become experience.

* * * *

EPILOGUE

My boyhood friend, O'Hara and I were both on the wrong side of fifty when we finally met again. He had the loan of his brother's house in East Hampton and chose to get in touch with us. Kate had been to see us a short while before, almost as a herald of this coming embassy. Kate had lasted. She was still an impressive presence. God knows what drives her or leads her for I certainly do not; but she was still very much in the game. She and O'Hara were still married but seemed not to live together at the time. O'Hara, in fact, spent a large portion of his time roaming the country in the Volkswagen camper in which he arrived at East Hampton. He was extremely fit physically and thought nothing of bicycling from East Hampton to Sag Harbor merely to deliver an invitation to dinner or drinks.

By this time of life, O'Hara and I had finally adopted— consciously or unconsciously—our various personae; his a distillation of his old style, a mixture of cynic and sardonic overlaid with a veneer of world weariness. Mine? I shall leave that to whoever has read these pages; some impression must by now have been gained.

O'Hara and I met again at a time when each of us had achieved about the same degree of success, in neither case very great. He had by then published a novel and two works of social history, the first of which had been taken quite seriously. To my mind, his most intriguing achievement was a series of juvenile novels about the adventures of a big, awkward, alienated rich kid. This kid was right out of the class of 1941 at the John Burroughs School, fit to be an honorary member of that odd assemblage. I believe these books were quite successful. I have not seen one recently but I am sure another will be along soon.

245

So it was that all between O'Hara and I ended reasonably well. As well as it could anyway. We corresponded briefly and did each other a few literary services. But time and long separation have cooled the great friendship of my youth. I keep watch for his works and wherever he is, I wish him well.

What eventually became of our farm? In the early seventies, we paid it a visit. When Anne, our youngest daughter was about eleven, she and Dorothy and I decided to take a motor trip through the southeast. A visit to the farm was, of course, on the agenda.

The closer we drew to the farm that day, the greater my nervousness became. We were going to see a place which, even though we had not owned it for many years, still remained a personal symbol of overwhelming importance. All of us want continuity; of this there can be little doubt. We want the objects we create, the children we breed and the thoughts we think to have bearing upon and use for the future. Yet we live face to face with the brutal fact that some things do not succeed, that people and ideas die.

Our farm was among those things that do not continue. My extreme nervousness as we approached it that day must have been a warning that we would find the place moribund. Such was in fact the case. As we rounded the last bend and saw the farm stretched out before us, it seemed fine. The great red barn we had caused to be built dominated the scene; the pastures, green and lush in that season, rose to the ridge in the distance. But then, as we rounded the bend by the Kegley place, it was clear that our first house had fallen into dreadful disrepair. Across the creek, it was equally clear that the grade A dairy farm we had left behind was no longer in operation. The house was occupied but high weeds surrounded the barns and filled the holding pen. Rusting cars—those prime symbols of futility—were parked near the house. We did not tarry. Hearts achill, we drove on, remembering an adventure that had held our hopes at a time when they badly needed holding: when we did not yet know that a sort of homecoming awaited us in the future.

PERTH AND KINROSS LIBRARIES